WHISPERING TRUTH TO POWER

AFRICA AND THE DIASPORA
History, Politics, Culture

SERIES EDITORS

Thomas Spear
Neil Kodesh
Tejumola Olaniyan
Michael G. Schatzberg
James H. Sweet

Whispering
Truth to Power

Everyday Resistance
to Reconciliation
in Postgenocide Rwanda

Susan Thomson

The University of Wisconsin Press

Publication of this book has been made possible, in part,
through support from the **Colgate University Research Council**.

The University of Wisconsin Press
1930 Monroe Street, 3rd Floor
Madison, Wisconsin 53711-2059
uwpress.wisc.edu

3 Henrietta Street

London WC2E 8LU, England
eurospanbookstore.com

Printed in the United States of America

Library of Congress Cataloging-in-Publication Data

Thomson, Susan M.
Whispering truth to power: everyday resistance
to reconciliation in postgenocide Rwanda / Susan Thomson.
p.   cm.
(Africa and the diaspora: history, politics, culture)
Includes bibliographical references and index.
ISBN 978-0-299-29674-2 (pbk.: alk. paper)
ISBN 978-0-299-29673-5 (e-book)
1. Rwanda—Politics and government—1994–.
2. Rwanda—Social conditions—21st century.
3. Government, Resistance to—Rwanda.
I. Title.   II. Series: Africa and the diaspora.
DT450.44.T46   2013
967.57104′3—dc23

Contents

Illustrations

Figures

Table

Preface and Acknowledgments

The Story behind the Findings

Writing a book was not even on my mind when I began my professional life. When I imagined my career back as I was completing my master's degree, in 1992, I was distracted by Africa. I was not ready to settle down in Nova Scotia, where I had been born and raised, and certainly was not keen on the desk jobs my friends were choosing. I wanted to go abroad and experience a part of the world that was rarely discussed in the lecture halls of my undergraduate political science courses but featured frequently on the evening news. The first Iraq war was raging at the time, and I was glued to CNN, whose reporting largely centered on the war in Somalia and the end of the apartheid regime in South Africa—topics that were framed as representative of the continent of Africa. I had yet to realize that the Africa reporting of major North American news outlets provided coverage of African events only in ways that would appeal to Western audiences. I knew only of an amorphous yet singular "Africa" that existed in the images and pages of English-language reports. I also did not appreciate that Western reporting on Africa was skewed in such a way that it both produced and reinforced stereotypes of the "dark" continent as a place of ethnic violence, famine, corruption, and big-man politics. Indeed, I did not even question how reporting on Africa could be anything but inaccurate given that the continent was at that time made up of fifty-three countries, covering a geographic area almost four times the size of the continental United States. I would not turn over in my mind how I learned about Africa and what it meant for my work in Rwanda and elsewhere for another few years.

Instead, I busied myself in securing a full-time position with the United Nations (UN) in East Africa. I believed in the UN as an organization dedicated to the security and development of individuals and states alike. I knew where this idea came from: as a Canadian, I learned in social studies classes in middle and high school that former prime minister Lester Pearson was the grandfather of modern peacekeeping—the quintessential Canadian value. That the UN was more often than not a source of insecurity in the lives of the civilians it claimed to protect would become clear to me soon enough. The civil war in Somalia was under way, and my first posting was as a "Nation-Building Officer" for the United Nations Mission to Somalia in Mogadishu starting in June 1993. The UN did not have the slightest clue about what was actually going on at the local level, so the mission ended shortly after Somali militias killed twenty-three Pakistani peacekeepers in July 1993. I took one lesson away from my three-week stint in the field: local knowledge matters, and the UN did not seem to have any access to it. It was quite the surprise to my young mind that local actors thought the UN an illegitimate entity.

In September 1993 I started to work in cyclone-ravaged Madagascar. I was supposed to monitor the gender dynamics of food distribution for ten months, but I completed only about three months of my appointment. The monitoring of the food distribution took place in rural communities, sometimes as far as forty or fifty miles off the main road. Madagascar has a rudimentary road network, and there is only one paved link between Antananarivo, the capital, and Tamatave, an eastern port city. Repeated cyclones in late 1993 washed the road away in many spots. Traveling the two hundred miles or so between the two cities could take up to twelve hours in a four-by-four that ferried me back and forth between "the office" (the UN office in Tamatave) and "the field." Every morning, I would be dropped off, with my translator, to trek from the main road back to the communities where I would spend my days monitoring food distributions organized by the United Nations High Commission for Refugees (UNHCR) and international nongovernmental organizations. My mission was cut short when I witnessed a murder. It was a surreal event, one that I struggled to make sense of for a long time.

One afternoon, my translator and I finished up about two hours early and had walked back to the pickup spot on the main road. My translator lived in a nearby community and left me alone, which was against UN policy as all staff members were supposed to check in at the office at the end of each day. I sat on an outcrop of the volcanic rock that characterizes much of the landscape and watched the comings and goings of foot traffic, motor bikes, private vehicles, and the UN pickups and four-by-fours that all vied for space on the narrow, muddy main route, which was basically a strip of cavernous potholes. There was a three-part funeral procession walking along the side of the road. The younger men and relatives of the deceased walked up front, where the shrouded body was carried in a burlap stretcher on the shoulders of six or eight men. Most of the population of the community walked behind, with children, dogs, and goats bringing up the rear. Suddenly there was a thud and then loud wailing and incessant screeching. The driver of a Renault 4 had hit a boy at the back of the procession, and it looked like he was badly injured. My heart pounded in my chest as I struggled to understand what I had just seen. I witnessed angry pallbearers drop the body they were carrying to run back and confront the driver. Loud, angry male voices filled the air. Time stood still as I watched the driver step away from his car and cross his wrists as he stretched out his arms toward the approaching group. No one seemed to be attending to the boy who had been hit by his car. Soon, I was off my perch and looking for safety, scanning in the distance for my now long-gone translator. I looked on in horror as the pallbearers began to dismember the driver. He yelped, and the crowd seemed to cheer. I saw his arm fall to the ground. His death ended with decapitation.

It was well past sunset before my driver appeared, three hours late, as I sat in the dark, shaken and alone, waiting for him to arrive. Those three hours felt like an eternity and I wondered if the dispatch folks at my UN office even noticed that I had yet to return to base for the night. I also thought about what I had just witnessed: obviously, what I had just seen was murder. But was it? It seemed so controlled, so methodical. All the parties to the event seemed to have a defined role. Why would the driver get out of his vehicle and offer himself with out-stretched arms? Why did the rest of the community cheer? What about the boy? I remained at the office for the next few days, in a state of shock and unable to articulate my feelings. It took me three days to tell my boss what I had seen. He was blasé about it. "Oh, okay. Um, you know that is how they solve problems between themselves. The driver probably gave himself up." I was dumbfounded. When I expressed my disbelief, he continued, "What you witnessed is nothing unusual. The tribes around here operate in an eye-for-an-eye way. The boy got killed, so the driver gave himself up to avoid turmoil between his tribe and the other one." This made some sense to me, vulnerable and shaken as I was from my experience. Eventually, I broke down, unable to function in this remote area in a high-stress position. I was medically evacuated to Sweden, where I underwent a period of "decompression"[1] to help me process the experience.

Following almost four months of therapy and rest, I had to undertake a trial mission, meaning a short two- or three-week mission back to Africa to assess my ability to continue working with the UN. I was still naively committed to the ideals of the United Nations that I learned in grade school. I was given the choice to either travel to Malawi or Rwanda as my first return to the field since leaving Madagascar. My UN handler, a German woman not much older than I was at the time, described both countries as "easy," with "good restaurants" and "pleasant people." "You'll have no troubles in either country" was her succinct summary of their merits. No other information on the politics of either country was provided, and I did not think to ask any questions about local conditions. My UN colleagues overseeing my return to the field provided no information on the ongoing ceasefire in Kigali, Rwanda's capital; indeed, I had no inkling that Rwanda was on the precipice of mass political violence that would end in genocide. So, I chose Rwanda, as only a twenty-three-year-old could, because of its proximity to my residence in Kenya—the flight from Rwanda to Nairobi had one fewer leg than the trip to Lilongwe, and I was eager to get home after an extended visit in Sweden. I arrived in Rwanda on March 26, 1994, to follow a team from the United Nations Development Program on its assessment of a women's cooperative in Gitarama. The mission was to end April 13, 1994. When I landed in Kigali, there was an obvious military presence as the civil war between the government and the then rebel Rwandan Patriotic Front (RPF) was ongoing. But I had not been briefed on the political situation and did not think much of the armed vehicles and the fifty-man troop patrols that walked the city—that is what ceasefires look like, right? I hopped into another white UN four-by-four and was taken to the office, where I met my team leader and was briefed on what we would be doing in and around Gitarama, some thirty miles southwest of Kigali. What struck me most during our meetings with the local cooperatives the UN was funding were the inequalities between the local representatives and the broader membership. The leaders were clearly drawn from the economic and social elites, given their covered shoes, stylish outfits, well-coiffed hairstyles, and perfect French. Ordinary peasant women were usually barefoot, spoke only Kinyarwanda, wore threadbare clothes, and had their children in tow. We never spoke to them, yet they were always present. I asked a few times during our interviews if we could speak to our "beneficiaries," but our hosts always replied with a polite "No, they have nothing to say; they are poor, you see. Our job is to take care of them for the development of the country." I did not question the UN's dismissal of these women as poor and thus without any knowledge or opinion worth considering. I also knew nothing of President Juvénal Habyarimana's development initiatives, which I later learned were grounded in an ideology in which only ethnic Hutu were the "real" peasants and that this ideology in part fueled the genocide that would engulf Rwanda just a few days later. Everything I experienced during my first week in the country was filtered through the lens of my UN colleagues and the local elites with whom we worked. I could see ordinary peasants everywhere I went but had no way to interact with them or engage them as individuals as I did not speak of a word of the local language, Kinyarwanda. Indeed, when I asked my UN boss why we did not travel with a Kinyarwanda language translator so we could talk to local people, he replied that it was not necessary to consult what the Rwandan authorities called "the masses" as their wellbeing was the responsibility of the government, not the United Nations.

Around 10:30 p.m. on April 6, 1994, the genocide started. I was safely ensconced in the UN headquarters in the center of Kigali. We had arrived back from Gitarama late and were still at the office when I heard the crash that launched the genocide. Habyarimana was returning from peace talks with the leadership of the then rebel RPF in Arusha, Tanzania, when his plane was shot down as it approached Kigali International Airport.[2] All passengers on board were killed, including the president of Burundi, Cyprien Ntaryamira. Road-blocks were going up around the city, and we received word from the UN Assistance Mission in Rwanda (UNAMIR) to stay put. I spent the next five or six days in the UN compound, waiting to be evacuated. The paralyzing fear I felt in Madagascar less than a year prior flooded my system. I spent the next few days numb, without words and without reaction, largely unaware and indeed unable to imagine the systematic and structured killing that was going on out-side the confines of the UN compound in Kigali. I gained a pretty good inkling when armed militia entered forcibly and killed some Tutsi staff members, including the UN driver with whom I had spent the last week. Their remains lay in the courtyard, and we had to step around and over their decomposing bodies to get to the cars that would take us by road to Uganda some five days later. The reentry mission to determine my ability to continue working for the UN would change my life. How could UN personnel not have known what was going on in Rwanda? How could I have been sent to a country on "the brink of civil war" (to quote the UN staffer who briefed us upon our safe arrival in Uganda)? The answers were not that hard to find: Rwanda was the darling of the international community for its commitment to good governance and economic development, and the implementation of the Arusha Accords was progressing well.[3] No one imagined a rupture as dramatic as genocide.

I returned to Nairobi in May 1994 to continue my work with the UN. But what I had experienced in Kigali became a constant preoccupation, which was fed by erroneous reports that atavistic ethnic hatred had erupted in Rwanda. Was it indeed genocide, as some sources were saying? How could genocide happen among neighbors? The United States certainly refused to say it was, and American inaction was a common theme of the reporting. Gruesome images of people dying by machete chop at roadblocks were interspersed with images of mass graves as bloated, decomposing bodies were piled high over one hundred days of genocide. The more I read, the less I knew. Since the RPF eventually stopped the genocide with a military victory, I, like many others, perceived them as the "good guys." I wanted to help rebuild the "new" Rwanda.[4] I first went to Ngara refugee camp in western Tanzania in mid-1995 and worked there alongside a team of delegates from the International Committee of the Red Cross (ICRC) who were investigating sexual violence in the camps. I had a naïve notion that criminal prosecution was a necessary part of understanding and explaining the genocide. Interfering in the lives of women who had lost everything seemed a good idea at the time. But the choice was ultimately about me—I needed to feel that I was doing something to help. I would not understand until years later that the help I offered was hardly the help people wanted or needed.

At the time, I was smitten with the RPF leadership. It had, after all, stopped the genocide, and for me it was a clear-cut affair. Ethnic Hutu had killed innocent ethnic Tutsis as a result of deep-seated hatred. That Hutu elites had manipulated ethnic identities for their own political and economic gain and that the RPF would do the same had not even crossed my mind. I trusted RPF rhetoric about socioeconomic inclusion for all Rwandans, not just RPF members. Like many others, I understood pregenocide Rwanda to be a place of ethnic discrimination and hatred that had resulted in the 1994 massacres. At the same time, I believed in RPF promises of a Rwandan rebirth rooted in ethnic unity and reconciliation. Their framing of the genocidal regime of then president Juvénal Habyarimana as unscrupulous and corrupt made sense, and I believed Paul Kagame, then the de facto head of the RPF, to be an ascetic, principled, and selfless leader. I suffered perhaps what many young people suffer, an implicit confidence in the value of leadership and charismatic political leadership in particular as a direct path to eliminate the structural conditions that result in unequal social, political, and economic institutions. That the cult of personality surrounding RPF leaders, including Kagame, could result in authoritarian rule was not something I would consider deeply until I witnessed firsthand the daily fear and insecurity that ordinary Rwandans felt with respect to their political leaders. Instead, like many others before and since, I understood postgenocide Rwanda through a narrow lens—that of the 1994 genocide, in which Hutu chauvinist leaders drove ordinary Hutu to commit acts of genocide against Tutsi. The RPF, led by the capable and visionary Kagame, is the hero of the Rwandan tragedy.

I eventually moved to Rwanda in July 1997, working for the United Nations Human Rights Mission for Rwanda (UNHRFOR). This was a ragtag bunch of young and often ambitious Westerners, with an occasional West African national thrown into the mix. We spent our days interviewing Rwandans about their experiences of violence since the genocide with the broad purpose of monitoring the human rights situation in the country. It did not seem to matter very much that many of my colleagues did not have the slightest clue what constituted a human rights abuse. Instead, we traipsed across the country, with armed soldiers as our escorts, to speak to ordinary Rwandans about the violence they had lived through or witnessed. We often met in hospitals, seeking to speak to people who had just been victims of violence. The hospitals stank: a pungent mix of dried blood, festering machete wounds, human waste, and charcoal smoke. Many of my UN colleagues would wait outside while those of us who were willing would go interview weakened, vulnerable, and frightened Rwandans. It did not take long to see that many of my colleagues were building careers, not caring for local people. The power dynamics inherent in these interactions were an equally unexamined aspect of our work.

I resigned from the Mission less than two weeks later. My last assignment was to monitor the public executions of twenty-two Rwandans at various sites across Rwanda. I witnessed the executions in Kigali of six people, including one woman, at Nyamirambo soccer stadium. As their bodies slumped over in the hail of bullets from six police AK-47s, I got really scared as many in the crowd cheered, others danced, some wept, while others remained stone faced. I knew I would have to resign. The situation in Rwanda was simply too complicated for me. I did not trust my UN colleagues to support or care for me. I had already been confronted with the bureaucratic incompetence of the United Nations. I could not image how public executions would facilitate national reconciliation in such a climate. What I was seeing and hearing in the hills when we interviewed ordinary people made no sense in the broader context of postgenocide Rwanda. I understood the executions as a political act designed to demonstrate that the RPF was squarely in charge of things but came to realize that I only superficially understood Rwandan politics. This lack of understanding was potentially dangerous for the people I interviewed and for me. A few weeks later, Kofi Annan, then UN secretary general, visited and held a town hall meeting with UN staff. We were invited to ask questions. I raised my hand and asked, "What do we tell local people when they tell us human rights don't matter?" Annan did not answer my question, and I was later called into the office of my team leader, who told me that my question was inappropriate given the prevailing political climate. I assumed he meant the political dynamic within Rwanda at large but later learned that he meant between the UN mission and the RPF-led government. The government shut down our Mission less than a month after Annan's visit in July 1998.

Since I had submitted my resignation letter to the UN some four weeks prior to Annan's visit, my name was not included in the list of active staff to the UN mission. As a result, I jumped at the opportunity when a United States Agency for International Development (USAID) representative asked me to work on their project at the National University of Rwanda. The project involved training Anglophone lawyers to take up genocide trials. I jumped at the opportunity; I would be working directly with Rwandans! I was "allowed" to stay in Rwanda, after a meeting with then minister of justice Gerald Gahima during which he made a few phone calls and ensured that I had a working visa. The government asked all UNHRFOR staff to leave, and only a few of us were able to negotiate permission to stay behind to take up other justice-related tasks. As Gahima said, "Our needs are many, and we want friends of Rwanda to work here, not those who criticize what they don't understand." I spent three and a half years in Butare town (now Huye since the administrative renaming exercise of 2006), working with students who had come to Rwanda after the genocide with their families. Many had never been to Rwanda before, and only a few spoke Kinyarwanda. Most of them spoke in glowing terms about the RPF; I must admit their earnest belief in the vision of the RPF swayed me greatly, and when I left Rwanda for Canada in January 2001 I was a strong supporter. I was not totally blind to the shortcomings of RPF rule but felt that their authoritarian practices were necessary to rebuild a peaceful and secure Rwanda. A benign dictatorship made sense particularly since so many of the Rwandans around me supported the government. I did not reflect much on the fact that I was helping to train the new elite and that the welfare of ordinary peasant Rwandans was not a priority for the RPF. It also did not occur to me that everything I had heard about or witnessed in the new Rwanda was again filtered through local elites.

All of these experiences eventually culminated in an intellectual journey that marked the beginning of this book project. When I first arrived home in Canada in early 2001, I was tired and fed up, and I could not make sense of what I had witnessed in Rwanda and elsewhere. I had heard about and seen an incredible amount of violence, and I had become cynical and bitter about these experiences. Eventually, I realized that this bitterness was not about "Africa," but instead was about my experiences with the UN. On multiple occasions, the UN had left me alone and vulnerable. And if the UN repeatedly and unnecessarily put me in dangerous situations, how much more so might their actions have put everyday Rwandans at risk? My critique of the UN did not, however, extend to the government of the "new" Rwanda. I took a second master's degree, focusing on the democratic transition in postgenocide Rwanda. My thesis provided a glowing tribute to the vision of the RPF.

In the ensuing years, I was able to reflect on what I had seen in Rwanda and elsewhere. I began to think more and more about what I had not seen. I had lived in Rwanda for almost five years, yet I knew next to nothing of the everyday lives of ordinary Rwandans and of how the nonelite peasants were coping in the aftermath of the genocide. Yet the ability of these ordinary Rwandans to adapt to the "new" Rwanda was a central feature of government discourse, which held that Rwanda was a nation on the road to recovery because of government policy combined with the resilient spirit of Rwandans. My wish was to design a project that would write the voices of peasant Rwandans into academic knowledge, to analyze the postgenocide political order from their perspective, and to understand the workings and effects of state power within Rwandan society. Others were analyzing how the genocide could have happened; although I devoured these works as they were published, I really wanted to understand the everyday politics of peasant Rwandans as they struggled to make sense of their lives in the aftermath of the genocide.

Also shaping my desire to understand the life worlds of peasant Rwandans were institutional politics at my doctoral institution, Dalhousie University. Myriad challenges arose with the Ethics Board, which required five written submissions over a period of nine months before I was granted ethics clearance, a mere two weeks before my fieldwork began in April 2006. My effort to explain and justify to the Board my choice of ethnographic methods in a postconflict society like Rwanda was compounded by Board members' lack of actual knowledge about Rwanda and the fact that political scientists do not "do" ethnography. One member even thought in 2005 that Rwanda was still at war and that conducting research would be impossible. The process was time consuming and frustrating but ultimately produced a stronger research proposal as I explained and reiterated my methodology, particularly my strategies for gaining access to peasant Rwandans. In fact, I am indebted to the members of the Ethics Board who made me think and rethink my research methods. I was forced to consider—patiently, cautiously, systematically—what my reality, as a foreign researcher in a potentially volatile context like that of postgenocide Rwanda, could be like. This understanding would later prove invaluable when the Government of Rwanda stopped my research and asked me to undergo "reeducation" about the "real" Rwanda since peasant people had "filled my head with negative ideas" (for more on this experience, see Thomson 2011d, 2013).

When officials at the Ministry of Local Government (MINALOC) summoned me to Kigali to meet with them in August 2006, I was very nervous for myself and for the thirty-seven peasant Rwandans who had volunteered to participate in my research. My physical safety was never at risk because such violence is not a regular tactic of the government for a foreigner like me. Instead, the government seeks to control the sociopolitical realm through fear, harassment, and intimidation. Indeed, I was dominated by fear when a MINALOC official took my passport, saying I would get it back once the government was satisfied that I had been adequately reeducated. What that meant or how long reeducation might last were not disclosed. After much discussion, the assistant to the minister told me that my methodology was "too kind to prisoners accused of acts of genocide"; I was not to treat them as I was treating Tutsi survivors (the only legitimate survivors in postgenocide Rwanda, a notion my research challenges). Did I not know that prisoners had killed and also had to be "re-educated" on what it means to be a good citizen in the new Rwanda?

The experience of having my planned year in Rwanda cut short affected the research in a number of positive ways. First, in offering to reeducate me, the government gave me a frontline look at the tactics and techniques it uses to control Rwanda's political and social landscape. Initial feelings of fear, for my safety and for that of my research participants, soon changed to a sense of privilege at being able to spend so much time in the company of Rwandan elites—something I had not included in my original research design. I learned to recognize the sweeping generalizations and oversimplifications of Rwandan history that the government relied upon to legitimize its rule. Since my research was grounded in the voices of peasant Rwandans, this recognition allowed me to further contextualize and situate the narratives of my participants in the analysis presented in this book. The government's attempt to influence my thinking on its reconstruction and reconciliation successes since the 1994 genocide was equally revealing as I was able to see firsthand how the government organizes the flow of information and determines what counts as the capital-T truth in postgenocide Rwanda. I wrote about this during the gestation of this book (e.g., Thomson 2009a, 2010, 2011d, 2013) and occasionally experience the wrath of the Rwandan government for doing so. A good example of the government's efforts to control the flow of information is its reaction to my contribution to Straus and Waldorf's (2011) edited volume on contemporary Rwanda. In May 2011, even before the book was published, a government-sponsored website dedicated to discrediting Straus and Waldorf as editors appeared, calling them the "pair in despair" and targeting select authors for their hatred of Rwanda (Butamire 2011a). The contents of my chapter on being reeducated at an *ingando* for released prisoners accused of genocide gained a page, where I was called a "fraud PhD" (Butamire 2011b). If foreign academics are subject to this sort of intimidation and censorship, how must the government treat ordinary Rwandans? I fear they are subject to considerably more harassment and intimidation and perhaps worse in a country where journalists and human rights defenders regularly disappear or flee into exile (Amnesty International 2011).

Despite the sometimes difficult path that my professional life has taken, I have also been fortunate to share in the lives of the thirty-seven Rwandans who formally participated in my research project and of the hundreds of other Rwandans who shared part of themselves with me. All of the Rwandans I consulted are identified only by pseudonyms in the pages that follow. I cannot properly acknowledge and thank any of the real people I write about without

potentially putting them in danger. It is this reality that makes my acknowledg-
ments difficult and important, as I cannot directly thank in print all of those
who made this book a reality, even though many of the Rwandans I spoke to in
the course of this research asked me to publish their names. Many of my participants simply wanted there to be some written record of their lives. Even the
worst violence cannot extinguish the basic human need to be recognized and
heard. As powerful as this need is for me, this book nonetheless chronicles the
postgenocide lives of ordinary peasant Rwandans without using their real
names, as it is my academic responsibility to protect my sources, not to reveal
them. Nonetheless, it is these people that I most want to thank.

There are individuals and institutions I can name. During the course of my
research, I benefited immensely from the generosity and kindness of innumer-
able people and organizations in Canada, Rwanda, and elsewhere. The research benefited from the funding support from the Canadian Consortium on
Human Security, the Dalhousie University Faculty of Graduate Studies, the
International Development Research Centre, and the Social Sciences and
Humanities Research Council of Canada. I do not name my Rwandan research
partners or assistants for fear of government retaliation against them. I am
likely unable to travel back to Rwanda to share my research with them anytime
soon, but I hope to do so one day. My research assistants and translators were
invaluable, and their friendship, particularly after the government stopped my
research, is something I will never forget.

Others have been generous in sharing their time and intellect. I thank in
particular David Black, Stephen Brown, Jane Parpart, and Tim Shaw. I also
thank everyone who commented on early drafts of my work or provided an
intellectual safe haven—there are too many of you to mention, but you know
who you are. David and Catharine Newbury provided much-needed moral
support and intellectual guidance during my Andrew W. Mellon postdoctoral
fellowship at Hampshire and Smith Colleges. Their combined commitment to
Rwandan studies and the Rwandan people is one I am trying to emulate in my
own work. Rwandan friends living across North America helped me make
sense of the intricacies of the Kinyarwanda language and the intrigues of
Rwandan proverbs and translations. Noel Twagiramungu and Séraphine
Mukankubito deserve special mention here, both for their language acumen
and friendship. Myriam Hebabi assisted with library research and Julia
McMillan helped update my bibliography. Anne Aghion, producer of the
documentary *My Neighbor, My Killer* (2009), provided the image of the woman
before the *gacaca* courts (figure 12). Thanks are also due to colleagues and friends
who provided some of the photographs that appear throughout the text. Jacob
Noel and Carie Ernst created the maps, which is no easy task in a country with

a habit of changing place names every now and then. J. Naomi Linzer Indexing Services crafted the index with fresh eyes—your work is much appreciated. Colleagues at my new institutional home, Colgate University, provided critical moral, financial, and administrative support. The students in my spring 2013 "Rwanda since the 1994 Genocide" course at Colgate University also provided much-needed good humor as I completed the manuscript. A number of colleagues and friends—An Ansoms, Jennie Burnet, Anu Chakravarty, Marie-Eve Desrosiers, Ellen Donkin, Bert Ingelaere, Etienne Mashuli, Rosemary Nagy, Jade Rox, Jacob Speaks, Noel Twagiramungu, and others who wish to remain anonymous—provided intellectual and moral support and deserve special mention here. Their support and insights, along with those of two anonymous reviewers, improved the book and perhaps even made me a bit smarter in the process of struggling to incorporate their constructive criticism into the text. Thank you all.

The text has also benefited from the suggestions and comments of editors and peer reviewers of the various journals in which I have published sometimes different versions of sections of the book. Parts of chapter 5 were published under the title "Whispering Truth to Power: The Everyday Resistance of Peasant Rwandans to Post-Genocide Reconciliation," *African Affairs* 100 (440): 439–56. Chapter 1 on my research methodology inspired an article on the challenges of working in highly politicized research settings, published under the title "Getting Close to Rwandans since the Genocide: Studying Everyday Life in Highly Politicized Research Settings," *African Studies Review* 53 (3): 19–34. In addition, parts of chapter 1 originally appeared in my chapter titled "'That Is Not What We Authorised You to Do . . .': Access and Government Interference in Highly Politicised Research Environments," published in *Surviving Field Research: Working in Violent and Difficult Situations*, edited by Chandra Lekha Sriram, John C. King, Julie A. Mertus, Olga Martin-Ortega, and Johanna Herman (London: Routledge, 2009), 108–24. Parts of chapter 6 were published under the title "The Darker Side of Transitional Justice: The Power Dynamics behind Rwanda's *Gacaca* Courts," *Africa: The Journal of the International African Institute* 81 (3): 373–90. A different version of chapter 6, coauthored with Rosemary Nagy of Nippising University, was published under the title "Law, Power and Justice: What Legalism Fails to Address in the Functioning of Rwanda's *Gacaca* Courts," *International Journal of Transitional Justice* 5 (1): 11–30. Parts of chapter 4 were published under the title "Peasant Perspectives on National Unity and Reconciliation: Building Peace or Promoting Division?," in *Rwanda Fast Forward*, edited by Maddalena Campioni and Patrick Noack (London: Routledge, 2012), 96–110. All of these papers were presented at conferences across Europe and North America, and I want to thank those panel organizers, discussants, and audience members who pushed me to think through my ideas and arguments.

The folks at the University of Wisconsin Press deserve special mention—Tom Spear, Matthew Cosby, and Logan Middleton—thank you all. Special thanks go to Gwen Walker, my acquisitions editor, and to Jeri Famighetti and Sheila McMahon, my copy and production editors, who patiently supported me as I rewrote and revised the manuscript for publication. Last but not least, heartfelt thanks go to my family, in particular my boys, Evan and Riley, who have put up with a lot over the years and have waited, sometimes patiently but often not, for me to finish "my work" so that I could come out and play.

Abbreviations

APROSOMA	Association pour la promotion sociale de la masse (Association for the Welfare of the Masses)
AFDL	Alliance des forces démocratiques pour la libération du Congo-Zaïre (Alliance of Democratic Forces for the Liberation of Congo-Zaire)
AI	Amnesty International
AIDS	Acquired Immunodeficiency Syndrome
ASF	Avocats sans frontières (Lawyers without Borders)
AVEGA	Association des veuves du génocide (Association of Genocide Widows)
BBC	British Broadcasting Corporation
CAURWA	Communauté des autochtones rwandais (Community of Indigenous Peoples of Rwanda)
CCM	Center for Conflict Management
CDR	Coalition pour la défense de la république (Coalition for the Defense of the Republic)
CNLG	Commission nationale de lutte contre le génocide (National Commission for the Fight Against Genocide)
CNS	Commission nationale de synthèse (National Synthesis Commission)
COPORWA	Communauté des potiers rwandais (Rwandan Community of Potters)
DANIDA	Danish International Development Agency
FAO	Food and Agriculture Organization
FAR	Forces armées rwandaises (Rwandan Armed Forces)

FARG	Fonds d'assistance aux rescapés du génocide (Genocide Survivors Assistance Fund)
HIV	Human Immunodeficiency Virus
HRC	Human Rights Commission
HRW	Human Rights Watch
IAI	International African Institute
ICG	International Crisis Group
ICRC	International Committee of the Red Cross
ICTR	International Criminal Tribunal for Rwanda
IFAD	International Fund for Agricultural Development
IMF	International Monetary Fund
IRDP	Institute of Research and Dialogue for Peace
IRIN	Integrated Regional Information Network
Kcal	Kilocalories
LDF	Local Defense Forces
LGDL	Ligue des droits de la personne dans la région des Grands Lacs (Great Lakes Region Human Rights League)
LIPRODHOR	Ligue rwandaise pour la promotion et la défense des droits de l'homme (Rwandan League for the Promotion and Defense of Human Rights)
MDR	Mouvement démocratique républicain (Republican Democratic Movement)
MIGEPROF	Ministère du genre et de la promotion de la femme (Ministry of Gender and Family Promotion)
MINALOC	Ministère de l'administration locale, de l'information et des affaires sociales (Ministry of Local Government, Information and Social Affairs)
MINECOFIN	Ministère des finances et de la planification économique (Ministry of Finance and Economic Planning)
MINIJUST	Ministère de la justice (Ministry of Justice)
MINITERRE	Ministère des terres, de l'environnement, des forêts, de l'eau et des ressources naturelles (Ministry of Land, Environment, Forests, Water and Natural Resources)
MRND	Mouvement révolutionnaire national pour le développement (National Revolutionary Movement for Development)
MRND(D)	Mouvement révolutionnaire national pour le développement et la démocratie (National Revolutionary Movement for Development and Democracy)

MSF	Médecins sans frontières (Doctors without Borders)
MSM	Mouvement social muhutu (Social Movement for Muhutu)
NGO	Nongovernmental Organization
NRA	National Resistance Army (Uganda)
NRM	National Resistance Movement (Uganda)
NSGJ	National Service of *Gacaca* Jurisdictions
NURC	National Unity and Reconciliation Commission
OECD	Organization for Economic Cooperation and Development
ORTPN	Office rwandais du tourisme et des parcs nationaux (Rwandan Office for Tourism and National Parks)
PAC	Presidential Advisory Council
PADE	Parti démocratique (Democratic Party)
PARMEHUTU	Parti du mouvement de l'émancipation hutu (Hutu Emancipation Movement Party
PCD	Parti chrétien démocrate (Christian Democratic Party)
PDI	Parti démocratique islamique (Islamic Democratic Party)
PL	Parti libéral (Liberal Party)
PPJR	Parti progressiste de la jeunesse rwandaise (Progressive Rwandan Youth Party)
PRI	Prison Reform International
PSD	Parti social démocrate (Social Democratic Party)
PSR	Parti socialiste rwandais (Rwandan Socialist Party)
PTSD	Posttraumatic Stress Disorder
RADER	Rassemblement démocratique rwandais (Rwandan Democratic Rally)
RPA	Rwandan Patriotic Army
RPF	Rwandan Patriotic Front
RSF	Reporters sans frontières (Reporters without Borders)
RTD	Rassemblement travailliste pour la démocratie (Labour Rally for Democracy)
RTLM	Radio-Télévision libre des mille collines (Thousand Hills Independent Radio-Television)
TIG	Travaux d'intérêt général (Works in the General Interest)
UDPR	Union démocratique du peuple rwandais (Democratic Union of the Rwandan People)
UNAMIR	United Nations Assistance Mission to Rwanda
UNAR	Union nationale rwandaise (National Rwandan Union)
UNDP	United Nations Development Program
UNHCR	United Nations High Commissioner for Refugees

UNHRFOR	United Nations Human Rights Mission for Rwanda
USAID	United States Agency for International Development
USCRI	United States Committee for Refugees and Immigrants
WB	World Bank

Note on Kinyarwanda Language Usage and Spelling

Throughout the text, I have used the current spellings for Kinyarwanda-language words, meaning that I omit double vowels (e.g., "Tutsi" not "Tuutsi" and "Uburetwa" not "Ubureetwa"). In general, Kinyarwanda words are used with their augment and prefix, changing only between the singular and the plural (e.g., *umudugudu*, sing., "village," and *imidugudu*, pl., "villages").

For categories of groups and people, I use the Kinyarwanda prefixes *umu-/aba-* (e.g., *umutindi*, sing., "destitute person," and *abatindi*, pl., "destitute people"; *umusazi*, sing., a "foolish" person, and *abasazi*, pl., a group of "foolish" people). I have also retained the prefixes for particular practices and actions where altering the form would introduce confusion. This means that I retain the augment and prefix for words like *ubuhake* (a traditional system of vassalage), *ubukonde* (practice of acquiring land through sweat equity), and so on.

References to ethnic/racial categories follow the conventions of the International African Institute (IAI), meaning that I omit prefixes. Thus, "Tutsi," "Hutu," and "Twa" instead of "Abatutsi," "Abahutu," and "Abatwa." Where readers see plural usage for ethnic/racial categories (e.g., the Bahutu Manifesto or the Bakiga people), this is to avoid modifying the language of the primary source document or to retain the original meaning.

WHISPERING TRUTH TO POWER

Introduction

STATE POWER AS LIVED EXPERIENCE

One Sunday afternoon in late September 2006, a genocide survivor I will call Jeanne came to my residence in Huye town in southern Rwanda.[1] Among Rwandans, elites and ordinary folk alike, Sunday is a day reserved for prayer and for visiting family and friends. Jeanne had never visited me before. I knew her well since she had participated in my research project, which sought to understand the effects of the postgenocide government's policy of national unity and reconciliation on ordinary peasant Rwandans living in the southwest of the country. I often received visitors on Sunday and continued to do so even after the government halted my project in late August 2006, stating that it "was against national unity and reconciliation" and "was not the kind of research they needed" (field notes 2006).

Given government scrutiny of my project and the precarious social position of most of my participants in the postgenocide order, I was rather surprised when people continued to drop by to show their support for the research and me. My astonishment was a reflection of my own state of mind—the postgenocide government was exercising its muscle, and I was its target. My visitors understood my feelings of powerlessness; some reveled in our mutual condition. I had "become one of them," and this newly acquired status was rooted in my detailed knowledge of the individual life stories of the thirty-seven peasant Rwandans who participated in my research. It was the sharing of secrets that structured my interaction with ordinary Rwandans, and many visitors subtly reminded me not to reveal anything that they had shared with me to the authorities.[2] Most acknowledged my "troubles" with the government and assured me that its interference was actually a good thing. As Martin, a Tutsi survivor of the 1994 genocide, stated prosaically just a week before I left the country: "My government knows what it will like and not like. You now know what it is like to fear because of them. It's good for you because now you know even better what we feel when the [local government official] comes to visit or when [President] Kagame issues an order that affects our life." Martin was referring to President Paul Kagame's July 2006 directive that all kiosks—the makeshift shops where ordinary peasant Rwandans buy their staple goods—be shut down. The directive was devastating not only to the economic lives of the owners of these kiosks but also for people who because of it had to travel further to market centers for their sugar, oil, and other basics, paying higher prices and losing the opportunity to socialize over a beer or tea.

Jeanne was initially reluctant to participate in the research, but as time passed she recognized that I was serious about listening to her life story. As our relationship progressed, she became adamant that her story be shared so that people "outside Rwanda" could learn about her everyday struggles and perhaps "storms like the war against Hutu and genocide against Tutsi" could be stopped and her surviving children would not suffer as she had. Jeanne came to be one of the most outspoken of the individuals who participated in my research. Ordinary people who have "nothing left to lose" have always spoken their truth to power; what is important is to know the "ways of doing it without provoking a reaction from the government" (interviews 2006). Before the genocide, ordinary people did so under the cover of madness, and these individuals are known as *abasazi* (plural, meaning "foolish"). They used their "madness" to give the impression that they were mentally unstable to justify their willingness to say "what regular people can't attempt" (interviews 2006). Since the genocide, ordinary peasant Rwandans like Jeanne, who no longer fear speaking out, are known as *ibyihebe* (plural, literally "fearless"). On our previous meeting, in June 2006, Jeanne had hugged me for a long time, perhaps five minutes, and when she broke our embrace she said,

> I am glad you have come into my life. You gave me a safe space to share my inner thoughts. It is not always safe in the new Rwanda to share what you really think. I had that with some people before the war. But Rwandese, we need secrets, we don't share easily. But with you, I shared, and my heart feels lighter. You understand because you want peace for all of us, even poor people like me. I am stronger because I met you, because we shared.
>
> But our time is now over. I can't see you anymore because people know that our official time together is now over. I want you to know you will always be my friend in here [*taps her chest*], but you must go and not greet

me if we meet, and do not visit. I sometimes told you more than I should have but I wanted to and you can tell my story in your book. But it is best for my family and I if you never come back here again. (Field notes 2006)

I understood why she asked me to keep distance, since our relationship was grounded in my knowledge of power relations in postgenocide Rwanda. As an "unimportant person" (meaning "a powerless subordinate") in Rwandan society, Jeanne likely wanted to distance herself from an (white-skinned, relatively wealthy, and foreign) "important person" like me, lest our continued relationship result in jealous neighbors or the renewed attention of the local official who would sometimes pop in during our interviews to inquire about "how things were going." So when she appeared at my gate a few months later, I assumed she had come to withdraw her consent to share her story in my book. To the contrary, and like many of my participants who heard the news of my "problems" with the government, she had come to rightly remind me that my "troubles" were far less severe than those that people like her experienced every day.

I also interpreted Jeanne's visit as an act of resistance, given the attendant risks of possibly encountering the handler the government had assigned to keep tabs on me or, perhaps worse, the member of the Local Defense Forces (LDF) who lived across the street and who was likely keeping an eye on me as well.[3] Before the government stopped my research, we greeted each other politely, sometimes even engaging in small talk about the security situation in our neighborhood. I still saw my LDF neighbor almost every day, but he no longer said hello—perhaps an insult in a society that prides itself on the formality of greeting other people, or perhaps he felt it best to no longer fraternize with me, as he was likely reporting back on whom I was with and what I was doing. His continued presence around my residence was not lost on many of my participants who came for a visit, as some joked about it with me. One individual summed up our shared condition with a proverb—the cracked pot laughs at the broken one (*ikimuga giseka urujyo*)—and further joked that all that was missing from my Rwanda experience was to be thrown in *cachot* (detention).

Jeanne's visit constituted an appropriate ending to a period of fieldwork that was fraught with challenges, most notably government interference in the research process (Thomson 2009a, 2013). During our visit, she spoke of how she valued our relationship and how she was "glad" to have been part of my project since the government stopped it. As a forty-seven-year-old Tutsi widow of the genocide, she did not expect that anything would change in Rwanda in her lifetime, but perhaps the "disturbance" I caused the government would "make them wake up to the hardships" of many peasant Rwandans. She continued:

The problems we have aren't just because we are poor. We know we are, but the government reminds us often that we are poor and that we need their help. We see new [local authorities] often. Kigali [the seat of government] changes them just as we are getting used to them, to their rules and ideas. They come in to our community, and we respect them. We do this because that is our culture. As peasants, we have no say in governance. Those who speak out can really get into problems. That is what happened to you. You made it easy for us to speak about our problems, and the [government] officials got really nervous and decided to stop your work.

This is the problem we suffer when the officials tell us about national unity and reconciliation. We can't speak out about our hardships. No [*shakes head*]. We must go to *gacaca* [neotraditional justice courts], and we must do what we are told, say what we are educated to say. We go to *umuganda* [community work], and we listen to their speeches. But they didn't grow up in our communities. They come from Kigali and don't understand what is necessary for us to live in peace. Some of them speak only a little Kinyarwanda [the language spoken by the majority of Rwandans]. The one who helped stop your work has only been our [appointed government] official these last six months.[4] He never asks us what we need. You understand that we peasants have few choices until the government says we do. That makes you a problem that must go away.

I am glad to be part of your research and I came to tell you in person that you are doing a good thing. If the government has noticed you among all the white researchers we see in [Huye] town, then I need to come and tell you to keep working and do your best when you get back to Canada. (Field notes 2006)

Jeanne's salvo was a great relief to me. She remained committed to the research and affirmed her continued consent. Her words also made me realize that the ordinary peasant Rwandans who had participated in my research and later visited me at my residence not only understood its purpose and goals but also knew that I would protect their life stories, despite the less than ideal conditions of my hasty departure. Jeanne understood the risks inherent in coming to visit me, but she came anyway and shared that I "made it easy" for the Rwandans I consulted to talk about their hopes, fears, and frustrations with the postgenocide social order.

Jeanne's narrative also speaks to a key finding of the research—ethnicity is not the most salient aspect of individual identity; levels of poverty as well as one's location in Rwanda's rigid and stratified socioeconomic structure before and since the 1994 genocide shape everyday life. When she speaks of "us," Jeanne does not mean other Tutsi but instead means others in her socioeconomic class. As a widow, she occupies a position in the postgenocide order that is exceedingly weak. Jeanne is poor and landless, without sufficient income to feed or clothe her children, let alone provide for their health care or schooling. Jeanne self-describes as "destitute" (*umutindi*), one of six categories of socioeconomic status that stratify Rwandan society (these are analyzed more fully in chapter 5). Vulnerable folks like Jeanne are near the bottom of the socioeconomic hierarchy, second only to those who are "most vulnerable" or living in abject poverty (the *abatindi nyakujya*), who must beg to survive as they often lack the family and kin networks that could offer them support (MINECOFIN 2001). Being vulnerable means that Jeanne and others like her rarely have the personal resources and autonomy to shape their own lives and livelihoods. They lack sufficient emotional or physical protection from the government, which in turn makes it difficult for them to anticipate, adapt to, resist, and recover from state-led interventions in their daily lives. In other words, individuals' interactions with the rules, regulations, and rituals of the postgenocide order are reactive, as government practices of surveillance and coercion essentially erase their ability to voice their discontent with its postgenocide policies and practices.

For Rwandans at the lowest levels of the socioeconomic hierarchy, their ethnic identity matters most when they are required to participate in state-led initiatives of national unity and reconciliation. National unity and reconciliation are the backbone of the government's reconstruction strategy and the defining features of state power in postgenocide Rwanda as it structures the interactions of individual Rwandans with the state as well as with one another. On paper, there is a set of mechanisms that "aims to promote unity between Tutsi and Hutu in creating one Rwanda for all Rwandans" (NURC 2000, 4). In practice, it disguises the government's efforts to control its population by using the language of ethnic unity and social inclusion while working to consolidate the political and ecomomic power of the ruling Rwandan Patriotic Front (RPF). From the perspective of the peasant Rwandans I consulted, it is a heavy-handed approach to postgenocide reconciliation that operates to create the necessary sociopolitical space for the government to engage in ambitious social reengineering aimed at "wiping the slate utterly clean and beginning from zero" (Scott 1998, 94). As is demonstrated in chapters 4 and 5, the policy of national unity and reconciliation is built on a bedrock of structural violence and economic inequality that places the burden of postgenocide reconstruction and reconciliation squarely on the shoulders of Rwanda's poor and largely rural population (Uvin 1998, 100–103; Zraly 2010).[5]

Broadly, the analysis that follows reveals the system of power that structure the lives of ordinary peasant Rwandans like Jeanne and the thirty-six other poor, rural Rwandans I consulted in 2006 and whose life stories form its backbone.

By "ordinary Rwandans" I do not mean those individuals who hold formal political power as a member of the political elite or those individuals engaged as agents of the state (e.g., police officers, civil servants, military personnel, local authorities). Instead, I conceptualize "ordinary Rwandans" as the nonelite and largely peasant citizenry, many of whom are subsistence farmers and/or day laborers. Postgenocide Rwanda represents a context where political power is firmly held by the state in a system where sociopolitical domination is common-place and accepted by ruler and ruled alike. When the power of the state is exercised at the local level, it takes the form of directives from "on high" (the regime in Kigali) and of strict monitoring of the ability and willingness of local officials to "implement government orders effectively and efficiently" (interview with MINALOC official 2006). RPF-appointed local leaders in turn keep an eye on the activities and speech of individuals within their bailiwick. Individual compliance with the demands of the policy of national unity is paramount. Indi-viduals are constantly and consistently reminded by appointed local officials of the need to "unify and reconcile" in order to consolidate present and future security. The density of the Rwandan state saturates everyday life with its strong administrative, surveillance, and information-gathering systems, resulting in minute individual forms of resistance when confronted with its various prac-tices of control and coercion (Longman 1998; Pottier 2002; Purdeková 2012b). Peasant Rwandans like Jeanne are subject to the exercise of power granted to appointed local leaders and must perform the prescribed rituals of national unity and reconciliation, regardless of their private realities.

More narrowly, this is a study of the individual lived experiences with state power of ordinary peasant Rwandans living in the southwest of the country—how does it make them feel and what does it make them say or do? Drawing on Weber (1946) and following Wedeen (2003, 680), the analysis distinguishes between the terms "state" and "regime." By "state" I mean the common set of public institutions capable of distributing goods and services and controlling violence within a defined, internationally recognized territory. By "regime" I mean the political order of a particular administration, in this case "the regime of the Rwandan Patriotic Front (RPF)" as opposed to "the state of the RPF." This distinction allows for a critique of the various mechanisms of the Rwan-dan state in pursuit of the twin goals of national unity and reconciliation as implemented by the RPF and its agents. In understanding and explaining the everyday practices of national unity and reconciliation from the perspective of ordinary Rwandans, I analyze their minute and subtle resistance to its many demands to illustrate the ways in which the policy goes against their interests as peasants.[6]

The analysis that follows examines the practices of national unity and reconciliation through an examination of three types of everyday resistance—staying on the sidelines, irreverent compliance, and withdrawn muteness—that some ordinary peasant Rwandans attempt. I examine some of the subversive and strategic ways in which Rwandans whisper their truth to the power of the postgenocide regime. I employ the concept of everyday resistance to identify and analyze the system of power to which ordinary Rwandans are subject to illustrate how individuals are positioned in relation to state power and how this positioning affects their life chances in the postgenocide order. I do not conceptualize individual acts of resistance as half of the unambiguous binary of domination versus resistance, which sees domination as a relatively static and institutionalized form of state power and resistance as organized opposition to it. Instead, I identify and analyze the everyday acts of resistance of ordinary peasant Rwandans—from silence and secrets to lying and foot-dragging—to show the many ways in which the policy of national unity and reconciliation represents an oppressive form of power in their lives through its various practices.

The Practices of the Rwandan State

My research is explicitly concerned with how the system of power that constitutes "the state" plays out in the lives of those subject to its disciplinary "technologies" that produce the power relations in which people are caught up (Foucault 1977, 202). My approach is thus not rooted in traditional political science approaches of statism or systems analysis that understand "the state" as an a priori conceptual or empirical object of analysis (cf. Abrams 1988; Jessop 1990; Mitchell 1991; Scott 1998). Instead of understanding the state as a unitary actor that controls how its institutions function, my analytical concern is to identify patterns of domination and control by mapping its constitutive practices and mechanisms in order to assess its impact on and reach into the lives of ordinary peasant Rwandans. Following Das (2004, 226), I study the ways in which the institutions and practices of the state "are brought into everyday life by the representation and performance of its rules" through the individual acts of resistance of ordinary Rwandans. As such, the analysis is focused on dissecting the power of the Rwandan state in identifying the often reinforcing and sometimes contradictory mechanisms of the policy of national unity and reconciliation at the level of the ordinary citizen (analyzed more fully in chapter 4). The complex relation between the practices of national unity and reconciliation and the strategic efforts of the RPF regime to ensure that Rwandans fulfill its many demands is the central theme that winds through the pages that follow.

Mine is a "state-in-society" approach (Migdal 2001) that analyzes the multiple ways in which the state employs disciplinary tactics to make Rwandans behave in ways they might not themselves choose and in ways that confirm one's location in the social hierarchy (cf. Bourdieu 2001; Foucault 1977; Scott 1985). I am concerned with how state actors establish and maintain their power and authority in ways that serve to legitimate oppressive forms of rule while shaping people's behavior to conform and obey the myriad requirements of national unity and reconciliation—in other words, its everyday practices that serve to reinforce the image of "the state" as a discrete and relatively autonomous social institution that is constituted through everyday social practices as an aspect of the power relations that legitimate its preeminence in society (Migdal 2001, 18; Mitchell 1991, 78). As such, I analyze the Rwandan "state" as the product of Rwanda's hierarchical, status-conscious bureaucracy in which political leaders see their right to rule as natural, structured by historical patterns of domination that lead "politicians [to] treat . . . citizens as objects they can manipulate at whim to serve their parochial interests" (Habimana 2011, 354). The postgenocide Rwandan state certainly seeks to change individual behavior through its top-down, state-led practices of national unity and reconciliation to prevent a "future recurrence" of events such as the 1994 genocide (Straus and Waldorf 2011, 8). As Purdeková notes, individual Rwandans, regardless of their location in the socioeconomic hierarchy, must do more than respect the authority of the state; they must also sacrifice individual preferences and sublimate private realities to work for the greater goal of unity and reconciliation (2012a, 192–95).

Two examples further illustrate this point of disindividuation. First, Sommers recounts a story from his 2011 fieldwork in which a Rwandan government official chastised his use of the Kinyarwanda word *umutindi* in reference to his own "destitution" (2012a, 51–52). Using descriptive language related to being very poor or destitute (*umutindi*)—whether jokingly as Sommers did or otherwise—is perceived by some local officials as criticism of the government. As such, it illustrates some of the pressures poor Rwandans can experience when interacting with government officials. How can they ask for what they need if they are unable to use words that best describe their poverty with those charged to alleviate it? Second, since 2006, it has been illegal to wear open-toed shoes in any of Rwanda's cities and town. This means that the rubber flip-flops that so many Rwandans favor because of their affordability are illegal. This rule, like the many other rules that structure the everyday lives of Rwandans, makes it difficult for urban and rural poor—the almost 68 percent of the population that earns less than US$1 per day—to acquire the covered shoes they need to take their goods to market, to bring their children to school, or to access health facilities.

These are but two of the many forbidden or obligatory practices that the RPF regime demands of its citizens (see Ingelaere 2011, 74, and Sommers 2012a, 245–49, for fuller lists). Identifying such disciplinary practices allows for an understanding of what "the state" is and what "it" does from a variety of viewpoints—political elites, government bureaucrats, and nonstate actors alike—and what effects the construction of "the state" and the authority it accords its representatives has on the operation of power throughout society.

By identifying and explaining everyday and often mundane practices of the state, we learn of the routine and repetitive actions that make "the state" real in the lives of ordinary peasant Rwandans. Administrative practices define the contours of everyday life without completely capturing it, because the very process of invading people's lives generates points of resistance and opposition. It also highlights the ways in which the command-and-control approach of the RPF regime at the lower levels of the administrative structure considers ordinary folks to be "vessels" or "implementers" of government policy without their input. Rwanda's dense bureaucratic state structure is made up of "webs of people" and is best conceptualized as a "chain, with 'cascade' potential," its nexus of action being primarily at the Sector and Cell levels (Purdeková 2011, 477; see also Ingelaere 2011).[7] Chapter 4 analyzes the webs of state actors and institutions as well as the practices and mechanisms of surveillance and coercion that make up Rwanda's bureaucracy to isolate where individuals "feel" the state.

Analysis of the mundane bureaucratic and institutional practices of state authority reveals what the entity known as "the state" means for people and how it makes them feel about its near constant and disciplining presence in their daily lives. In the Rwandan case, the state has different meanings for different people, and its meaning is best determined by one's socioeconomic status and not necessarily by one's state-imposed or self-perceived ethnicity (see also Chakravarty, forthcoming).[8] This tends to mean that politically connected elites and other urban and educated Rwandans have overall a rosier perception of Rwanda's remarkable postgenocide recovery than do the majority of poor, marginal, and rural dwellers that I consulted in the course of my research. Those at the higher levels of the socioeconomic hierarchy are more likely to have benefited from Rwanda's postgenocide economic and development policies (Ansoms 2008, 2009; Ingelaere 2011). Purdeková astutely refers to those who benefit from government policies as "the captivated minority." She continues, "There is the excitement and elation of relatively privileged young people who believe the future that government paints in front of them" (2012b, 16). Indeed, it appears as if this "captivated minority" is one of the few groups to benefit from RPF rule since the genocide. Wimmer et al. (2009) find that

Rwanda has the third-highest rate of socioeconomic and political exclusion in the world (following Sudan and Syria), concluding that Rwanda "has a higher probability of a return to war than any other country in the world" (Wimmer et al., quoted in Sommers 2012a, 227). In addition, since 2006 the Rwandan economy is only adding an annual average of 8,800 private-sector jobs, instead of the 120,000 annual jobs needed to support current levels of economic and population growth (Gökgür 2012, 32)

The popular and predominant narrative of Rwanda's postgenocide success is one that is largely attributed to the visionary leadership of President Paul Kagame (1999–present).[9] And indeed, there is no denying Rwanda's robust economic growth. Under Kagame's leadership, Rwanda has become a leader on the African continent in terms of service delivery in education and health. International donors—notably the United Kingdom, the United States, the European Union, and the World Bank—consistently cite Rwanda as a country with low levels of corruption and high levels of institutional accountability (Zorbas 2011). The recovery of the formal economy has been nothing short of outstanding. Not only has urban poverty decreased as national income rises, but since 2001 the economy has continued to grow at an average of 7 percent per year (Ansoms 2011). President Kagame regularly receives international awards and accolades for his visionary leadership in Rwanda's recovery from war and genocide (Sommers 2012b). Rwanda since the 1994 genocide is a place where the government is renowned for increasing women's rights and includes the highest percentage of female parliamentarians anywhere in the world; it has also reduced corruption and overseen innovative local justice processes that have resulted in ethnic reconciliation (Burnet 2008b, 2011; Cooke 2011). President Kagame regularly boasts that less than twenty years since the 1994 genocide, peace and security reign again for all Rwandans (Kagame 2011, 2012). By most accounts, under the visionary leadership of Paul Kagame, Rwanda is an African success story to be admired and emulated by other post-conflict societies (Crisafulli and Redmond 2012; Clinton Foundation 2009; Dagan 2011; Gourevitch 1998, 2009; Kinzer 2008; UN-OHRLLS 2006, 130; Warren 2009; Zakaria 2009). The question that is rarely asked is: to whose benefit are Rwanda's economic gains accruing?

At the same time, Rwanda's postgenocide rapid reconstruction and reconciliation have been criticized for its heavy-handedness (Ingelaere 2011; Longman 2011; Reyntjens 2004, 2011. For the impact of the strategy on youth, see Sommers 2012a, 143–55). The RPF seeks to dominate all levels of sociopolitical life, from the office of the president down to the lowest levels of administration through its policy of "decentralization" (MINALOC 2004, 2006, 2007). The government maintains a tight rein on political expression and, in 2003, banned any public manifestation of "ethnic divisionism" (between Tutsi and Hutu), "promoting genocide ideology" (against Tutsi), or "preaching genocide negationism" (that is, questioning claims that only Tutsi died in 1994). These laws are vaguely worded and arbitrarily applied to anyone who makes public statements that the government perceives as critical. They also have the effect of removing ethnic Hutu from the public sphere as the genocide ideology and negationist laws represent a near total and "undifferentiated accusation" of presumed Hutu participation in the 1994 genocide (Chakravarty, forthcoming; Waldorf 2009, 2011). The government also targets journalists as the purveyors of divisionist opinion and strictly controls civil society organizations and other forms of associational life, including churches and mosques (Adamczyk 2012; Gready 2011; Longman 2011; Sommers 2012a). While Human Rights Watch and other international human rights advocacy groups highlight the government's lack of commitment to basic human rights such as the right to life and to free expression, President Kagame stresses the importance of state control and authority to maintain the ethnic unity that he claims to be the basis of present and future security of Rwanda.[10]

When confronted with such starkly contrasting points of view, it is important not to throw up one's hands and declare that the truth lies hopelessly somewhere between the polar extremes of Rwanda's glowing economic success and its denial of political liberties. Such an approach is misguided for analysts on both sides of the divide. Since both sides offer some insights into how "the state" manifests in the lives of ordinary peasant Rwandans through its practices of authority and control, my research methodology matters greatly. It is one that focuses on process rather than conclusive outcomes. As such, my analysis is best understood as a snapshot of everyday life in 2006 for a handful of ordinary peasant Rwandans resident in the southern region of the country.

Political Ethnography:
Identifying Everyday Acts of Resistance

My research joins a growing movement within political science that draws on ethnographic methods to illuminate different ways of analyzing the everyday practices of state power. Political scientists have fruitfully employed ethnographic approaches to "get close" to people's everyday experiences. For interpretivists, ethnography is "the art and science of describing a group or culture" (Geertz 1973, 5). For positivists, it is a tool used to explain the causal story (e.g., Allina-Pisano 2007). Despite this epistemological distinction, both camps agree on a minimal definition of ethnography as "the process of learning through exposure to or involvement in the day-to-day or routine activities of participants in the research setting" (Schensul et al. 1999, 91).

In order to bring in the everyday acts of resistance of ordinary peasant Rwandans, I drew upon ethnographic methods: living in southern Rwanda for six months in 2006; learning Kinyarwanda, the national language; participating in daily life through everyday interactions and conversations; observing events and places such as meetings, festivals, *gacaca* justice trials, *ingando* citizenship re-education camps, and so on; examining gossip, rumors, proverbs, and jokes for their underlying meaning; recording field notes to produce everyday accounts of sociopolitical life; and letting trust and emotional engagement be of benefit to the research.

As a tool for political analysis, I understand ethnography as both an activity and a sensibility, an approach that squarely situates my research within the interpretative tradition of political science (Schwartz-Shea and Yanow 2012). It is closely tied to fieldwork, where the researcher physically and emotionally enters the space she seeks to understand. Ethnography seeks to allow "the original researcher and subsequent readers to make sense of local knowledge, expert knowledge and the researcher's and reader's own knowledge (among others) in a manner that has potential to accord more equal weighting among different bases" (Pader 2006, 163). The ethnographic stance is a commitment to what Geertz calls "thickness" to produce meaning through nuance, texture, and detail (Geertz 1973, 5–6, 9–10). This should not be read as "exhaustiveness," as there is an inherent hubris in seeking to analyze every nook and cranny of a given subject. Instead, my ethnographic stance is an epistemological statement that aims to portray ordinary people as "knowers" and as "recorders" of their own life stories, rather than to build on existing portrayals of these individuals as "powerless" victims of the 1994 genocide, willing "to do whatever the RPF tells them to do" (interview with RPF official 2006). Such an approach renders visible the power relations that structure the ways in which the peasant Rwandans I consulted understand and react to the options available to them in the face of the official goals of national unity and reconciliation.

My approach to political ethnography is grounded in an understanding of "knowledge," be it the local knowledge of ordinary Rwandans like the folks I consulted, that of Rwandan elites, or that of the "specialist" knowledge of outsiders as historically situated and enmeshed in relationships of power. Knowledge is socially constructed, meaning that the categories and classifica-tions that refer to particular phenomena—for example, who is a "survivor" of the genocide and who is a "perpetrator"—are manufactured for political gain rather than naturally occurring as a result of the 1994 genocide (more on these constructed categories in chapters 5 and 6).

An ethnographic approach also positions resistance as an analytical category. Everyday resistance is a useful concept as it highlights the scope and nature of power in most forms of relationship (Abu-Lughod 1990, 42–43; Ortner 1995, 175). I conceptualize acts of resistance as acts that individuals undertake knowing that there is a risk of sanction from "the state." This means not that individuals necessarily violate a law against the act in question but more simply that they take a calculated risk to maintain or enlarge their position vis-à-vis the state. In the relationship of power, the dominant group will do what is necessary to maintain its positions of power, which in turn gives the subordinate many grounds to resist the relationship (Scott 1990, 9). Indeed, the ways in which the RPF, as the dominant political class, justifies the routine repression of its subordinates — ordinary Rwandans as well as its political opponents and journalists — emerge more clearly when everyday acts of resistance are identified. This also exposes the exaggerations of the RPF, who, like members of the Habyarimana regime before them, strategically situates peasant people as "passive," "powerless," and "like infants" to justify continued authoritarian control of the population in the name of peace and security (Desrosiers and Thomson 2011).

Routine surveillance is a tactic of the RPF regime, and it includes exaggerating the "urgent need to reeducate [ordinary Rwandans] on the purpose and goal of national unity and reconciliation" (interview with Rwanda's ombudsman 2006). Government surveillance in the name of national unity and reconciliation seeks to justify the economic and political domination of the RPF. It allows the RPF regime — as Rwanda's current elite — to maintain the barriers between social classes and ethnic groups that its vision of national unity and reconciliation claims to eliminate. An ethnographic approach reveals that peasant people are far from apolitical, "passive," and "ignorant" individuals who need to be "taught what it means to be Rwandan" (interview with Rwanda's ombudsman 2006). This challenges exaggerated claims by the elite that ordinary peasant people lack the necessary consciousness to actively and productively engage in politics or that they need to be "educated" or "sensitized" if they are to be adequately equipped to do so (Desrosiers and Thomson 2011; M. C. Newbury 1980; Purdeková 2011, 2012a). The nonconsciousness of ordinary people is assumed to render them unable to participate in the political arena, which in turn leads to the conclusion that "obedience is part of Rwandan political culture" (NURC 2004, 16).

An ethnographic sensibility further reveals the everyday lived realities of ordinary peasant Rwandans to show that the forms of obedience they practice are tactical as they seek to limit their interaction with the imposed requirements of the policy of national unity and reconciliation. It also opens up an opportunity to both acknowledge and explain numerous instances of resistance to state power in Rwanda since precolonial times. For example, African Rights (2003g) shows how peasants ignored the orders of elites to burn Tutsi bodies during the genocide. Burnet (2007) states that peasants in southern Rwanda refused to cut down their banana plantations to plant crops that the post-1994 government considered more productive. Des Forges (1986, 2011) analyzes instances of resistance against the German colonial authority as well as against the Tutsi king in the late nineteenth and early twentieth centuries, while Berger (1981) analyzes local resistance to state expansionism led by Rwandan religious elites in the precolonial period. Longman (1995) describes how peasants burned woods to resist elite directives before the genocide. C. Newbury (1992) shows how peasant farmers destroyed coffee bushes in the late 1980s and early 1990s to grow food for their families instead. Burnet (2012, 121–26) analyzes the ways in which Rwandans resist state-imposed silences about what happened to them and their loved ones during the 1994 genocide.

Situating Lived Experiences of State Power in Postgenocide Rwanda

This book opens up the life worlds of peasant Rwandans since the 1994 genocide. Specifically, it analyzes the interactions with state power of thirty-seven ordinary peasant Rwandans at the lowest rungs of society—notably the destitute (*abatindi*) and the poor (*abekene*). Taken together, these groups represent approximately 66 percent of Rwanda's peasantry (Howe and McKay 2007, 200). Eighty-two percent of Rwanda's entire population lives in rural areas and is considered by the government to be peasants (World Bank 2012). The Rwandan peasantry is made of four categories of differing degrees of poverty (see table 1 for the full list). Lowest in the socioeconomic hierarchy are those living in "abject" poverty (*abatindi nyakujya*; sing. *umutindi nyakujya*); next highest are the "destitute" (*abatindi*; sing. *umutindi*); above them are those identified simply as "poor" (*abakene*; sing. *umukene*). Taken together, these three categories represent "the poorest of the poor" in Rwanda and make up, in socioeconomic terms, the majority of those living in rural areas. The fourth and highest category of the peasantry consists of the poor with economic means (*abakene bifashije*; sing. *umukene wifashije*), the socioeconomic class of many elected local officials. *Abakene bifashije* represent about 14 percent of the 82 percent of Rwandans identified by the government as peasants (Howe and McKay 2007, 200).

The analysis that follows also underscores the historical continuities in both the nature of socioeconomic hierarchy and elite governance in Rwanda to show that the policy of national unity and reconciliation does not represent "a new way forward to assure peace and security for all Rwandans since the genocide" (President Paul Kagame, quoted in Jha and Yadav 2004, 69). Chapter 2 shows that a careful reading of the precolonial, colonial, and pregenocide

Table 1. Rwandan socioeconomic classifications

Group	Socioeconomic status
umutindi nyakujya (pl., *abatindi nyakujya*)	Abject poor/most vulnerable
umutindi (pl. *abatindi*)	Destitute
umukene (pl. *abakene*)	Poor
umukene wifashije (pl. *abakene bifashije*)	Salaried poor
umukungu (pl. *abakungu*)	Rich without money
umukire (pl. *abakire*)	Rich

Source: Ministry of Finance and Economic Planning (MINECOFIN) 2001.

literature highlights the deep historical roots of the policy. The complex machinery of tactics, hierarchies, and direct and indirect practices of control operates to ensure the integrity of the state system. The policy of national unity and reconciliation, which has its roots in the precolonial governance structures, highlights the ethnic unity of Rwandans under Tutsi monarchs with no regard for the sociopolitical complexities of the court (Berger 1981; Des Forges 2011; Vansina 2004). The policy also adopts an official history that starts with an already established Tutsi monarchy, glossing over Rwanda's distant origins and romanticizing the ethnic harmony of the precolonial period.[11] It also effectively erases the presence of ethnic Twa in Rwandan history and undermines their legal standing as an indigenous population (Adamczyk 2011; Beswick 2011; Thomson 2009b).

Individual experiences of the 1994 genocide are tied to both personal histories and the grand narrative of national unity and reconciliation. Understanding these individual experiences is important as there are multiple and sometimes contradictory layers of victimhood and perpetratorhood that go back for decades among individual Rwandans, rarely meshing with government-imposed practices of national unity and reconciliation. Most notable of these is the RPF's focus on creating a unified Rwandan identity or "Rwandan-ness." Rwandan-ness is the official rejection of ethnic identity—of being Hutu, Tutsi, or Twa—in favor of creating "one Rwanda for all Rwandans." In attempting to wipe away ethnicity, the policy produces two broad simplifications that portray all Tutsi (whether or not they were in Rwanda during the genocide) as innocent victims or "survivors" and all Hutu (whether or not they participated in the genocide) as guilty perpetrators (known in 2006 as *génocidaires*) and "violent killers who need to be reeducated (on what it means to be 'Rwandan')" (NURC 2007d, 2007e, 2007f).

Recent studies have produced insightful theoretical work on individual motives for committing acts of genocide against neighbors, friends, and family to show that the genocide is not rooted in "long-standing ethnic hatred between Hutu and Tutsi," as the RPF contends (NURC 2004, 19). Instead, recent micro-level studies show that individual decisions to commit acts of genocide are grounded in intra-ethnic social pressure or personal grudges and in feelings of fear, insecurity, and anger, as well as poverty (André and Platteau 1998; Fujii 2009; Mironko 2004; Straus 2006; Uvin 1998; Verwimp 2005). As a whole, these analyses constitute a significant contribution to the microdynamics of mass violence grounded in both local knowledge and analysis of the prevailing social and political climate in a context of Rwanda's civil war (1990–94). In particular, Fujii's (2009) research shows that the collective categories of killers, survivors, bystanders, and rescuers are often incomplete, with individuals frequently inhabiting a variety of these categories. This has practical implications for how practices of justice and reconciliation play out at the level of the individual. Straus's work challenges the wisdom of the government's postgenocide strategy of "maximal prosecution" of ordinary Hutu men for crimes that many committed either under duress or as a survival strategy (2006, 244).

Together these works also speak to the climate of intimidation and fear on one hand and the coercive social pressures on the other that left some ordinary Hutu with little option but to commit acts of genocide against their Tutsi brethren when instructed to do so by their political and military leaders. Read in conjunction with existing knowledge of the prevailing political climate and the RPF stratagems to gain state power, this microlevel research also challenges dominant RPF narratives about the genocide and the RPF's role in both precipitating and stopping it (Dallaire 2003; Prunier 1997, 356–89). In one-on-one interviews with senior members of the RPF's inner circle, Kuperman (2004, 63) identifies mass killing as a possible response of the then rebel RPF to the demands of the Habyarimana regime for political and military power sharing, with the broader goal of state power trumping other considerations, including loss of life among the Tutsi. Ruzibiza's (2005) recounting of his role in downing the plane that killed then President Habyarimana, sparking the genocide that ended with the RPF taking state power, is particularly damning to the RPF's version about its role in "stopping" the genocide.

The official RPF regime position is that Hutu extremists within the Habyarimana government shot down the plane because they feared Habyarimana's apparent willingness to share state power with the RPF (Gourevitch 1996, 184–86; NURC 2004, 45; Reed 1996, 480). Challenging the regime's official narrative becomes even more important as the postgenocide government amends its version of events, presumably for an uninitiated audience, and its account of its role in the genocide (see Pottier 2002 for analysis of the media savoir-faire of the RPF). It is well documented that the genocide occurred in the context of civil war (1990–94) and that the RPF entered Rwanda from Uganda on October 1, 1990, with the stated purpose of overthrowing the Habyarimana government and gaining the right of return for Tutsi refugees (Straus 2006).

Research prepared by international organizations can also be productively read through an ethnographic lens in seeking out points of reference about why current state practices of national unity and reconciliation are so damaging for a large number of peasant Rwandans. African Rights (1994) produced a significant volume that is grounded in local testimonies and eyewitness accounts, and numerous nongovernmental organizations (NGOs) based in Rwanda (e.g., *Cahiers lumière et société* 1995, 1996; *Dialogue* 2004) have compiled similar accounts. Combined, these accounts provide useful empirical evidence on individual experiences of the genocide across time and space. African Rights has documented individual experiences of genocide in its reports on the history of genocide in various administrative sectors (African Rights 2000, 2003a, 2003b, 2003c, 2003d, 2003e, 2003f, 2003g, 2005). The reports also reveal some of the silences that the recent administrative restructuring has created in showing how the *gacaca* jurisdictions do not necessarily overlap with pregenocide administrative units. This is a significant development, as the postgenocide government claims that it reconfigured Rwanda's administrative boundaries to "decentralize the power structures that led to genocide" and to "foster ethnic unity as people will have to live together" (field notes 2006). In practice, it appears more likely that the RPF has redrawn administrative boundaries to further consolidate its own power and to enable it to deploy administrative and security personnel in all corners of the country (Purdeková 2011; Reyntjens 2004, 187–94; 2011, 8–18).

Human Rights Watch (HRW), in a meticulously prepared report compiled under the supervision of Alison Des Forges (1999), produced the most complete and thorough analysis of the genocide and its historical antecedents, including an analysis of the strategy of genocide from the inner circles of the Habyarimana regime, through its military and militia groups, down to the lowest level of administrative *fonctionnaire* (bureaucrat). HRW continues to provide excellent locally situated analysis of the causes of genocide as new evidence comes to light (e.g., HRW 2006a, 2006b), just as it has sought to understand the postgenocide social and political order and its impact on ordinary people, notably the rural poor (e.g., HRW 2000, 2001b, 2008, 2011). HRW maintains its "watchdog" practices, much to the chagrin of the current government, in reporting on key developments, including the 2003 and 2010 presidential elections and the political and social climate before and after (HRW 2003a, 2010). Along with Amnesty International (AI), HRW has released a multitude of reports, press releases, and briefing papers that are replete with locally grounded collective and individual testimonies that speak to the everyday challenges of peasant people as they seek to navigate the postgenocide social and political order.

Accounts from journalists add nuance to our understanding of how individuals survived the genocide, notably from the position of Tutsi survivors of the genocide. These accounts are not representative of individual experiences of the genocide but instead are better interpreted for how they present the stories of individual Rwandans (e.g., Gourevitch 1998; Keane 1995; Koff 2004). These accounts provide insight into the nature of the moral discourse surrounding the genocide that lumps all Hutu men into the category of evil perpetrators and presents all Tutsi survivors as hapless victims. An ethnographic reading both highlights the folly of collectively victimizing perpetrators and survivors and reveals the many silences that such an approach entails (see Burnet 2012 on "amplified silence" since the genocide). In addition, these journalistic accounts further complicate efforts to understand the multiple motivations that individuals had for killing and tend to conflate acts of genocide against Tutsi and politically moderate Hutu by militias, the military, and some ordinary Rwandans with the killing of civilians in the course of the war between the Forces armées rwandaises (FAR) and the RPF (1990–94) and the killing of civilians (Hutu, Tutsi, and Twa) by the RPF in the immediate postgenocide period (1994–96).

Equally subjective is the witness literature, meaning the corpus of personal stories written by individuals who survived the genocide (e.g., Aegis Trust 2006; Hatzfeld 2005a, 2007; Ilibagiza 2006; Kayitesi 2004; Mujawayo and Belhaddad 2004, 2006; Mukagasana 1997, 1999, 2001; Mukasonga 2006; Rucyahana 2007). Taken together, these works provide direct testimony of the experience of genocide and provide some insight and a greater sense of context for those interpreting individual experiences of genocide. Of particular value are testimonies that focus on the reconciliation process from the perspective of survivors, including critiques of the *gacaca* court trials that show that what the government perceives as sincere reconciliation is actually forced coexistence between survivors and perpetrators (see also the survivor stories published by Médecins sans frontières [MSF] [MSF 2003, 2004a, 2004b, 2006a, 2006b, 2006c, 2006d]). Nonetheless, these accounts are to be read with caution, as most of them present individual stories of survival that not only are designed to shock and horrify the reader but also draw on simplified versions of history that make it sometimes difficult for the uninformed reader to situate these narratives in broader context. As a whole, these books are written by members of Rwanda's educated elite (save Hatzfeld, an outsider), who write authoritatively of individual experiences without adequately situating their interlocutors within Rwanda's social hierarchy and without due regard for other salient forms of identity (e.g., gender, occupation, political affiliation, and class) that could have shaped individuals' chances to survive and that consequently enhance or constrain their ability to reconcile with family, friends, and neighbors.

Testimonial accounts from Hutu voices add much-needed nuance to our understanding of how many ordinary peasant people lived through the genocide and of the diversity of their experiences of survival in its aftermath, when millions of Hutu quit Rwanda, sometimes forcibly, to refugee camps in neighboring countries, notably in eastern Zaïre (now Democratic Republic of the Congo). They were later returned to Rwanda, often against their will, by the RPF and/or the United Nations (Hatzfeld 2005b, 2009; Lyon and Straus 2006; Umutesi 2004). Umutesi's (2004) work is particularly powerful, as her story is representative of the lived experiences of hundreds of thousands of individuals who fled the genocide in Rwanda only to find themselves trapped in crowded, unsafe refugee camps. As such, it is an important antidote to the simplified historical narratives of Tutsi as the only legitimate "survivors." It provides a more complex version of reality, showing the multiple and fluctuating constraints that shaped individuals' options for survival. Umutesi's story is also representative of the everyday experiences that all Rwandans—Hutu, Tutsi, and Twa alike—lived through before, during, and after the genocide. Tutsi are rightfully and correctly survivors of genocide as they were targeted by virtue of their ethnicity, but all Rwandans are survivors of conflict, jostled and shaped by events over which they had little control. Umutesi's account also shows the folly of analysts new to the region who rely on stereotypical generalizations about ethnic conflict and simplified accounts that seek to explain the genocide in the language of atavistic ethnic enmity.

Paul Rusesabagina's *No Ordinary Man* (2006) is an example of a "Hutu" version of events that the government actively tried to suppress by denouncing him as "a liar" and "a genocide revisionist" for his account of saving more than 1,200 Tutsi lives during the 1994 genocide (field notes 2006; also Adhikari 2008; Waldorf 2009). His book, which was made into the Hollywood movie *Hotel Rwanda*, illustrates the importance of personal networks and the strategic use of resources as salient determinants of survival in narrating how he negotiated and bargained with senior members of the Habyarimana regime to save the lives of Tutsi who sought refuge at the Hôtel des Mille Collines in central Kigali. Much to the chagrin of the RPF, his account has been internationally acclaimed and Rusesabagina deemed a "hero" in North America and Europe for his actions during the genocide. He has also used international forums to speak out about the current political climate of authoritarianism in Rwanda and to call for a truth and reconciliation commission to bring RPF crimes committed during the genocide to book. The RPF has responded by saying that those soldiers who broke rank and perpetrated revenge crimes against individuals are being dealt with "accordingly" (field notes 2006). The RPF has further contended that Rusesabagina is lying because "there are no *Mille Collines* survivors" and that his status as a hero is something that "only the people of Rwanda can decide" (field notes 2006).

Rusesabagina's international notoriety and the government's reaction to it matter because they are emblematic of how the RPF seeks to control the political landscape in postgenocide Rwanda (cf. Adhikari 2008). The RPF works hard and employs a variety of tactics to ensure that its version of "how things really are in [postgenocide] Rwanda" is the only one that circulates and the one presented to foreign audiences (interview with RPF official 2006). Rusesabagina is considered "an enemy of the state" because his book and his movie directly challenge "the moral authority of the RPF" to rebuild Rwanda in its vision of national unity and reconciliation (field notes 2006; also Waldorf 2009). The RPF continues to discredit Rusesabagina to international and domestic audiences alike and has sponsored the publication of a book, *Hotel Rwanda or the Tutsi Genocide as Seen by Hollywood* (Ndahiro and Rutazibwa 2008). The book, which was written by President Kagame's press secretary and a senior member of Rwanda's Information Agency, alleges that Rusesabagina is "trading for personal riches" and that his account "distorts the true history of what happened during the genocide" (Kezio-Musoke 2008, 1).

Ndahiro and Rutazibwa's book is also part of the growing list of "approved by the RPF" publications that are produced by domestic think tanks, nongovernmental organizations, and government offices. The RPF sees itself as the guardian of "Rwanda's culture and destiny" and has subsequently made "its own contribution to the crafting of an intellectual image about [Rwanda] and its heritage" (Pottier 2002, 109). To this end, once-exiled intellectuals, many of whom have returned to Rwanda since 1994 and who now hold positions of authority in government, universities, and churches, have produced numerous publications. These publications have the RPF seal of approval and are useful as they reveal at length the RPF's interpretation of Rwandan history and the causes of the 1994 genocide.

The substantive content of this body of work is remarkable only in the similarity of its message wherein ethnicity is deemphasized and historical unity among Rwanda's ethnic groups prior to the arrival of colonialists is invoked to justify current policies, notably the policy of national unity and reconciliation. The leading example of this is Jean-Paul Kimonyo's *Revue critique des interprétations du conflit rwandais* (2000), a Center for Conflict Management (CCM) publication and a document that numerous elites told me during my reeducation that I "must read" as it is the "truth about how people came to kill one another." Other noteworthy examples include the reports and surveys produced by the CCM, the Institute of Research and Dialogue for Peace (IRDP), the National Unity and Reconciliation Commission (NURC), the National Service of *Gacaca* Jurisdictions (NSGJ), the Human Rights Commission (HRC), and the Office of the President. Read together, these works not only reveal the official narrative of national unity and reconciliation but also point to reasons behind the paucity of published works from Rwandan academics on the causes and consequences of the 1994 genocide. This is perhaps not surprising, given that "the issues are too fresh, the society too divided, the community of scholars too small, and the political situation too tense" (Uvin 2001, 76).

Organization of the Book

The thirty-seven ordinary peasant people from southern Rwanda who participated in my research in 2006 have four things in common: (1) they think of themselves as "survivors" of the 1994 genocide, regardless of their ethnicity; (2) they are poor and live in rural areas across southern Rwanda; most are landless and are unable to meet the minimum basic needs of their families; (3) they have been required, in most cases forced, by the government to perform acts of national unity and reconciliation and have tried to resist in indirect and non-confrontational ways; and (4) they have acted or spoken against the postgenocide government despite the known risks. Through a detailed exploration of these four elements, the book identifies the various forms of resistance employed by ordinary Rwandans as they seek to rebuild their lives in the face of a strong and centralized state power. Chapter 1 provides an overview of the methods used to research the everyday lives of ordinary peasant Rwandans as they seek to rebuild their lives following the 1994 genocide. In particular, the chapter discusses site selection, access to research participants, interview procedures, and safeguards, as well as how I interpret the raw narratives of peasant Rwandans from across southern Rwanda. The focus is on my use of life history interviewing.

Chapters 2 and 3 contextualize the historical role of the state in everyday life to introduce readers to the structural foundation of political hierarchy and socioeconomic stratification that characterizes the Rwandan state. I ask for your patience as both chapters 2 and 3 lay the groundwork that allows for detailed and bottom-up analysis of the policy of national unity and reconciliation that begins in chapter 4 and of everyday resistance to its demands in chapters 5 and 6. Chapter 2 begins the historical detour to identify the various practices of elite contestation for state power to highlight that the policy of national unity and reconciliation is rooted in particular mechanisms and practices of state power. It also analyzes the historical foundation of contemporary forms of sociopolitical exclusion to introduce the reader to the traditional patron-client forms of oppression that the RPF government relies on to rationalize the version of history found in the policy of national unity and reconciliation. The chapter further illustrates the ways in which successive regimes in Rwanda have manipulated ethnic identity to seize or consolidate their power. Finally, chapter 2 introduces the reader to the broader historical context in which the policy of national unity and reconciliation operates. The purpose is to illustrate the ways in which the policy fits within a long-standing pattern of political elites maintaining their power through practices that result in obvious assaults on the individual dignity of the ordinary "masses."

Chapter 3 brings in the experience of ordinary peasant Rwandans with state power into the 1990s. The aim is to deconstruct the official version of the genocide found in the policy of national unity and reconciliation to illustrate how it seeks to both simplify and shroud the individual acts that, in the aggregate, make up the 1994 genocide. The genocide did not occur in a power vacuum, nor was it the result of ancient tribal hatred, as the current government contends. This chapter illustrates the ways in which the RPF-led government has sought to silence dissent and control the political sphere since taking power in July 1994. The chapter also examines the extent to which the policy of national unity and reconciliation suppresses open and frank discussion by Rwandans of the physical and structural violence of the 1990s, including that meted out by the RPF in the context of the civil war that began in October 1990 and ended with the launch of the genocide in April 1994. Chapter 3 further illustrates the extent to which the policy of national unity and reconciliation fails to acknowledge how Rwandans of different backgrounds recall and make sense of the various forms of physical violence they experienced between 1990 and 2000, when the RPF-led government officially adopted the policy of national unity and reconciliation.

Chapter 4 identifies and analyzes the various practices of control and coercion of the policy of national unity and reconciliation to illustrate the extent to which it is a source of oppression in the daily lives of rural Rwandans. In deconstructing the various practices and mechanisms of national unity and reconciliation that make up the system of power that the policy embodies, the chapter makes clear the extent to which the RPF controls the political and social landscape in postgenocide Rwanda. Chapter 4 sets the stage for the analysis of the everyday acts of resistance of ordinary peasant Rwandans living in the south that are the subject of both chapters 5 and 6 as it sets out the discursive and structural elements of the policy of national unity and reconciliation that they seek to resist.

Chapter 5 introduces the everyday acts of resistance of ordinary peasants resident in southern Rwanda. Specifically, the chapter explores the dynamics between local government officials and ordinary Rwandans as both sides of the relationship endeavor to perform acts of national unity and reconciliation. It situates the discussion within the Africanist resistance literature to show how an analytical focus on the everyday acts of resistance of peasant Rwandans illustrates how they are not only enmeshed in but also positioned differently in relation to the mechanisms of national unity and reconciliation. I discuss the generalities of resistance—from talking back to a local police officer (irreverent compliance) to defying orders to remember and mourn lives lost during the 1994 genocide in accordance with state directives. In this chapter, we see how resistance includes maintaining silence (withdrawn muteness), as well as identifying when ordinary people push to open up space to bring dignity to their lives or the lives of their loved ones. The chapter also illustrates how acts of everyday resistance include "staying on the sidelines" in tactical and clever ways to avoid having to perform state-prescribed acts of national unity and reconciliation. The chapter demonstrates that where the policy of national unity and reconciliation forces peasant Rwandans to live within its lies, they in turn confront it in ways that seek to restore their personal dignity while subtly attempting to live their own truth of what they experienced before, during, and after the genocide.

Chapter 6 explores one specific mechanism of national unity and reconciliation—the now-closed *gacaca* (ga-cha-cha) courts. Specifically, it illustrates the extent to which the postgenocide government and its agents controlled the *gacaca* process. The chapter analyzes the power of the state and its efforts, through appointed local officials, to control the *gacaca* process to identify the myriad constraints that the policy of national unity and reconciliation imposes on individuals and how this limits individual opportunity for resistance. It focuses mainly on the everyday acts of resistance of Tutsi survivors, as the primary actors in the *gacaca* process, to demonstrate the subtle and creative ways in which they revealed their discontent toward government policy before the courts. The chapter finds that the *gacaca* courts were more than an instrument of state power that created an atmosphere of fear and insecurity in the everyday lives of many ordinary Rwandans; the courts also helped the RPF consolidate its political power in ways that are contrary to the stated goals of the policy of national unity and reconciliation.

The conclusion summarizes the argument while highlighting its utility in assessing the likelihood of a return to mass political violence in contemporary Rwanda. It also focuses on the implications of the research for theories of the state, highlighting the power of the state to impose its will even in the face of individual resistance. By identifying and analyzing the practices of the state, I

assess forms of domination that condition obedience by virtue of political authority from the perspective of those subject to what they themselves perceive
to be an illegitimate form of state power (Weber 1946, 80–86). The conclusion
analyzes the methodological importance of bringing in the individual lived
experiences of ordinary peasant people. It also examines what the everyday
acts of resistance of ordinary peasant Rwandans teach us about the broader
stability of the policy of national unity and reconciliation as the basis for Rwanda's
"present and future peace and security" (interview with NURC official 2006).
Finally, the conclusion highlights some areas for further comparative research
given the potential for renewed mass political violence in Rwanda.

A Note on Field Notes and Interviews

Readers will have already noticed that I distinguish "interviews" from "field
notes" in the text. I do this to help readers understand and interpret who has
said what. The material gathered in formal interviews, which I define narrowly
to include only the stories and observations of my thirty-seven research participants, usually in the presence of a translator and in full view of family, neighbors, and even local government officials, are cited as "interviews," while the
experiences and observations in my everyday interactions with Rwandans from
all walks of life—peasants and elites alike—that I inscribed every evening in the
format of "field notes" are cited that way. These distinctions are used so that
the reader can make sense of how I turned personal narratives into "findings,"
using both descriptive accounts of everyday life in postgenocide Rwanda from
a variety of actors and my own observations to reveal broad patterns of state
activity from the perspective of the ordinary peasant Rwandans I consulted. I
maintain different standards of consent for state elites as I was almost always
the weaker party in the exchange. Interacting with them was a perfunctory part
of the research process as there were always layers of administrative approval
required to access the remote areas where ordinary Rwandans live. In the early
stages of the research, I had to cultivate rapport and trust with local officials in
order to be allowed to enter rural regions within the bailiwick of the official in
question.

    I also ascribe the observations and experiences of state agents, be they local
officials or government elites in Kigali, to the "field note" category, as most of
my interactions with them were unplanned informal exchanges that took place
as part of my reeducation process (Thomson 2011d). I had conversations with
representatives of the Ministries of Defense, Foreign Affairs, Finance, Gender,
Internal Security, Justice, Local Government, and Youth, Sports, and Culture;
the attorney general; the head of the *gacaca* courts; judges on the Supreme
Court; the heads of the Constitutional Reform, Human Rights, National Unity

and Reconciliation, and National AIDS Control Commissions and of the Office of the Ombudsman; leaders of the RPF; and Catholic, Pentecostal, Presbyterian, and Muslim leaders. Material gathered from these formal interviews before my research was stopped is cited as interviews with a representative of a particular government ministry or body (e.g., "interview with NURC official 2006" or "interview with senior RPF official 2006"). Pseudonyms are used throughout the text. As an additional safeguard against any potential government backlash or reprisal against the peasant Rwandans who participated in the research, I do not cite the specific date or location of interviews.

1

Bringing in Peasant Rwandans through Life History Interviewing

In studying peasant Rwandans as active subjects, my research is designed to allow for inquiry into their past, present, and future. The task is not to predict but rather to illustrate the knowledge that peasant Rwandans possess as a result of their lived experiences and to situate those individual realities within a broader historical, cultural, and institutional context. At issue is how state practices and mechanisms of national unity and reconciliation affect people's relationship to the state and its agents. The research does not seek to establish a knowable "truth" but instead illustrates what counts as truth, who or what evokes it, how it circulates, and who gains and loses by particular nominations of what is true, real, and significant. The research brings in thirty-seven peasant Rwandans as "knowers" of their own life stories, rather than building on existing portrayals of these individuals as powerless victims. Life history interviews are the backbone of the research, and this chapter focuses on the techniques and procedures of conducting life history interviews in the course of interviewees' everyday life, as well as the challenge of translating these experiences into knowledge. This approach is developed over four sections. I first conceptualize life history interviews as a method to identify personal stories; I then discuss the choice of southern Rwanda as the research site, the process of identifying the individuals who shared their stories with me, and the broader context of discreet government surveillance. In the third section, I set out the procedures I used to conduct life history interviews with ordinary peasant Rwandans. I also address specific ethical and practical challenges and solutions that arose in the research process. The last section sets out my approach to interpretative research and the methods used to analyze the stories told to me in the course of the research.

Conceptualizing Life History Interviewing

I use the life history interview method as a way to bring in the life stories of ordinary peasant Rwandans to both counter and contextualize the official narrative of national unity and reconciliation. Through life history interviewing, we learn more than how they see themselves in relation to others—we also see how they represent their own lived experiences of violence. As Plummer writes, "stories are the pathways to understanding the bases of identity" (1995, 19). The narrative approach that is inherent to life history interviewing has much to offer political scientists as they provide a way to make sense of language, including that which is not spoken (Riessman 1990). In addition to increasing readers' awareness of a variety of viewpoints and opinions, life history interviews provide ways to understand the interactions that occur among individuals and groups— important insights when seeking to understand and explain any society, let alone a postconflict one (Brounéus 2008; Jackson 1998; Plummer 1995, 2001). They are also useful in helping us understand the art of truth telling about life under authoritarian rule (Bilbija et al. 2005).

With their capacity to contextualize and situate individual stories within broader societal discourses, both symbolic and material, life history interviews provide much-needed nuance to the dominant narrative of national unity and reconciliation as crafted and forcibly maintained by the RPF-led government. Life history interviews are able to provide this contextualized nuance through the stories that ordinary people tell (McCabe and Bliss 2003). As a method of knowledge production, life history interviews do not "ignore the politics of narratives and the extent to which they support or contest social structures and practices" (Jackson 1998, 62). The knowledge produced from life history interviews with ordinary people does more than just reflect their lived reality; it also challenges taken-for-granted beliefs, assertions, and assumptions of life before, during, and after the 1994 genocide, such as those found in the RPF's policy of national unity and reconciliation (Worthington 1996). These histories also highlight the importance of understanding that lives lived through violence do not neatly correspond to the conceptual boundaries of "pre-" and "post-" conflict periods. Instead, individual experiences of violence reside in specific socio-historical and political legacies that in turn shape postconflict "peace" processes. As Nordstrom notes, "War doesn't end and peace begin in a unilinear process. . . . Peace begins in the front-line actions of rebuilding the possibility of self (which violence has sought to undermine) and society (which massacres and destruction have sought to undermine)" (2004, 183–84). In situating the lived experiences of peasant Rwandan men and women, my research privileges their individual agency, circumscribed as it is, in producing a text that is grounded in the narratives that they use to "explain to outsiders what practices, places or symbols mean to them" (Young 1997, 72). This is accomplished by retaining an awareness of the socioeconomic conditions and the broader political context in which lives are lived as one considers how culture and social structures shape the stories that life history interviewees tell (Lawler 2002).

Site Selection and "Sample"

As I sought to uncover the everyday experiences of Rwandans from all ethnic groups—Tutsi, Hutu, and Twa—before, during, and after the 1994 genocide, it was important that research participants live in and be surrounded by more or less a largely unchanging group of people. This was my primary motivation in basing the research in southern Rwanda, home to the largest pregenocide Tutsi population (Des Forges 1999, 432, 489, 593; Guichaoua 2005, 19–21). Many Rwandan communities have undergone profound changes as a result of the civil war of 1990–94, the genocide, massive population displacement during and after the genocide, government pressure to relocate to *imidugudu* (villages) since the genocide, and the January 2006 administrative reorganization of the country (HRW 2001b). Villages are not a traditional feature of the Rwandan landscape, as rural folks live in dispersed homesteads (see fig. 1); government efforts to relocate individuals to villages since the genocide have been met with much resistance, with Tutsi in the south the most vocal about their unwillingness to move (De Lame 2005a, 12–16; field notes 2006; van Leeuwen, 2001).[1]

Tutsi survivors of the genocide represent a small minority in many communities, and indeed many have relocated since the genocide. IBUKA (Kinyarwanda, "to remember"), the main survivor organization, estimates that 70 percent of survivors have relocated (interview with IBUKA representative 2006). Waldorf, citing a representative of AVEGA (Association of Genocide Widows), estimates 65 percent of survivors have relocated (Waldorf 2006, 76n457). Southern Rwanda, however, notably in and around Butare town, has not changed demographically and is much the same after the genocide as it was before (MINALOC 2002). All of the thirty-seven ordinary peasant Rwandans who participated in my research were resident in what is now South province before the genocide, and all but six of them had an experience of flight and return brought on by the 1994 genocide, whether they moved internally within Rwanda or went to the refugee camps in the neighboring Democratic Republic of the Congo (DRC), known as Zaïre at the time. Of the 400 Rwandans I

Figure 1. Mud and thatch homes like these, most of which were rebuilt since the genocide, are now illegal under the government-led *nyakatsi* campaign to modernize Rwanda's housing sector. (photo by Bert Ingelaere, © 2006)

consulted in the course of participant observation, 321 individuals had this experience of flight and return.

Butare province (now part of South province) also had a tradition of resistance to the genocidal politics of the previous regime, and there are documented instances of Hutu and Tutsi working together to resist the genocide in its early days (Des Forges 1999, 216–20, 494–99; Guichaoua 2005, 250–58; 2010, 409–53). There are also documented instances of Hutu who resisted the plan to kill Tutsi and who were threatened with death themselves by the Interahamwe militias that initiated much of the killing (Des Forges 1999, 555–91; Fujii 2009, 124; Straus 2006, 122–52). Also living in and around Butare town are Rwandans who lived through the humanitarian assistance offered by the French and those who fled to the relative safety of Burundi or were pushed into the camps along the border in Zaïre (Pottier 2002, 1–8; Umutesi 2004, 103–63). By the end of the genocide, in July 1994, an estimated one million Rwandans were internally displaced, and about 1.7 million had taken to the roads and fled to neighboring countries. There are also many survivors of the double massacre at the Kibeho internally displaced persons camp in what was then Gikongoro province: first the massacre of Tutsi and Hutu opposed to the genocide in April 1994 by the Interahamwe and then, in April 1995, a second attack when the military wing of the RPF, the Rwandan Patriotic Army (RPA), opened fire on a largely but not exclusively Hutu population (Prunier 2009, 38–42).

The choice of southern Rwanda is also grounded in my own experiences in the region during an extended period of residence from July 1997 to January 2001, when I worked first as a human rights investigator with the United Nations High Commissioner for Human Rights Mission for Rwanda (UNHRFOR) in Gitarama and Kibuye préfectures (now located in South and West province, respectively) and then as the resident coordinator of the US Agency for International Development (USAID)/National University of Rwanda Anglophone Law Project, based in Butare town (now Huye). Knowledge of place names from the period before the postgenocide government restructured Rwanda's administration was critical during the research as the government changed the names of all provinces and collapsed smaller units into bigger units with new names (see figs. 2 and 3). Place names, notably those of towns and districts, were either changed or dropped altogether. The government justified the renaming as necessary for the healing of Tutsi survivors as the invocation of place name is "just too upsetting for them" (field notes 2006). Throughout the research period, however, ordinary Rwandans from all walks of life continued to use the old place names, while government officials, many of whom returned to Rwanda after the genocide, used the new names.

Given the diversity of individual experiences before, during, and after the genocide and the demographic and administrative realities in southern Rwanda, I opted to follow individuals through their social and political networks, rather than limit the research to the goings-on in a specific community. Everyday life in Rwanda, like that in rural areas in other countries, is not confined to a geographical entity, despite government efforts to formalize village life through its *imidugudu* program (HRW 2001b; C. Newbury 2011). Consequently, I chose to follow the paths between individuals, and this approach took me across the country as the linkages between individuals were revealed. For example, the first participant in the research was born in South province, and her genocide experiences occurred in and around the place where she grew up, just to the south of Butare town. As she shared her story with me, and with her permission, I made notes about the individuals she referred to. She spoke of family, friends, and neighbors as well as of her interactions with government officials before and after the genocide. Some of the experiences with the people were positive, others negative. Regardless of the quality or nature of the relationship, I tried to follow up with each of the named individuals. In this way, I was able to trace

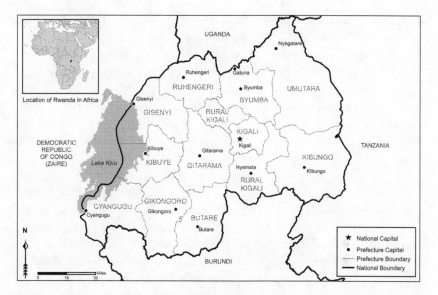

Figure 2. Rwanda, pre-2006 administrative boundaries. (map by Jacob Noel and Carie Ernst, © 2013)

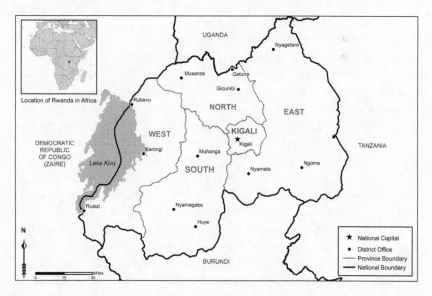

Figure 3. Rwanda, post-2006 administrative boundaries with new place names. (map by Jacob Noel and Carie Ernst, © 2013)

the private and public relations of the individuals who agreed to participate in the research. This method provided 167 names. I contacted 95 individuals, of whom 37 agreed to participate. In addition to these individuals, I spoke with or observed approximately four hundred Rwandans in the course of their daily lives in spontaneous, casual conversations that resulted from everyday inter-actions near my base in Butare (now Huye) town and elsewhere, from Cyangugu (now Rusizi) in the west, north to Gitarama (now Muhanga), and northwest to Kibuye (now Karongi) and Gisenyi (now Rubavu), as well as at myriad points in between (see figs. 2 and 3).

I have a basic knowledge of Kinyarwanda and was aware of the cultural norms and codes that would frame my presence in the lives of peasant Rwan-dans. I kept a book of Rwandan proverbs (Crépeau and Bizimana 1979) that served as a useful way to understand euphemistic comments about cows, drums, cooking pots, and warriors. I also kept Kinyarwanda language books with me at all times (Overdulve 1975; Shimamungu 1998), both as learning tools and to demonstrate that I was trying my best to speak to Rwandans in their mother tongue. I was able to speak about everyday things, such as shopping in the market and people's family or work, and to order a drink at a local kiosk. This language facility also provided unparalleled day-to-day access to ordinary peasant Rwandans as I was able to repeatedly interview individuals in locations of their choosing—for example, in homesteads, banana groves, grazing pastures, kiosks, or pubs, on the bus or at the taxi stand, or simply during long walks through the hills—without a translator.

Knowledge of the quiet resistance of peasant Rwandans also helped me to dig deeper when consensus versions of events inevitably arose, to go beneath the accepted standards of what could be safely discussed with an outsider. For example, a senior representative of one of my two local partner associations recommended many participants that I could interview, which I did but only because they were presented to me as "interviewable." I later learned that the representative told these recommended participants what they could and could not say to me. For example, the cousin of the older sister (by a different father) of one of my participants was one of the individuals brought to my home by one of my local organizational contacts. She said that members of the organiza-tion in a community where some of my participants live had been told by my contact what they could and could not say during the interview. If the participant spoke on themes other than those "authorized" by the staff member, he or she would likely lose the privileges of membership, including access to health care and funds for school fees (corroborated by Chakravarty 2012, 257–59, 262–63). These narratives are not excerpted in the book but instead speak to broader processes of surveillance of foreign research projects and to local power dynamics within survivor organizations in particular and at the community level more generally (cf. Begley 2013; Purdeková 2011; Thomson 2009a, 2013).

My formal "sample" consisted of thirty-seven individuals, consisting of three ethnic Twa, twenty ethnic Hutu, and fourteen ethnic Tutsi, all of whom were "survivors" of the genocide. I averaged seven meetings with each individual, resulting in an average of 9.4 hours of recorded interview data per participant, for a total of 348 hours of recorded material. Of the Hutu individuals I interviewed, six had been through the *gacaca* process, while another six individuals—three who had confessed their crimes and three who had not—were in prison on charges of genocide. None of the thirty-seven participants identified as mixed Hutu-Tutsi. All declared a "single" identity of being Hutu, Tutsi, or Twa, which may be a reflection of kinship ties, as Rwandans take the ethnicity (or *ubwoko*) identity of their father. It may also be a function of socioeconomic class; all but two of my participants self-identified as poor or destitute. Ethnic identity did not shape their daily existence until the "law" of genocide singled out Tutsi for death (Straus 2006, 245). Indeed, nine participants to the research who self-identified as Hutu told me, in the words of one man, that "we all ran together when the killing mobs came. It wasn't until later that we realized only some of us [Tutsi] were being killed" (interviews 2006).

Sixteen women participated in the research. Two participants were under the age of sixteen. The average age was forty-three years for women and thirty-nine years for men; one participant was past seventy, and one was past ninety. None of my participants had finished primary school; the average length of schooling was three years. Two had salaried jobs. The rest were subsistence farmers, day laborers, or unemployed. Twelve individuals considered themselves homeless as they lived in newly created *imidugudu* (villages), not in their communities of origin. All considered themselves Christian and attended church regularly. All of my participants participated in the *gacaca* courts on several occasions, and all but twelve had been through *ingando* citizenship reeducation.

All but two of the individuals who agreed to participate reside in rural communities, and their social and political outlook was oriented to hillside life. The social and economic diversity within the sample resulted in my decision to subdivide it into three broad categories: (1) members of peasant families *without* sufficient land to be economically self-sufficient (the destitute *abatindi*), (2) members of peasant families *with* sufficient land to be economically self-sufficient (the poor *abakene*), and (3) members of peasant families with sufficient land and cash income to satisfy basic needs (the salaried poor *abakene bifashije*). Such an approach allows variations in the themes of the life stories of peasant Rwandans to be further contextualized as their experiences are organized according to their location in the social structure (de Lame 2005a, 168–243). It also allows nuanced distinctions among individual life experiences to emerge as the range of social roles played by peasant people is shaped by their agency as structured within a range of limited, circumscribed choices.

I did not sample on ethnicity despite an obvious temptation to do so, as individuals lived or died during the genocide on the basis of this identity. One reason why discussion of ethnicity was avoided is that the policy of national unity and reconciliation makes it illegal (Legal and Constitutional Commission, Republic of Rwanda 2003, articles 13 and 33). I also did not want to frame individual experiences of the genocide in ethnic terms; instead, I sought to gain the widest possible representation of participants regardless of ethnicity and across diverse forms of identity, including kin, friendship networks, class, and gender.

Interview Procedure and Protocol

At the heart of the research is oral testimony, which speaks to my epistemological commitment to voicing ordinary peasant Rwandans as possessing knowledge that is the direct result of their life experiences. The life history method provides "an analysis of the social, historical, political and economic contexts of a life story" (Hatch and Wisniewski 1995, 125). In many ways, the life history interview allows for a history of the present; it also centers the individual in his or her own narrative, as the researcher becomes an instrument to voice the told story (Alevesson and Sköldberg 2000). The goal is not to elicit specific information but rather to allow individuals to speak, at their own pace and in accordance with their comfort level, to the topics and issues that are important to them (Bondi 2002).

The task of the researcher is to turn a life story into a life history by situating the individual narrative in a broader context (Borland 1991) and in ways that may cast doubt on official accounts and established theories (Olson and Shopes 1991; Stanley and Wise 1991). In turn, the "findings" produced can lead to the development of new theories that resonate more closely with people's lives (Hyden 1993). In addition, by entering into conversation with others, researchers can elicit stories that result that have the potential to validate the knowledge of ordinary people as subjects that tend to be omitted from academic research and policy formulations alike (Benmayor 1991; Smith 2004). The life history interview is a critical tool for developing new ways of knowing and of developing new frameworks and theories based on the lived realities of ordinary people, particularly those rooted in individual experiences of conflict. For this reason, I do not use the language of "informants" or "respondents" but instead use "participant" to acknowledge the important individual role of ordinary peasant people in sharing the knowledge that makes the production of this text possible.

I usually made initial contact with potential participants alone, usually in Kinyarwanda or, more rarely, in French. During this contact, the participant and I discussed the possibility of working together. My goal was to produce a written document that would allow readers to better understand the life world of thirty-seven ordinary peasant Rwandans resident in the south of the country. Several participants saw this as important to avoid future violence in Rwanda; others felt a sense of pride in that a foreign researcher would spend so much time with them, letting them talk. Many voiced a feeling of anonymous security in sharing experiences with someone with no formal links to Rwanda. Aimable's words are emblematic: "Madam, I am so happy that you have come into my life. Never before have I been able to speak with such openness, and to a young stranger like you. There is no hope for me, I am an old man and the future is for youth. But maybe the work you are doing will help other young ones avoid storms like the genocide again. I am glad that you ask my stories and even more proud that you will write them down for others to see" (interview 2006).

Once the participant and I established a formal working relationship, the next task was to determine which translator would accompany me to the first interview. Some individuals sought an alternate translator to the one I proposed. For example, in one case I presumed that a Tutsi woman who was raped during the genocide would want to be interviewed by a woman translator who had also been raped. Instead, she opted for the male returnee because she felt she would feel less ashamed to "tell a boy" who would not know much about her life before or after the genocide and who had no knowledge of her personal ties or alliances (interview 2006).

Obtaining the informed consent of participants was a challenge. Most of the "formal" life history participants, as well as the ordinary people I would meet and talk with in the street or in the hills, were unable to understand the concepts associated with informed consent. I had two ways of dealing with this. First, I always explained my presence as a Canadian researcher and my interest in voicing the lived experiences of ordinary peasant people before, during, and after the genocide. I also explained that I was particularly interested in how national unity and reconciliation processes were progressing for them. This approach invariably resulted in anecdotal evidence about a friend, relative, or associate of the person I was speaking to—the genocide touched everyone in Rwanda, even those who returned after 1994 and particularly those who were in the country during the genocide but who are not considered "survivors" by the government. Even the most nonchalant beginnings to conversation—"It is really hot today" or "Who won the [World Cup] soccer game last night?"— often resulted in a story of someone who had to deal with the local authorities in pursuit of unity and reconciliation, as individuals wanted to know what I was doing in Rwanda and why.[2] Second, with the life history participants, I tried to make it clear that their voices (in the form of text) would be quoted at length and verbatim and that it was my job as the researcher/writer to contextualize their stories within broader social, political, and historical trends in Rwanda. Consent or, perhaps more appropriate, conditions of use were always under negotiation.

I worked with four different research assistants to transcribe what my digital voice recorder captured before translating the material into English. I carefully considered whom I would hire as research assistants after interviewing twenty individuals. We were all aware of the politically sensitive nature of the research, and their assurances of confidentiality led to increased trust and rapport between us. I did not allow the assistants to meet one another, and all interview files were transferred through me. In the end, the team consisted of a male returnee whose family had been exiled to the Congo in the 1960s and who was born abroad and did not experience the genocide directly, one man who lived through the genocide as a young teenager, and one middle-aged woman who was raped during the genocide and lost her entire family. The fourth member of the team was a young woman who survived the 1995 attack at Kibeho and lost several family members after the genocide officially ended in July 1994. Two of the assistants were of mixed ethnic heritage, having one Tutsi and one Hutu parent. Two were senior students enrolled in Translation and Interpretation studies at the University of Rwanda. Both women were mothers, and this was a factor with many female participants as we were able to share experiences of motherhood and continue our discussions about their lives long after the voice recorder had been turned off. None of this postinterview material is quoted in the research, but it did result in a deeper and more nuanced interview process as we spoke about topics that might have been off limits without this personal rapport. Of particular interest and a real icebreaker were my own children, the youngest of whom was born in Kigali in 1999. That I had chosen to deliver my child in Rwanda made me more approachable, and some women felt "I was one of them" despite clear class, racial, and other differences (field notes 2006).

I never used the names of participants during the interviews, nor did I type or write their names in the transcripts or field notes. When a name appeared in an audio recording, I blanked out the name before the interview was transcribed by a member of the research assistance team. I also blanked out any information that could be used to identify a participant, such as the names of relatives or friends, associational memberships, or place names (Thomson 2009a). Safeguards enacted to protect individual confidentiality were critical as one of my two local partner organizations repeatedly requested a summary of what was being said by whom. As a colleague in one of my partner organizations became more forceful in requesting this information, I was glad that these safeguards were in place to protect the identity of participants and to ensure their confidence as part of the trust-based relationship I shared with both my participants and my research assistance team. Anonymity during the research process, particularly with individuals who shared their life history with me (and my translator), was virtually impossible. I followed these safeguards meticulously to ensure that, despite any potential backlash that might occur during the research process or as a result of any publications based on the research, Rwandan government officials would be unable to locate the ordinary peasants who participated in my research. I eventually learned that one of my local partner colleagues was concerned that the Rwandans I consulted were making negative comments about the government. Although few of them did, as the narratives reported in this book attest, the perception of peasant criticism of the government was sufficient to raise the threat of sanction against this colleague's organization. All researchers require a local partner, and my "colleague" was likely accountable to the government for my actions. Once this concern became apparent, I interviewed all of the individuals that he brought to my doorstep, treating them as a collective voice about the power dynamics between the government and civil society and also between civil society and its membership.

No two interviews with the same individual unfolded in the same way. Some interviews lasted for hours and included sharing a drink or a meal with the participant and his or her family, while others lasted only a few minutes. Only one individual did not complete the life history interview, saying that it was "too hard to relive it all" after the third meeting. The first interview opened with the question "Where did you grow up?" Subsequent interviews opened with a theme from our previous discussion, unless the participant had something specific to share. All the participants responded with a long narrative about either the genocide itself or its aftermath—where they were, whom they were with, what they saw, what they heard, and how "everything" changed after "that" (meaning the genocide). Others spoke about their trauma, still others about the experience of living with HIV/AIDS (analyzed in Thomson 2011c). Some spoke at length about how they killed. Most complained about their increasing poverty and about living in constant fear of the future. All spoke about a loss of personal safety and a sense of increased insecurity in their home communities since the genocide.

I never asked questions about individual experiences during the genocide both as a matter of respect and to ensure that the individual remained in control of the conversation as much as possible in the power-laden relationship between a foreign researcher and an ordinary peasant Rwandan. Some participants revisited narratives about specific acts of violence during the genocide at the beginning of subsequent meetings, which further facilitated analysis as each meeting revealed slightly more or different information. Sometimes subsequent meetings were gripe sessions, where the participant complained to me about a friend or relative or about the abuses of an "important person," meaning some-one higher up on the social ladder. Stories of the excesses of local officials or the lack of morality of religious leaders often filled our conversations.

Multiple meetings with the same participants not only made it possible to revisit events but also allowed both parties to the research relationship—researcher and researched—to develop more relaxed interactions. I sometimes used photographs, usually from local newspapers, as a prompt, a technique borrowed from Codere (1962). The research was entirely open ended, with few closed questions posed, except to clarify statements or events I did not under-stand. I worked with two of my translators before arriving in Rwanda to translate key concepts and to strengthen my understanding of the nuanced meaning of such concepts in Kinyarwanda. For example, some peasant people, because of their low social status, were surprised the first time I asked them if "they felt that they had a choice." I initially translated the word "choice" as a command, rather than as an option, and my research team and I had long conversations about the meaning of such words in Kinyarwanda, words that we refined and redeployed over the course of the research. In much the same way, I spent several hundred hours with each team member poring over the interview material, carefully working through meaning and context to ensure that the translations were as accurate as possible.

There was an element of caution early in the interview relationship, with participants maintaining distance until a rapport was established and we began to establish a relationship. The usual cultural wariness of an outsider was some-what mitigated by my having lived in Rwanda from 1997 to 2001 and by my continued (but often feeble) attempts to communicate in Kinyarwanda. Ulti-mately, my ability to conduct research depended on the various permission letters that constituted my official authorization to justify my continued presence in rural areas and which implied a tie with the government. That I had official permission was of no surprise to anyone. It was assumed and expected. I was unsure how ordinary Rwandans would interpret my obvious ties to the govern-ment and the frequent visits to the offices of my local partners in their home communities. I was required to record my presence in a community with a visit to the local authority office and an additional courtesy visit to the local office of my local research partners. Once this had been done and the local official recorded that I had come to speak to "peasants" or "unimportant people," they all but ignored my presence in the community. Over time, my interactions with local authorities inevitably became a topic of conversation and a point of shared experience, as individuals recounted their own experiences in navigating their relationship with local officials before and after the genocide.[3] My willingness to come to the homes of individuals, sit with them, and listen to their stories was an obvious benefit once the initial ice breaking had been completed. Indeed, thirty of my thirty-seven participants said that part of the reason they agreed to take part in my project was that I did not find them through formal organizational contacts and that I made an effort to meet them in places "where we live" or "in the fields were we work" (field notes 2006).

Part and parcel of my research process was one that Rwandans from all walks of life are well familiar—government surveillance. I needed to show the appointed local government officials with whom I worked that I had the sponsorship of local organizations that would "help me navigate rural areas" (interview with Rwanda's ombudsman 2006). I knew that my "choice" of local partner would affect to whom I could speak and when. For this reason, I decided to pursue partnerships with two local organizations, one of which had clear ties to the government (Partner A) and one of which (Partner B) had more autonomy and was sometimes subtly critical of government policy. I nurtured relationships with both organizations about eighteen months prior to beginning my actual interviews with Rwandans. Surveillance appeared early in my relationship with Partner A. I was required to meet with eight senior RPF representatives, including two ministers and three senators, before I was "allowed" to apply for a research permit from MINALOC. During each of these meetings, I presented each official with a list of interview topics for them to approve, my curriculum vitae to illustrate my ability to carry out the proposed project, and a one-page overview of the research and its expected outcomes. The one-page overview included a paragraph on my chosen local research partners and the nature of our working relationship to illustrate how my research project would benefit their development mandate.[4] Each meeting ended with the official waxing lyrical on the success of the government in restoring peace and security since the genocide. Most government officials I met also reminded me to maintain regular contact with my appointed Partner A representative. Perhaps foreshadowing the eventual cessation of my research by MINALOC representatives, I was also advised not to believe everything I heard in rural areas (Thomson 2011d, 2013).

During May 2006, the first full month of a planned year of field research, it became clear that my Partner A colleague was checking in on me as he repeatedly urged me not to believe anything I learned from the peasant Rwandans to whom I spoke. At first, I perceived this as small talk, but I quickly came to appreciate the role of his organization, as well as my own role, in Rwanda's information economy. Research involves making choices about which voices are heard and whose knowledge counts. The government was not particularly keen on learning about how rural Rwandans live or understanding their daily hardships. Its representatives were interested in hearing only from those who support its vision of economic development and ethnic unity (corroborated by Chakravarty 2012, forthcoming). My Partner A colleague understood this, and I soon did as well, engaging in a cat-and-mouse game in which I tried to gauge what he wanted to hear during our weekly reporting sessions, during which I updated him on my activities. My strategy was to tell him no more than was needed to satisfy his curiosity while at the same time asking ordinary Rwandans I knew about the best ways to avoid having others—be it neighbors, government officials, or civil society representatives—observe our conversations. I did not try to hide from my participants that my Partner A colleague was asking about what we had discussed in our formal interviews. Instead, I shared with some of them the kinds of questions that he was asking about our conversations, asking for suggestions on how to avoid telling him much of anything. This usually resulted in a deepening of the interview relationship, as some participants were delighted that I seemed to understand the role of the government in their daily lives and was willing to discuss how to avoid the glare "of people who make decisions in Kigali that affect us [at the local level]." As Joseph N., a destitute released prisoner, told me, "Those people from Kigali tell us what to do when they come here. You ask me what I think and I can tell you. Then you tell me next time how you took my 'news' [*smirks*] to [Partner A representative] in Kigali. It is very good" (field notes 2006).

Another element of the research design was critical to building rapport and maintaining trust. I tried to live, as much as a white foreigner possibly could, as peasants Rwandans lived, albeit in Butare town. I had no hot water, no telephone, none of the "conveniences" of town life as a matter of choice. I walked everywhere and took public transportation only when I had to go any extended distance (I traversed distances of less than ten miles on foot; my translator for the day would often meet me at the agreed site rather than walk). This gave me a certain cachet as it became evident to many people that I was ready and willing to travel considerable distances on foot over steep hills, on hot, humid days and during the rainy season. Some of the most revealing conversations took place in the hills surrounding the valley where I lived and walked every evening after dinner. During these walks I always met a broad cross-section of ordinary peasant Rwandans, some of whom were participating in the life history aspect of the research. When I ran into participants outside the formal interview setting, I did not greet them unless they greeted me first. This was out of respect for them, as questions about how and why we knew each other would inevitably arise. Sometimes, I was met with shouted greetings, such as "So nice to see you out here [in the hills]," "I forgot to tell you this when we met last time," or "Now you can come and meet my sister that I told you about."

I did not pay any of my participants for the time spent interviewing, although I did provide soda and tea, and sometimes we would share a meal if appropriate, although when that did happen, I was the one being hosted by my participants. There was an in-kind payment for every participant as I provided FRw 2,500 (approximately US$7 in 2006) phone cards for use at public phone booths in the event that a traumatic event manifested during or after any interview (per my partnership agreement with my Partner B organization). Some individuals required more than one phone card, and others did not use them at all. One person returned the card to me after our last formal interview. Participants often asked me for money for school fees, one asked for a dowry, and a few times people asked for funds for funeral expenses or to buy livestock, but I always respectfully declined, stating that I had to save my resources to raise my own two children. Eventually, people began to see that I was "the one with the notebook" and that, although a white foreigner, all I had to offer were my time and some kindness. The only time I offered any form of payment was when the child of one of my participants fell into a pit latrine during our interview and required medical care. I gave FRw 1,500 (approximately US$4 at the time) toward his emergency care so that he could be ferried by car to the nearest medical facility, twelve miles away.

Participants and I built mutual trust and confidence over time, and they came more readily with some than with others, but I was mindful to treat everyone the same: with humility and respect. I knew from prior experience that Rwandans would speak their minds when they felt secure and comfortable. I was sensitive to the reality that learning about the lived experiences of a cross section of Rwandans would require that I leave some topics untouched and that I listen empathically to what individuals deemed important and demonstrate my trustworthiness by not prying where my presence was not wanted. I never pressed anyone to speak about anything he or she did not want to discuss. The close relationships that developed were a reaction to my interest in people's understanding of and feelings about different events and changes in their lives, particularly since the genocide. I was interested only in what individuals were willing to share.

The research also had therapeutic effects for many individuals. In fact, many people thought that if I was a researcher and so interested in their lives as few before had been, then I must by definition be a therapist. Most individuals were aware of the role of therapists since the genocide because the postgenocide government had organized posttraumatic stress counseling units for survivors of the genocide and for individuals who needed emotional support following their participation in the *gacaca* courts (Bagilishya 2000; Ndayambajwe 2001). "Therapist" was a role I could not escape, and many individuals asked me during the long walks to and from interview sites if their behaviour was "normal" or confided in me their troubles and heartaches. This was an added layer of stress for me as I spent most of my days listening to the narratives of individuals who had survived the genocide, who had been raped or tortured, or who had witnessed killings or had killed. While this was personally difficult as I often took on the pain and suffering that individuals shared with me, the therapist image also meant that the combination of my empathy and respect made me privy to significant and intimate details of people's lives that would have perhaps been unobtainable otherwise.

In anticipation of the trauma that I expected people to exhibit during the research, I set up two safeguards. Prior to beginning fieldwork, in October and November 2005, I spent six weeks in Rwanda at a trauma counselor training session, organized by one of my local partner organizations, and lived in a homestead that a local women's group had built to provide a safe home for widows of the genocide who were too traumatized, too poor, or too old to return to their home communities. During my interviews in 2006, trained trauma counselors from one of my Partner B organizations were available to each of my participants, either in person or by telephone.

Interpretation

All this material about the feelings and perceptions of ordinary peasant Rwandans about their lives before, during, and after the genocide leaves the problem of translating the "raw" material into a workable and academic document that is clearly intended for audiences far removed from the everyday lives of participants. Moreover, individual lived experiences are embedded in social and cultural forces that can constrain some and enable others (Scott 1991). What standard of "truth" and "validity" can possibly be attributed to information generated by the life history interview method and triangulated with participant observation, Foucauldian genealogy, and historical analysis? Ultimately, the veracity will be determined by the reader, not the text, which is why I made the decision to quote the narratives of ordinary Rwandans at length. As Kellehear writes, interpretative research "is a 'reading' of the world, and the task is always on persuasion rather than proving" (1993, 25). It is the work of the author to ensure the logical coherence of the argument being advanced, as well as the cogency of the supporting evidence and of the historical contextualization of the narratives presented (Schwartz-Shea and Yanow 2012, 78–89). My commitment is to voicing ordinary Rwandans as active subjects, so it should come as no surprise that I embrace the contradictions, exaggerations, and perhaps outright fabrications that the life history method entails. Seeing Rwandans as "agents" means situating them within the complex and ambiguous arena that makes up political and cultural relations in postgenocide Rwanda. My task is to piece together and to make sense of the multiple and often contradictory presentations of self that constitute the life worlds of thirty-seven peasant Rwandans.

I have not verified the narratives that were generated through the life history method except to ascertain the commitment of the individual speaker to his or her own life story. Instead, I acknowledge that the individual narratives are historically situated and enmeshed in relationships of power. In addition, I understand that each narrative is shaped by each person's selective and often self-interested memory. Some elements of what was narrated to me may actually constitute something that happed to a friend or relative of the speaker. I do not try to distinguish what is actual lived experience and what is lived-through-someone-else experience. For example, in my interviews with survivor women, it was common to learn early in our relationship that a sister or neighbor had been raped during the genocide. Sometimes, later on, the individual reported that she had been raped during the war and that it was important to her that I know it was she, and not, for example, her sister who had been attacked. Instead, I seek to ascertain and understand the interconnections between who sees what as important, when and how. My role as the author is central, and a core assumption driving my use of the life history method is that the material gathered is mutually constituted. Together, the researcher and the researched bring the life history stories to life—the text is coproduced.

Central to this coproduction is the idea that memory is important and the idea that the individuals living in the present sometimes develop a historical amnesia, particularly in a country like Rwanda, where a plurality of histories exists, each corresponding to a political agenda of its own. History in this sense is hidden from memory, although it can be recaptured through the life history method, with its ability to frame, construct, and define what is seen or obscured by individuals in the course of their everyday lives. In this way, life history is an entryway through which both researcher/author and reader may begin to understand a political system other than their own. The purpose is to contextualize and situate the lived experiences and memories of individuals within the literature, to add a nuanced layer of knowledge, rather than to correct or revise the existing material—literature is a tool for fieldwork. The life history narrative exists somewhere between history and memory, as it is spoken interaction that creates memory from the perspective of the present; the life history is, after all, that which is made real through being spoken about. As Feldman notes: "The event is not what happens. The event is that which can be narrated" (1991, 14, quoted in Ross 2003, 77).

Memories are recalled for reasons that are important to the individual, which perhaps explains in part why each of my participants started our research relationship with his or her own experience of the genocide. It is still an event from which individuals are emerging and that continues to shape the range of options available to them and the ways in which they choose or choose not to engage those options (Roth and Salas 2001). In many cases, particularly around processes of national unity and reconciliation, ordinary Rwandans are circumspect in their engagement with state agents. Yet, through the material gathered through the life history method, individuals reveal sites of political and social struggle about what is "real" to them and its meanings. The life history method also reveals that personal interpretations of the past are founded on experiences of the present, and the two are often in "deep and ambiguous conflict with the official interpretative devices of a culture" (Steedman 1987, 6).

My task thus is to sift through and analyze these narratives while keeping in mind the broader political and social context in which they were shared. Chapter 4 marks the beginning of this analysis, in deconstructing the various mechanisms of the system of power that is the Rwandan "state." Before moving on, however, historical background is necessary to situate the broader sociopolitical context in which ordinary peasant Rwandans currently live.

2

The Historical Role of the State in Everyday Life

I don't understand why the government is always telling us to forgive those who killed and to reconcile with those who are not like us. We can decide who to forgive and with whom to reconcile. Things happened here during the genocide. But things [violence] happened before and things have happened more and more since the *gacaca* courts started sending people to prison. Before 1994, we heard about this problem or that problem in Kigali when the burgomaster [mayor] would come and tell us there were problems. When politics eventually comes to our door like it did during the genocide, we have problems because the government always likes to pretend that we [poor] will do what they tell us to do.

The government gives orders to show us they are in charge. Before the genocide, I was a Hutu who lived in the same community as Tutsi, and we shared sometimes. But mostly within families, not with people we didn't know. Or if someone got wronged, we ignored that family too. But now it is different. Everyone is different since the genocide. Some of us lived, some of us died. Some are still living, but they say they are dead inside. We hardly share at all now because we don't know whom to trust to keep our safety.

Now, I am a former Hutu because the new government says that we have to get unified. I never thought about being a Hutu before, but now I wonder why they want to wipe that idea out of our heads. We were unified before; we were poor then and we are poor now. But now our problems include forgiving and reconciling with people we don't even know or talking about things we never saw. [Because I am a former Hutu,] they [the government] expect me to go and "tell my truth." As a Hutu [man]

who was just in prison, I just want to keep quiet. I would say something [to
the local official], but I have kids and I want them to grow up without
interference so it is best that I just keep quiet about my frustrations. I have
seen what happens to others who speak out. I just want to live in peace
without interference. (Interview with Tharcisse, a destitute Hutu man,
2006)

Tharcisse is a very poor "former Hutu" with limited options to exercise his
agency, yet his narrative shows political acumen. He was accused of acts of
genocide in his home community in 2001. He spent almost two years in prison
and was released for lack of evidence in 2003. His struggle to reestablish the
semblance of a normal life has been compounded by constant reminders from
RPF-appointed local officials to reconcile with his neighbors. His is a "small
statement of dissent" (Scott 1990, 192), as he and others in his marginal social
position are hardly able to openly challenge the postgenocide order of national
unity and reconciliation. Instead, he shows us the ways that the power of the
Rwandan state, through its appointed agents, enters into the everyday lives of
ordinary peasant Rwandans as he questions the state-imposed need to "forgive,"
"reconcile," and "get unified." The excerpt also highlights the intersection of
ethnicity and socioeconomic location, the two factors that structure Rwandans'
experiences of lived violence as the state decides who is targeted and for what
reason.

Immediately before and during the genocide (1990–94), the Rwandan state,
led by the Habyarimana regime, targeted ethnic Tutsi and politically moderate
ethnic Hutu (broadly meaning elite Hutu who did not support the plan for killing
the Tutsi). Since the genocide, whether or not individuals are targeted by "the
state" has depended on where they were during the genocide and what acts of
violence they are perceived to have committed. For example, Hutu men like
Tharcisse have been targeted for their presumed participation in the 1994 genocide. Tutsi who returned after the genocide, many of whom occupy appointed
local government positions, view Tutsi survivors of the genocide as suspect;
their rationale is that they must have colluded with Hutu in order to survive.
The structural violence that individuals have experienced since the genocide is
less obvious because the current regime has eliminated references to ethnicity
from public life.[1] Individuals are no longer Hutu, Tutsi, or Twa but instead are
simply Rwandans. How individuals perceive their own identity matters less—
both historically and today—than does the power of the state to shape individual realities through the careful and strategic use of competing historical
interpretations of ethnicity and statehood. The broader point is that violence of
some kind forms a definitive backdrop to the everyday lives of ordinary Rwandans, as is demonstrated more fully in the next chapter. What changes is the

Figure 4. A survivor of the political violence of 1959, 1963, and the 1994 genocide walks to tend to the field of his "patron" (*shebuja*) in northern Rwanda, August 2006. (photo by Frank V. McMillan, © 2006)

type and intensity of violence depending on one's social location and ethnic identity, as categorized by the state.

This chapter places the power of the Rwandan state to categorize everyday life in historical perspective. The purpose is to illustrate that there is nothing new or different about the structural forms of violence that ordinary peasant Rwandans have experienced since the genocide. The policy of national unity and reconciliation represents a continuation of both the various forms of oppression experienced by ordinary Rwandans at the hands of state agents and the imposition of ethnic identities by the state on their everyday lives. As such, this chapter introduces the reader to the sociopolitical structures of Rwandan society to highlight the historical forms of elite relations with nonelites. It introduces the historical foundation of contemporary forms of sociopolitical exclusion by identifying traditional patron-client forms of oppression, concluding with an analysis of the ways in which these practices were used in the postcolonial period by the then political leadership of presidents Grégoire Kayibanda (1962–73) and Juvénal Habyarimana (1973–94). Finally, it examines the processes through which contrasting interpretations of ethnicity and statehood have been manipulated by successive regimes in Rwanda to justify and maintain policies of exclusion, the most recent manifestation of which is the policy of national unity and reconciliation. Such an approach matters because elite characterizations of ethnicity and the contours of the state "can be traced to intense struggles over power carried out by leaders—struggles involving the politicization of ethnicity and a perverse dynamic of violence and fear" (C. Newbury 1998, 7).

The Strategic Roots
of National Unity and Reconciliation

The government's policy of national unity and reconciliation is grounded in a specific interpretation of more than two centuries of history. According to "historical" documents produced by the National Unity and Reconciliation Commission (NURC), Rwandan society was essentially unified before the arrival of colonial powers and the Catholic Church.[2] Precolonial social categories did not matter because the three groups were unified by language, religion, loyalty to the Tutsi king, clan lineages, and socioeconomic interdependence. Conflict between groups was rare, and when it did arise it was rooted in regional or clan identities, not ethnic ones. Also implicit in this interpretation of social unity are precolonial class distinctions, with Tutsi being the richest and therefore the most important: "Ethnic groups are . . . characterized by wealth or poverty; they were not based on blood. One could shift from being a Twa or a Hutu and become a Tutsi if he got rich, if he became poor while he was a Tutsi, he was called a Hutu or Twa" (NURC 2000, 19).

The RPF's strategic interpretation of "official" history is that it was colonial rule, first by the Germans, then by the Belgians, that divided Rwandan society and transformed the categories of Hutu, Tutsi, and Twa into ethnic categories. The policy of national unity and reconciliation posits that the ethnic divisions imposed on Rwanda by colonial rule are the primary cause of the 1994 genocide: until the arrival of the white man, who "threw down the seeds of ethnic division that caused the [1994] genocide," the categories of Hutu, Tutsi, and Twa had limited social importance, being occupational differences rather than status-based ones (NURC 2004, 11). According to the policy of national unity, the postcolonial Hutu-led governments of Kayibanda and Habyarimana used ethnicity as a tactic to divide Rwandans. These regimes taught that "all Tutsi were foreign invaders who always subjugated and exploited the labour of the Hutu majority" (NURC 2004, 22). It was these false teachings that created the hatred of "*all* Hutu for *all* Tutsi" (President Kagame, quoted in Jha and Yadav 2004, 67, my emphasis). This false history also "dehumanized Tutsi," which resulted in a "widely-held belief that minority Tutsi were less deserving of basic rights than the majority Hutu" (Kimonyo 2000, 107). The official narrative of national unity and reconciliation also sees the 1994 genocide as rooted in bad governance and weak leadership, which manipulated ethnic identities to hold onto state power (NURC 2004, 5–6). The postcolonial regimes encouraged an obedient and tractable population, which allowed an ideology of genocide "to take hold in the minds of Hutu" (Office of the President 1999, 54).

To counteract the ingrained teachings of the postcolonial regimes, the current government teaches an ideology of national unity and reconciliation through a variety of social and political mechanisms (discussed at length in chapter 4). Significant state resources are dedicated to ensuring that the population understands the importance of unity. The postgenocide government has established mandatory solidarity camps known as *ingando* to "reeducate" the population. Politicians, church leaders, ex-combatants, released prisoners, *gacaca* judges, and incoming university students attend *ingando* for periods ranging from several days to several months. *Ingando* lecturers, all of whom are RPF loyalists, teach participants the official interpretation of history presented in the policy of national unity and reconciliation (NURC 2006a, 2006b, 2006c, 2007d, 2007e; field notes 2006). The government also encourages a collective memory of the genocide through memorial sites and mass graves that double as genocide museums to show the end result of ethnic divisionism. In many sites across the country, the bodies of victims are on display, exposed on shelves, in semi-open tombs, or in the rooms where the killing took place. Every year, annual commemorations are held during national mourning week (April 7–14) to remind Rwandans of the "pernicious effects of ethnic divisionism" (interview with NURC official 2006). The RPF-led government has introduced new national holidays—Heroes Day (February 1), Day of Hope (April 7), Liberation Day (July 4), and Patriotism Day (October 1)—to support its vision of ethnic unity and to act as platforms for leaders to remind Rwandans of the need to fight the ideology of genocide. The RPF also adopted new national symbols in 2001— flag, anthem, and emblem—as the existing ones "symbolized the genocide and encouraged an ideology of genocide and divisionism" (interview with NURC official 2006). The revised 2003 Constitution made illegal public references to ethnic identity (article 33) and criminalized "ethnic divisionism" and "trivializing the genocide" (article 13). These constitutional provisions reinforce a 2001 criminal law on divisionism and sectarianism that punishes public incitement to ethnic discrimination or divisionism by up to five years in prison, heavy fines, or both. The RPF also changed place names at all administrative levels, from villages to provinces, in 2006 as part of Rwanda's administrative restructuring to "protect genocide survivors from remembering where their relatives died" (interview with Ministry of Culture official 2006). The restructuring is officially a part of Rwanda's decentralization policy, whose rationale is to dismantle the highly centralized administrative system that made the genocide possible (BBC 2006; field notes 2006). In practice, the policy of decentralization appears to cover up the deployment of RPF loyalists throughout the lowest levels of the bureaucratic administration (see Ingelaere 2011, 68–75; Purdeková 2011; and Reyntjens 2011 for analysis of the centralizing effects of the policy).

The policy of national unity and reconciliation is grounded in a strategic vision of history that differs from that taught by previous regimes. The pre-1994 regimes taught that Tutsi, Hutu, and Twa were distinct racial groups that migrated into the territory now known as Rwanda at different times. That the Tutsi are foreign invaders who conquered Rwanda centuries ago and who have since oppressed and exploited the majority Hutu in myriad ways was a key aspect of the ideology used to incite the 1994 genocide and is one that the current government claims to be undoing (Waldorf 2011). It came as no surprise to many of the peasant Rwandans I spoke with that the official interpretation of history had changed since the genocide. As one man who claims to have been born during the 1959 social revolution noted caustically, "Whoever has power are the ones that shape our national history" (interview 2006). Many ordinary Rwandans understand that those who hold state power shape the official interpretation of history; in this case, it is the RPF's version of history that forms the official one. The version of history found in the policy of national unity and reconciliation is the "politically correct" one and is the one that most ordinary Rwandans parrot in public even if they disagree in private (field notes 2006, corroborated by Chakravarty 2012, forthcoming).

In promoting a singular version of Rwandan history, the policy of national unity and reconciliation fails to acknowledge the multiplicity of historical interpretations and individual lived experiences that constitute Rwandan history. The postgenocide government has effectively disseminated a message of national unity and reconciliation that seeks to reshape the collective memory of Rwandans about the causes of the genocide (Burnet 2012, 74–109). Many peasant Rwandans understand the version of history put forth in the policy to be a product of the RPF elite designed to safeguard their own positions of power rather than the result of a sincere effort to unify and reconcile the country. As Emmanuel, a poor Tutsi man who survived the genocide, whispered as we shared tea at a roadside kiosk near Butare town:

> I can hardly support this notion of national unity when I know it is meant to keep us [Hutu and Tutsi neighbors] apart. If they [the RPF] left us alone, we could find our own ways to reconcile. Now, we have to do it publicly, and when we are told to do so. The RPF doesn't care about if we truly reconcile, they only care about their own positions. Reconciliation is

for "important" people; it is not for people like me. I am Tutsi, and I can say that because I am a survivor. My [Hutu] brothers cannot speak for fear of being accused of supporting genocide. Who in their right mind supports genocide? It is those who love power who love genocide. . . .

I don't know if Hutu and Tutsi like me [meaning peasant] were unified before the white man came. That is what they [the RPF] say. But how does it matter? I want to eat every day and I want to send my children to school. If they tell me that you [whites] brought division, then of course I agree.

Peace is for those with power, not [poor] people like me. All I can say right now is that I don't know any Hutu who hold hatred for their Tutsi brothers like the government says they do. If they did, how would I even know? Rwandans keep secrets easily. And my [Hutu] brothers are hardly going to tell me about their inner secrets. All I know is that history is for our leaders; we just try to live our life without attracting extra problems. Even the genocide, how they say it happened at *gacaca* is not like it really happened. (Interview 2006)

This excerpt shows that for some ordinary peasant Rwandans, the policy of national unity and reconciliation has adopted a historical narrative that is but one version of a sequence of inventions and reinventions about ethnicity and state power. Fabricating continuity with the past in order to socially engineer the future is a common strategy of political elites (Hobsbawn 1983, 1–14). The policy of national unity and reconciliation ignores the carapace of power of the state to coerce ordinary Rwandans to participate.

The remainder of this chapter puts the policy of national unity and reconciliation in a broader historical perspective to show that the official version of history it presents to ordinary Rwandans is not only inaccurate but rather strategically revisionist and designed to allow the ruling RPF to maintain control of Rwanda's political and social landscape in much the same way that previous regimes in Rwanda have done. Specifically, the chapter focuses on the origins of the labels "Hutu" and "Tutsi" and the way successive generations elites have manipulated these terms for political gain to highlight the continuities in bureaucratic structures of the Rwanda state under the policy of national unity and reconciliation. It also lays the necessary analytical groundwork to challenge the RPF's carefully managed image as the sole political entity capable of saving Rwandan society from its genocidal past, suggesting a radical break in leadership between the pre- and the postgenocide periods (Desrosiers and Thomson 2011). President Kagame, as the self-proclaimed harbinger of the "new" Rwanda (meaning Rwanda under RPF rule), consistently claims to be the only leader capable of leading Rwandans along the "right" path to peace, security,

ethnic unity, and development (Kagame, quoted in Kouyate 2011). Placing the
president's claims in a broader historical context, as the remainder of this
chapter does, illustrates that there is little new about the "new" Rwanda from
the perspective of the nonelite and largely peasant majority.

Elite Exaggerations, Ordinary Realities

In Rwanda, as elsewhere, elites have creatively revised history to justify their
policies and actions, and the RPF's policy of national unity and reconciliation
is certainly no exception. Two distinct histories have emerged. The first focuses
on the distinct origins of Rwanda's "racial" groups—the Hutu, Tutsi, and Twa.
The second focuses on historical patterns of unity among Rwandans, noting
that any differences were occupational (class based), rather than ethnic. The
latter version is the one that the policy of national unity and reconciliation has
drawn on to justify its policies and actions since the genocide. Both interpretations rely on the selective amnesia of elites about what ethnicity may have
meant to individuals and local communities once upon a time and what ethnic
labels have come to mean over time. Neither version is reflective of the objective
history of this complex state, whose political elites have written and rewritten
official history for political gain (Chrétien 2006, particularly 201–90; D. Newbury, in Des Forges 2011; Vansina 2004, 67–98, 126–39). Central to both ficti-
tious yet strategic versions is any discussion of the nature of precolonial state
structures and the role of history in creating and propagating ethnic antagonisms
between Tutsi and Hutu. The Twa, Rwanda's third social group, are not discussed in much depth given their marginality: they make up about 1 percent of
the population and are "universally disregarded as well as disdained in state
politics," thereby minimizing their political impact then and now (D. Newbury
and C. Newbury 2000, 840).

Imagining Precolonial Rwanda

Before being colonized by Germany (1894–1916) and Belgium (1916–62), the
Rwandan state was a highly centralized monarchy. The *mwami* (king) ruled
through divine authority. He was the embodiment of political power, which
was bestowed by *imana* (God). The good fortunes of the royal court were linked
to the king's well-being and supreme intellect in determining what was best for
his subjects—ordinary Rwandans (Des Forges 2011, 7; Reyntjens 1985, 24–25).
The first of Rwanda's official histories was compiled by historians attached to
the royal court and was a reflection of power interests, not empirical fact. Official
oral histories (*ibitekerezo*) were mechanisms used to glorify the Tutsi dynasty
known as the Nyiginya kingdom, which held monarchical power for hundreds
of years prior to the arrival of the Europeans (Vansina 2000, 375–77). According

to Vansina (2004, 46), "Rwanda's past was the history of a nearly uninterrupted progression of chosen people, the Tutsi, whose royal dynasty descended from the sky."

Official histories, narrated by the official interpreters of custom and history (*abiru*), situated the three groups—Hutu, Tutsi, and Twa—into specialized roles that were based in each group's innate and natural characteristics. The official court story stated that prior to the arrival of the Tutsi in present-day Rwanda, the Nyiginya kingdom (the pre-Rwandan state) was home to dispersed groups of cultivators (Hutu) and forest dwellers (Twa). In the tenth century, a group of pastoralists, the Tutsi, arrived from the north and easily conquered the region and its inhabitants through their cunning military prowess. The Tutsi, advanced as they were, introduced a centralized form of government along with pastoralism and ironworking. It was the Tutsi—specifically the members of the Nyiginya clan—that brought the Hutu and Twa together to create Rwanda (Vansina 2004, 45–46). The Hutu were assimilated through a system of vassalage known as *ubuhake*. To submit to an *ubuhake* contract was to acknowledge submission to the king. The king ruled through a complex hierarchy of subordinates responsible for controlling the population, settling disputes, and collecting revenue, and the vassalage contract was a key instrument in the consolidation of his power (Codere 1962, 50). The patron (*shebuja*) gave more cattle to the client (*umugaragu*) but maintained ultimate ownership. In return, the client became the servant (*umuhakwa*), and the patron ensured his financial and physical protection (*umukuru w'umuryango*) (Vansina 2004, 47, 152). Indeed, control over cattle was a key element of acquiring power for the royal court. Extension of control over land, another important aspect of power and political relationships, emerged later, in the first quarter of the nineteenth century (C. Newbury 1988, 99).

According to this official narrative, Tutsi rule is natural since it is grounded in a benevolent relationship that respects the innate skills and attributes of each group (Des Forges 2011, 13). Various proverbs and myths tell tales of Tutsi supremacy in all things intellectual and administrative. The predominant myth states that Kigwa, the first-born son of the heavenly king Nkuba, entrusted each of his three sons—Gatutsi, Gahutu, and Gatwa—with the safekeeping of a calabash of milk overnight. In the morning, Kigwa found that Gatwa had drunk his milk. Gahutu had spilled his. Only Gatutsi had kept his milk safe. Kigwa therefore entrusted to him command over the gluttonous Gatwa and the clumsy Gahutu (Vansina 2004, 12–13). During my reeducation period, in September 2006, several of the RPF leaders to whom I spoke invoked this founding myth of Tutsi superiority to legitimate the government's postgenocide reconstruction and reconciliation policies (field notes 2006).

Careful study of Rwandan historiography finds that this RPF version of what its representatives call "official history" of preordained Tutsi rule is built on a foundation of half-truths. Many court rituals and institutions were "fundamentally Hutu in nature" and ignored "the role played by leading Hutu" in shaping the growth of the state (Des Forges 1995, 45). Vansina's research (2000, 2004) exposes the claim that "more enlightened" Tutsi introduced governance, noting that Hutu lineages had developed forms of social and political organization long before the Nyiginya clan arrived. The history of Rwanda is better understood as one of lineages (*umuryango*),[3] both Hutu and Tutsi, which enjoyed significant autonomy under the ultimate authority of its leader or head (C. Newbury 1988, 95–98). The other major kinship group in precolonial Rwanda was clans (*ubwoko*), which are more a social category than a corporate entity. Members of a clan cannot usually trace their ancestral links to one another, and clans have no political function "apart from social identity" (D. Newbury 1980, 391). Each clan includes members from all three ethnic groups, which challenges the idea found in the policy of national unity and reconciliation that Rwanda's ethnic groups are rigid to the point of resembling castes (Office of the President of the Republic 1999).

The Hamitic Myth

The arrival of European explorers and missionaries in the late nineteenth century paved the way for the first written histories to emerge. Catholic missionaries, known as les Pères Blancs (White Fathers), were encouraged by the Church to study local customs and to learn Kinyarwanda; early written accounts were thus a result of their work (D. Newbury and C. Newbury 2000, 844). Their historiography was grounded in the racialized worldview of Europeans, informed as it was by the "Hamitic hypothesis." A pseudo-scientific and fundamentally racist theory, the Hamitic thesis ranked all races according to each group's innate intelligence and skills.[4] In Rwanda, the hypothesis maintained that members of a superior Caucasoid race from northeastern Africa was responsible for any signs of civilization that the Europeans found upon their arrival in East and Central Africa (Chrétien 1985, 131). Through the Hamitic lens, European colonizers saw obvious evidence of Tutsi superiority in their natural ability to lead, their tall and slender builds, and their aquiline noses and fine hair; they were black Europeans. In reality, these characteristics are hardly universal among Tutsi. It must also be stressed that the Europeans interacted almost exclusively with the Tutsi aristocrats, and their view was shaped by their relationship with the Tutsi political elite. Tutsi members of the political classes "accounted for less than 10 percent" of all Tutsi in Rwanda at the time of the arrival of the Europeans (D. Newbury and C. Newbury 2000, 839).[5]

Similarly, the Hamitic lens assumed that Hutu (presumed to be about 85 percent of the population, both then and now) were sturdy, short, and dark. These physical features invariably meant that the Hutu were best kept as a subordinate class of laborers as they were seen as "naïve" and "easily duped" (Rwabukumba and Mudandagizi 1974, 13). In fact, the Hutu were never a homogeneous group, and numerous lineages, particularly in what is now North province, were headed by Hutu political elites (Des Forges 2011, 112–13; Vansina 2004, 145, 162). A third social category was also defined by the Hamitic myth— the Twa (presumed to compose less than 1 percent of Rwanda's population, then and now). Like the Tutsi and Hutu, the Twa were hardly a homogenous social group; some were attached to the royal court as entertainers and story-tellers, but most were on the margins of society, relegated to the status of "exotic appendages to Rwandan society" (Kagabo and Mudandagizi 1974, 76). Sadly, such imagery is used today to "attract attention to the plight of Twa. We can no longer organize as Twa because of the politics of national unity. We need to keep our people in the imagination of Westerners and that [as exotics] is how you whites know us" (interview with Prosper, a poor Twa man, 2006; see also Beswick 2011; Thomson 2009b).

Creating Ethnic Distinctions

Contra another of the core tenets of the "official" history found in the policy of national unity and reconciliation, Rwanda's social groups did not "arrive" as rigid ethnic categories, nor were they "found" as static entities. Instead, the categories of Tutsi, Hutu, and Twa "emerged as part of the larger processes of social flux, individual action and political power across the territorial region that would become Rwanda" (D. Newbury and C. Newbury 2000, 840). Indeed, there was significantly more individual mobility and interchange than any official version of a collective and ethnically unified Rwandan past can possibly present. The state was hardly created by a single lineage, royal or otherwise. Power and ethnicity did not coincide originally; they took shape and salience in cadence, not in confrontation with each other (C. Newbury and D. Newbury 1995, 16). Before the arrival of the Germans, region was more important than lineage (royal or not) in defining identity and the lived environment and ecology more influential than ethnicity in shaping the lives of ordinary people (D. Newbury 1991, 43–64; D. Newbury and C. Newbury 2000, 864–66). Precolonial historiog-raphy emphasizes royal history—essentially a history of Tutsi elites—that was narrated by historians appointed by the king, notably Alexis Kagame (no known relation to the current president, Paul Kagame). The current official history of the precolonial period relied on the Hamitic hypothesis that favored the Tutsi as natural rulers.

In reality, the terms "Hutu" and "Tutsi" did not refer to clearly demarcated, static groups; instead, their meaning varied by context, particularly in regional usage. The nature of the ties to the royal court of a given lineage shaped the everyday meaning of "Hutu" and "Tutsi." In regions where there were loose or nonexistent ties to the royal court, the terms rarely had any meaning in everyday life. In northern Rwanda, where lineage heads and their subordinates carefully guarded their autonomy from the royal court, individuals referred to themselves not as Hutu but rather as *bakiga* (meaning people from the Kiga region) (Lemarchand 1970, 99). In southwestern Rwanda, along the shores of Lake Kivu, individuals identified themselves in terms of clan affiliation, which was largely shaped by kin and clientship ties, not ethnicity (M. C. Newbury 1978, 18). Residents in this region used the term "Tutsi" but in ways that did not accord with its usage in other regions (C. Newbury 1988, 11).

In parts of Rwanda where the everyday use of both "Hutu" and "Tutsi" was common, their meaning leaned more toward identifying wealth or region of origin than ethnicity. In southeast Rwanda, "the origin of the terms Tutsi and Hutu is obscure, but in fact 'Tutsi' refers to a 'noble,' as 'Hutu' refers to a 'commoner' and not to different tribes" (Gravel 1968, 165). Wealthy and hence powerful Hutu lineages that commanded the respect of their neighbors acquired local influence to the extent that they often were "absorbed into the upper class" (Gravel 1967, 329; 1968, 170). Economically successful Hutu clients could adapt their identity to become Tutsi, which was a marker of socioeconomic status. The meanings of "Hutu" and "Tutsi" were fluid in that individuals could become influential and important (Tutsi) or remain common (Hutu). "Tutsi" was used to indicate a certain level of power and wealth (particularly in the form of cows) and was generally associated with those lineages linked to the royal court. Even Alexis Kagame recognized that "whoever possesses many heads of cattle is called Tutsi, even if he is not of the Hamitic race" (quoted in C. Newbury 1988, 253n34).

Thus, "Hutu" and "Tutsi" were terms whose meanings varied according to context and did not represent static and rigid categories as set out in the policy of national unity and reconciliation. Most important were lineage affiliations as these structured the elements of identity that were relevant in daily interactions as well as economic and political obligations to the state (through local chiefs). Tutsi, particularly those closest to the royal court, were members of the ruling elite. Many chiefs were Hutu, and they held important positions as confidants to the royal court (Franche 1997, 18).

The policy of national unity and reconciliation relies on static meanings of "Hutu" and "Tutsi" in hopes of harkening back to the imagined unity of the precolonial period. What the policy fails to appreciate is that state building marked an increasing intrusion into the everyday lives of rural Rwandans. The meaning of "Hutu" and "Tutsi" began to take on a more fixed and uniform meaning under a period of state expansion led by *mwami* Kigeri Rwabugiri (ca. 1865–95). Rwabugiri was determined to expand the territorial reach and political influence of his kingdom by expanding the network of lineage chiefs to bring more ordinary Rwandans into contracts of servitude and submission (Des Forges 2011, 12–14, 67–68, 75–76, 99–100, 226–29).

State Power and the Politicization of Identity

It was in the middle of the nineteenth century that the royal court began to centralize political power under the expansionist political and military approach of King Rwabugiri. The diversity of political lineages and the high degree of autonomy they enjoyed from the royal court were soon a thing of the past. Rwabugiri sought to maintain tight administrative control through central chiefs, many of whom he handpicked (Vidal 1969, 391). The modern equivalent is the RPF's policy of decentralization (Purdeková 2011; Reyntjens 2011). Peripheral regions that had previously enjoyed significant autonomy from the royal court soon found themselves governed by a complex network of chiefs appointed by Rwabugiri from Tutsi-headed lineages. Rwabugiri freely disposed of incumbents and appointed chiefs directly dependent on him, just as Kagame has done in appointing RPF loyalists at the local level (C. Newbury 1988, 108). Direct central administrative control was the hallmark of Rwabugiri's reign. Under his rule, domination of Hutu by Tutsi through clientship mechanisms began to take on political meaning, particularly as royal control spread administratively across the kingdom and down to the lower levels of society (M. C. Newbury 1978, 19). Three related processes in particular shaped the everyday life of ordinary Rwandans: the growing ascendance of chiefs appointed by Rwabugiri at the expense of the authority of lineage heads, shifts in land rights, and a move toward greater social stratification. In particular, Rwabugiri sought to exercise influence through chiefs loyal to him via a patron-clientship practice called *umuheto*.

Before Rwabugiri extended his reign to the regions, *umuheto* was a practice in which lineage heads in the peripheral regions maintained ties to central chiefs loyal to the court. *Umuheto* ties were grounded in reciprocal alliances, sometimes even characterized by strong affective ties (M. C. Newbury 1978, 18). It was a bond between elites that was limited to cattle-owning lineages, and its defining characteristic was the social and political cohesion it created among elites (Vidal 1969, 390). With the extension of the power of the royal court and the appointment of provincial chiefs loyal to the court, *umuheto* became a tool of ethnic differentiation. Under Rwabugiri, differences between the heads of Hutu and Tutsi lineages were sharpened as his provincial chiefs in turn appointed their subordinate hill chiefs. Most provincial chiefs were Tutsi, and the category began to take on "hierarchical overtones" (M. C. Newbury 1978, 21). "Tutsi" became a term associated primarily with central administrative power, particularly the exactions of chiefs, which were arduous for many ordinary Rwandans, Hutu and Tutsi alike. Dispossessed chiefs of both ethnicities were relegated to the sidelines of political activity, as they were increasingly unable to protect their subordinates from the continued demands of court-appointed provincial chiefs (Des Forges 2011, 100).

Rwabugiri's policies led to significant changes in land rights related to both tenure and distribution. *Ubukonde* was transformed from a collective endeavor through which property rights were vested in a lineage as a whole into *isambu*, a system in which land was owned by hill chiefs, who guaranteed land tenure to subordinates in exchange for payments and corvée labor (Vansina 2004, 42).[6] Dispossessed lineage heads and their membership found that under *isambu*, their ability to work the land—either through pasturage or cultivation—was compromised as the whim of the hill chief determined when and by whom the land could be used (M. C. Newbury 1978, 20). This system also marked a dramatic shift away from the practice of young lineage members addressing the lineage's head to request their own land; instead, it became a form of coercive political control as hill chiefs sought to extend their political authority over existing lineage members (Meschi 1974, 44–49; Vansina, 2004, 97).[7]

By the end of the nineteenth century, "Tutsi" came to identify those individuals associated with central power, notably through the exactions of Tutsi hill chiefs who served the interests of the court, not those of everyday lineage members. "Hutu" came to be associated with and defined by inferior status. The political salience of membership in one category or the other came to depend on who held power through clientship mechanisms and who did not (M. C. Newbury 1980, 100). It is doubtful that Rwabugiri's policies were specifically designed to transform the meaning of the labels "Tutsi" and "Hutu." They were developed with the goal of enlarging the power of the royal court, not to favor Tutsi as a group and not to anoint them as Rwanda's natural leaders. Most important was the changing nature of power and the increasing authority with which subordinates of the court in turn treated their subordinates in the hills.

The Internal Politics of the Royal Court

It is important to understand the internal politics of Rwabugiri's court for two reasons: to understand the politicization of the terms "Tutsi" and "Hutu" and to appreciate the political uses of the "unity" of the precolonial period in the policy of national unity and reconciliation. His reign, particularly in the ten years right before his death, in 1895, gave rise to a period of increasing violence among prominent lineages, all of which vied for royal power in violent ways. Rwabugiri did not discriminate and killed Hutu and Tutsi rivals, including his own mother (Des Forges 2011, 14, 23; Linden and Linden 1977, 20). The effects of the violence among and within lineages affected court relations with the German colonizers. Rwabugiri's successor, Musinga, shaped relations among the various lineages. According to Catharine Newbury, it was the Rwandans "who largely determined the ways in which colonialism influenced the trans-formation of clientship ties" (C. Newbury 1988, 59). The politics of the court and its rivals were intense, characterized by waves of executions and persecu-tions among various factions (Des Forges 1972, 22–23; D. Newbury 1991, 145–226; Vansina 2004, 164–95). The intrigues of the court culminated in a coup d'état that overthrew Rwabugiri's legitimate successor, King Mibambwe Ruta-rindwa, and put Musinga on the throne in December 1896. It resulted in a "nearly permanent recourse to violence" that created a climate of insecurity and fear among ordinary Rwandans and elites alike (Vansina 2004, 181). It also succeeded in dissolving the cohesion of the most basic social groups, from the smallest unit, the *inzu* (house), up to the court itself. The coup also was marked by intense violence between elite lineages within prominent clans as the Aba-hindiro (of the lineage of the Abanyiginya royal clan) were soundly defeated by the Abakagara (of the Abeega clan). The shift in power from the elites of one royal clan to another generated significant changes in local patron-client ties, "since those with links to a central patron who was on the losing side . . . found it necessary to switch allegiances" (C. Newbury 1988, 59).

Military activity intensified, as did the politics of denunciation and accusa-tion, two practices that are equally prominent in everyday contemporary life in Rwanda (Amnesty International 2011; Weinstein 1977; see also chapter 4). Both practices were common (then and now) among elites as tools for eliminating adversaries, either for the purpose of obtaining their wealth (in the form of land, cattle, or people) or out of simple hatred or revenge (Codere 1962, 71; Vansina 2004, 184). Acts of denunciation by lineage heads could culminate in the death of one or both men, adding to the sense of insecurity among the members of lineages as their protection by their patrons could not be ensured. Patterns of disgracing or shaming hill chiefs by competing élites was devastating to ordinary people, as Musinga replaced these chiefs with people drawn from his own power base, in violation of the chiefs' contractual rights. The new chiefs routinely abused their power and extorted as much as they could from local people (Meschi 1974, 49). This inevitably led to often violent conflict in the hills as the newcomers sought to exercise their authority over the existing chiefs.

Ordinary people did not know where to look for protection, further heightening their everyday sense of fear and insecurity. The internal politics of the royal court served to further institutionalize a "humiliating differentiation made between Tutsi and Hutu" in the exploitation of the population, including the imposition of unpaid corvée labor on farmers but not herders and the increasing interference of the court in local administration (Vansina 2004, 192). *Ubuhake* contracts were particularly affected as once powerful patrons fell in disgrace, with the result that some ordinary people were unable to establish relations with a new patron; others, particularly in northern Rwanda, no longer looked for a patron, preferring to "go it alone" (Meschi 1974, 44).

The dissolution of *ubuhake* relationships was but one aspect of the ever-increasing exploitation of the population by the leadership. *Uburetwa*—manual labor at the service of Tutsi authorities—applied only to Hutu and quickly became "the most hated and humiliating [of practices as it] symbolized the servitude of the Hutu vis-à-vis the dominant minority" (Rwabukumba and Mudandagizi 1974, 21). *Ubuhake* affected only a small percentage of ordinary Rwandans, while *uburetwa* put thousands of people in "direct contact with political authority through an extractive relationship" (M. C. Newbury 1980, 108). The centralization of control over land, the loss of autonomy for ordinary people dependent on patrons, and the multiplication of local authorities linked to the royal court, combined with the violent politics of the court, were all ongoing on the eve of European arrival.

Colonial Transmutations

Rwabugiri died in 1895. Shortly after, Germany established a military presence in northwest Rwanda, and its colonial rule began in 1898 with a minimal presence of five administrators for the entire country (Louis 1963, 204; Reyntjens 1995, 17). The political and social impact of their presence was substantial. A German officer named von Ramsey proposed an alliance with Musinga that his mother, Kanjogera, readily accepted. Kanjogera was a member of the Abakagara lineage and was influential in court politics, notably in orchestrating her son Musinga's accession to the throne following the coup at Rucunshu.[8] As queen mother, she held a vaunted position and used her power to shape court ritual obligations as well as important political prerogatives. Her efforts to concentrate royal power in her own hands continued well into Musinga's reign, resulting in continued violence among competing elites seeking to gain power (Des Forges 2011, 72–97; C. Newbury 1988, 58–59; Vansina 2004, 176–77, 190–91, 202).

Musinga ascended to the throne at the age of thirteen or fourteen in 1897, and his enthronement was heavily contested by chiefs, warriors, and lineage heads seeking either to maintain a position of influence with the royal court or to seize its power (Vansina 2004, 179). The Germans did not interfere in domestic affairs for the next twenty years, which allowed the political intrigues and violence of Rwabugiri's era to continue (Des Forges 2011, 125–29). It was German policy to rely on the "traditional" rulers, which meant that they used Tutsi chiefs as intermediaries to the population (Reyntjens 1985, 97). This greatly enhanced the power of these chiefs, further adding to the violence and intrigues surrounding the court, which in turn heightened the fear and insecurity of ordinary people. Chiefs appointed an additional layer of administrators (the *ibirongozi*) to perform "particularly unpopular functions for the hill chiefs, such as extracting prestations, services and taxes from the population" (C. Newbury 1988, 115). These new officials usurped the functions previously carried out by lineage heads. Hutu, who had once enjoyed autonomy and authority as lineage heads and local leaders, saw their status diminished as power became increasingly concentrated in the hands of Tutsi chiefs (Linden and Linden 1977, 124).

At about the same time in the late 1800s, Catholic missionaries arrived in Rwanda. The White Fathers also tried to establish good working relations with Musinga but were met with a mixture of resistance and quiescence. Under pressure from the Germans, upon whose firepower Musinga relied to consolidate his power, he granted the Fathers land for their missions (Des Forges 2011, 92). The parcels of land Musinga granted the White Fathers were strategically located far away from the court to provide a modicum of distance while superficially appearing to facilitate their mission. Musinga was uneasy about the presence of the White Fathers and advised Tutsi chiefs not to send their children or subjects to missionary school—religious teaching was to be only for Hutu and Twa (Des Forges 2011, 29). The result was the unintentional creation of a largely Hutu church, since the first converts were nearly all poor Hutu (Linden and Linden 1977, 52). Indeed, many Hutu and ordinary Tutsi sought the protection of the White Fathers against increasingly extractive Tutsi chiefs and their new deputies, the *ibirongozi* (Des Forges 2011, 66–68).

Rwanda came under Belgian control in 1916 following the advance of Belgian troops across Rwanda. German forces retreated, leaving Rwanda to the Belgians, altering local power relations. During the first year of Belgian rule, its military administration regarded Musinga with suspicion. Prominent regional chiefs took the opportunity to defy royal authority and deal directly with the Belgians. Musinga was unable to punish these renegade chiefs, which further undermined his personal prestige and political power (C. Newbury 1988, 129). Belgian policy initially favored the Hutu, notably in the northwest of Rwanda (the *bakiga* region). Like the Germans, the Belgians relied on Tutsi chiefs as agents of their rule but tried to influence their conduct to "conform to standards of administrative, rational behaviour" (M. C. Newbury 1980, 102). Chiefs astutely recognized that loyalty to the Belgians was critical for their own survival as Musinga was no longer "the top of the clientship chain" (Linden and Linden 1977, 157). The Belgian authorities backed the power of Tutsi chiefs, in turn allowing for a greater proliferation of chiefly dominance through administrative practices such as obligatory cultivation, unpaid corvée labor, and the imposition of additional taxes, which were levied on individuals rather than on lineages as they had been in the past (M. C. Newbury 1978, 23). These changes in the power equation were further underscored by the hardship experienced by ordinary Rwandans, who were suffering from severe famine (known as Rumanura) in the northwest (Des Forges 2011, 137–38). With these new bureaucratic powers concentrated in the hands of Tutsi chiefs, two parallel systems of exploitation emerged under Belgian rule—clientship linkages and administrative powers. The role of "patron" and "chief" were conflated in ways that "much reduced the capacity of clients to bargain and manoeuvre" (M. C. Newbury 1978, 22). Moreover, the Belgian authorities appointed chiefs from above and usually chose individuals who were not resident in the community they were to control. The primary responsibility of the chief became to ensure that the local population met its labor and tax obligations; his loyalty was to his political superior (C. Newbury 1988, 110–14). When the Belgians consolidated small administrative units into larger ones, the distance between chiefs and the population was increased (M. C. Newbury 1978, 22).

Belgian policy required chiefs to ensure that every adult man paid taxes and performed corvée when requested. In practice, the Belgians often arbitrarily administered their policies to serve the interests of the chief, who had great discretion in determining who paid or participated and in what capacity. The type of work that chiefs assigned to individuals for corvée often depended on that ordinary individual's standing with the chief. Those of low or no status were called upon more often and assigned the more exploitative and oppressive tasks (Codere 1962, 51; C. Newbury 1988, 127–28, 136–37; Vidal 1974, 55). An oft-cited reason for a chief to dispossess an individual of his land was nonperformance or nonpayment of taxes. Even where the work was completed or the payment made, it was the chief who reported to his Belgian superiors who had "paid" or "refused" corvée (Pottier 2002, 183–84). The arbitrary use of power by the chiefs, who were the most effective intermediaries between the central government and the local populations, was usually overlooked so long as "the chiefs met the requirements placed on them" (M. C. Newbury 1978, 24). This put ordinary people in a bind as they consistently found themselves in increasingly oppressive client-patron relationships in which they were the weaker party but in which they were required to seek to gain the favor of the chief in their community. Ordinary Rwandans who had strategically abandoned client relationships after Rwabugiri's reign were forcefully brought back into patron-client relationships, the most important of which was the land clientship practice of *uburetwa* (C. Newbury 1988, 134).

The Belgian authorities were particularly fond of *uburetwa* (manual labor in the service of Tutsi chiefs) because it ensured the submission of the population to their chiefs. In practice, *uburetwa* was a specifically Hutu obligation, particularly as those of Tutsi status could more easily defend themselves against the whims of chiefs. The services performed "were usually of the most menial kind" (C. Newbury 1988, 141). More significant, *uburetwa* directly shaped the relationship of ordinary persons to their land since nonperformance could provoke the chief to seize that land. The Belgian authorities did not abolish the practice, which they saw as an expression of the obedience of the population to their chiefs, who owed their privileged position of power to the Belgians. Catharine Newbury argues that pressure from the chiefs themselves to uphold the practice likely contributed to *uburetwa*'s longevity, because "the unpaid labour available could . . . contribute substantial enrichment of the chiefs" (C. Newbury 1988, 142). It also fueled continued insecurity among Hutu and "further bitterness" toward the capricious rule of Tutsi chiefs, backed as it was by the Belgian authorities (M. C. Newbury 1978, 25).

Colonial rule thus resulted in a more pronounced centralization of power at the top while creating group awareness among elite Hutu, the primary victims of the political, social, and economic changes that allowed elite Tutsi to use the state apparatus to forward their own interests. These changes meant that elite Tutsi identity was formed before the colonists arrived, backed as it was by the rich oral tradition of the royal court and its historians. Hutu group awareness emerged in relation to the colonial state as it formalized the leadership of Tutsi. Hutu were not given a national political role in a restrictive colonial context that favored elite Tutsi; it was the use and abuse of power by Tutsi chiefs that created Hutu consciousness. As Catharine Newbury argues, "It was in fact oppression in its many different forms that brought about the cohesion among Hutu" (1988, 209). Those Hutu who became political leaders in the 1950s pursued higher education through seminary school offered by the White Fathers where they were exposed to the ideals of equality and social justice (Linden and Linden 1977, 209, 198). Hutu leaders were able to tap into this consciousness to call attention to socioeconomic inequalities in Rwanda and gave a voice to their grievances as the country moved toward independence at the end of the 1950s. Ordinary peasants—Hutu and Tutsi—suffered under the bureaucratic expansionist policies of both the royal court and colonial authorities. The growth of the colonial state meant greater intrusion and increased extractions, which in turn threatened peasants' security. Ethnicity was less salient in their daily lives than was their relationship to their patron and the ways in which they were able to navigate the labor requirements of that relationship, which was in turn shaped by the relationship of their patron to the Belgian authorities. Most devastating to many ordinary Rwandans was the loss of kinship ties; if anything, the dual colonial practices of the Belgians and Tutsi authorities heightened awareness among peasant Rwandans of their lack of control over key resources, namely their own land, cattle, and labor.

Decolonization and the 1959 Revolution

The bitter resentments and political consciousness of rural Rwandans— ordinary peasant Hutu and Tutsi alike—resulted in a movement for Hutu liberation, led by educated Hutu (M. C. Newbury 1980). Ordinary peasant folk shared hopes of releasing themselves from the oppressive nature of the existing clientship relations and labor control mechanisms. The movement called for the transformation of the oppressive political and economic structures before independence (Lemarchand 1970, 112). Belgium was under pressure from the United Nations to decolonize. In July 1952, it issued a decree setting out the procedures for the formation of elective councils from the level of the subchief up to the highest positions in the state (Lemarchand 1970, 79–81; Linden and Linden 1977, 230–31). Elections were held in 1952 and 1956; both times, Hutu candidates were virtually shut out as Tutsi authorities rigged the vote to ensure that their incumbents held onto their positions (Linden and Linden 1977, 231; Lemarchand 1970, 83).

Defeat had a significant impact on the corps of Hutu local leaders as neither the Belgians nor the Tutsi authorities introduced reforms that could pave the way for elite Hutu participation in the structures of power (C. Newbury 1988, 190). For example, the High Council (Conseil supérieur) included only three Hutu members, who constituted less than 6 percent of its members. The HC was the highest advisory body of the state and "was expected to assume legislative functions when Rwanda was granted self-government by Belgium" (C. Newbury 1988, 191). In response, Hutu leaders issued the "Manifesto of the Bahutu."[9] This manifesto "vociferously asserted the centrality of the 'Hutu-Tutsi problem,'" which lay directly in the "political, socioeconomic, and cultural monopoly" of the Tutsi elite and its continued oppression of ordinary people (C. Newbury 1988, 191). The manifesto identified the source of rural grievances, noting the disaffection of rural Hutu and impoverished Tutsi youth and their inability to continue to accept the coercive practices of the Tutsi authorities. The only plausible solution was the implementation of changes to Rwanda's entrenched political and social system that would allow for the inclusion of rural issues. In contrast to the interpretation of the radical roots of the manifesto found in the policy of national unity and reconciliation, Hutu leaders did not call for revolution or overthrow of the colonial political system. Instead, their primary request was inclusion in the existing system, not its overthrow.[10] Calls for change fell on deaf ears among both Belgian and Tutsi authorities (Lemarchand 1970, 114). Instead, the High Council blamed Hutu oppression on Belgian colonizers (d'Hertefelt 1964, 229).

Hutu leaders responded by creating organizations that could defend Hutu interests in anticipation of the first national elections. Grégoire Kayibanda formed the *Mouvement social muhutu* (MSM), which later became a political party, Le parti du mouvement de l'émancipation hutu (PARMEHUTU), with the purpose of promoting the objectives articulated in the Hutu manifesto (C. Newbury 1988, 192). Another prominent Hutu leader, Joseph Gitera, formed L'Association pour la promotion sociale de la masse (APROSOMA), whose stated objectives were not framed in ethnic terms. Instead, it sought "to represent the interests of all poor groups, Tutsi as well as Hutu" (C. Newbury 1992, 196). Parties led by Tutsi elites also emerged, notably the UNAR (Union nationale rwandaise), which wanted to crush Hutu resistance to maintain the monarchy. Younger, educated, and politically moderate Tutsi joined RADER (Rassemblement démocratique rwandais), which favored institutional reform and a constitutional monarchy (Lemarchand 1970, 160; C. Newbury 1988, 194).

Tensions between elite Hutu and Tutsi continued, fueled as they were by PARMEHUTU's appeals to ethnicity. Violence erupted in central Rwanda in November 1959 and later spread to the north and south of the country (Lemarchand 1970, 159; Reyntjens 1985, 196). The Union nationale rwandaise (UNAR), a Tutsi monarchist party, sparked local violence when a group of its militants attacked one of the few Hutu subchiefs in Rwanda. Rumor quickly spread among the population that he had been killed (which was not true). In protest, a group of Hutu went to the residence of a Tutsi subchief and killed him, along with two other Tutsi notables (Reyntjens 1985, 260). In the aftermath, the resentment of the population reached the point where many Tutsi chiefs and subchiefs were forced to resign. The Belgians further fueled this climate of insecurity in November 1959 when they switched their allegiance from the Tutsi authorities to the Hutu counterelite in declaring their commitment to majority rule (Reyntjens 1985, 278). They then filled these newly vacant posts with "interim" Hutu appointees, many of whom showed little administrative aptitude (Lemarchand 1970, 173–174). A climate of fear and insecurity once again prevailed in the everyday lives of ordinary Rwandans as political elites postured to secure their political positions.

The transfer of power from Belgium to the Hutu elite normalized routine violence in the everyday lives of Rwandans. Communal elections were held in June and July 1960 to select burgomasters (mayors) and local councilors to replace the existing subchiefdoms, which were restructured into larger units, and chiefdoms were combined into provinces (C. Newbury 1988, 198). The elections were violent; UNAR thugs tried to use intimidation tactics to prevent victory for Hutu parties, which won 83.8 percent of the vote anyway (C. Newbury 1988, 198; Lemarchand 1970, 179–80). PARMEHUTU won 71 percent of the vote (Reyntjens 1985, 283). These elections were instrumental in placing Hutu leaders in key administrative positions. Despite this apparent "ethnic" victory, the identities of ordinary Hutu remained tied to tradition, extending only as far as one's family and clan; group consciousness and references to Hutu ethnicity were an elite affair (Lemarchand 1970, 182). Newly installed mayors, unconditionally supported by the Belgian authorities, used their new-found power to intimidate former Tutsi authorities, notably through arbitrary arrest and imprisonment. In some areas, mayors fabricated rumors of night raids and other disturbances to initiate "retaliations" against the old Tutsi authorities. Many fled with their families to other regions of Rwanda or to neighboring countries, laying the foundation for the RPF's eventual return to Rwanda in 1990, when it invaded the country from Uganda (Linden and Linden 1977, 160; Reyntjens 1985, 289).

The Belgians ensured a quick transfer of power to the PARMEHUTU leaders despite the disquiet surrounding the communal elections. On January 23, 1961, Joseph Gitera assembled the recently elected burgomasters and councilors to "declare the abolition of the monarchy and the birth of the newly independent Republic of Rwanda" (Lemarchand 1970, 192). The Belgians named PARMEHUTU's Grégoire Kayibanda as the country's second president, which was later confirmed when Rwanda gained its independence from Belgium on July 1, 1962.[11]

Postindependence Politics, 1962–1990

Despite the pristine image of national unity that the Belgians thought they had created in transferring their loyalty to the majority Hutu, dissension among Hutu elites was rife in the immediate postindependence period (1962–73). A regional rivalry emerged almost immediately, with northern Hutu showing "unmitigated disdain" for their counterparts from the southern and central regions of Rwanda (Lemarchand 1970, 266). In an effort to unite the various Hutu factions, Kayibanda's government identified a common threat—the *inyenzi* (or cockroach) raids that began in late 1961. The so-called *inyenzi* was an armed faction of the UNAR (Reyntjens 1992, 172). Small bands made frequent forays with the aim of "creating a sense of insecurity within Rwanda, and the prime targets were Hutu officials and European administrators" (Weinstein 1977, 61). The worst attack was in December 1963 when between 250 and 1,000 *inyenzi* rebels crossed into Rwanda from Burundi and came within twelve miles of Kigali, after a foot trek of some 140 miles (Lemarchand 1970, 220; Weinstein 1977, 64). The reaction of the Kayibanda government was swift. Authorities rounded up twenty Tutsi leaders affiliated with UNAR and RADER (a moderate and ethnically inclusive party) and publicly executed them (Lemarchand 1970, 225). Local militias were created in each province to guard against future Tutsi attacks. In some areas, Hutu authorities attacked Tutsi homesteads, burning, looting, and pillaging (Weinstein 1977, 65). By the time the attacks were contained, more than ten thousand Tutsi had lost their lives (Lemarchand 1970, 225). The national police rounded up a few hundred influential Tutsi and some Hutu; some were executed, others charged with treason or held without charge (Reyntjens 1985, 463). By the end of 1963, between 130,000 and 300,000 Rwandans (mostly Tutsi, along with Hutu and Twa who followed their patrons) had fled to neighboring countries (Lemarchand 1970, 172; Reyntjens 1985, 455).

In identifying the *inyenzi* rebels as the common enemy, Kayibanda was able to unite the Hutu leadership. His tactics, however, eventually backfired as the population—both ordinary peasant people and the educated class— recognized that government-led efforts to unify against the *inyenzi* threat were designed to consolidate Kayibanda's position, rather than actually addressing the sources of fear, insecurity, and dissatisfaction that had motivated Hutu to participate in the 1959 revolution in the first place. Ordinary people continued to suffer the same abuses of power that their local officials (now of Hutu ethnicity) had exacted upon them in the past. Educated Hutu—students, teachers, and junior civil servants—felt shut out of the rewards of the revolution, from which much had been promised. Despite their initial commitment to Kayibanda's cause of Hutu unity, many educated Hutu quickly saw corruption among state elites, recognized that the promises of increased pay would not be honored, and judged that opportunities for career advancement were virtually nonexistent (Lemarchand 1970, 238–41). The response of the Kayibanda regime to these grievances was to blame all Tutsi, regardless of social status or economic class.

Kayibanda expanded PARMEHUTU's reach into local communities in an effort to "mould the loyalties of citizens" (Lemarchand 1970, 247). Kayibanda retained the identity cards that the Belgians introduced in 1931 to label Rwandans as "Hutu," "Tutsi," or "Twa," and he instituted a quota system to ensure proportionality in education and employment. The Kayibanda regime also limited Tutsi to 9 percent of the total number of seats in schools, the civil service, and even the private sector (Reyntjens 1985, 501). Contrary to the version of history found in the policy of national unity and reconciliation, elite Tutsi continued to populate the ranks of the educated elite because of their historical advantage. In addition, Kayibanda's quota system was regularly bypassed as close-knit intra-ethnic kin and local networks procured prominent positions in government and private sector employment for elite Tutsi. This was possible because colonial policy had limited access to formal education to Tutsi, which meant that few Hutu had the necessary skills to compete for these jobs (C. Newbury 1992, 197). It also meant that close to 50 percent of the teachers and students at secondary school and in universities were Tutsi (Reyntjens 1985, 501). At the National University, the primary training ground for the civil service, Tutsi accounted for 90 percent of the student body (Lemarchand 1970, 260). The residual effect of these colonial practices prompted members of the Hutu elite from the northern region of Rwanda to call for radical reforms to remedy this ethnic imbalance.

Individuals from central Rwanda, where Kayibanda grew up, dominated his government (C. Newbury 1992, 197). Corruption was the order of the day; Kayibanda's long-term associates and family held key administrative positions, which caused a rift among Hutu elites. Northern factions "began to openly criticize the regime" (Jefremovas 2000, 303). In efforts to protect his power, Kayibanda reframed regional dissent as ethnic violence. Rumors of Tutsi attacks against Hutu like those of the *inyenzi* in 1959–63 spread quickly. The population was quick to believe them, relying on the stories of refugees from Burundi who had fled that country's 1972 Hutu genocide, in which an estimated one hundred thousand to two hundred thousand individuals died (Lemarchand 1998, 6). As Burundian Hutu streamed into Rwanda, Kayibanda instituted public safety committees, which were essentially vigilante groups created to monitor the civil service, universities, schools, and businesses to ensure that the ethnic quota regulations were being followed (Des Forges 1999, 40).[12] In late 1972 and early 1973, almost all Tutsi students were run out of schools and the national university (Reyntjens 1985, 503). Anti-Tutsi sentiment affected elites and ordinary people alike. The public safety committees ensured that educated, salaried workers were fired, and blacklists were posted in offices to intimidate local Tutsi. Ordinary folk were asked to leave their homes, which were looted and burned by members of public safety committees (Reyntjens 1985, 503). In the hills, the violence was not directed solely at Tutsi as it was in economic centers like Kigali, Butare, and Gitarama. Instead, the wealthy, rural elite Hutu and Tutsi alike— not ordinary peasant Tutsi—were the victims. Those from the north targeted southerners, while those with outstanding grievances against the local authorities used the opportunity to exact payback (Reyntjens 1985, 504).

By July 1973, the violence had abated, and Major-General Juvénal Habyarimana, the most senior officer in the northerner-controlled army, took power from Kayibanda in a "bloodless" coup (Des Forges 1999, 41; C. Newbury 1992, 197–98; Reyntjens 1985, 506).[13] Under Habyarimana, the ethnic question took a backseat, and his coup was "welcomed" because it reduced both ethnic violence and rampant government corruption (Jefremovas 2000, 303). Habyarimana was popular with Tutsi, and some Hutu groups accused him of favoring Tutsi. Relations between elite Hutu and Tutsi were amicable early in Habyarimana's rule, although top positions in government were reserved for northern Hutu. There was also considerable intermarriage, "not only between southern Tutsi and Hutu but also between northern Hutu families and economically powerful Tutsi families" (Jefremovas 2000, 303).

Peace and the semblance of stability nonetheless came at a cost. Habyarimana consolidated a highly centralized state apparatus to monitor and control the activities of the population that today is part and parcel of the RPF regime (Purdeková 2011; Reyntjens 2011). Habyarimana banned political parties in the name of ethnic unity and national security in much the same way that Kagame has (Amnesty International 2011; Cooke 2011; Reyntjens 2011). In 1975 Habyarimana created the Mouvement révolutionnaire national pour le développement (MRND), of which all Rwandans were members (Des Forges 1999, 41). The party structure was then extended down to the most local levels of government as the central party apparatus appointed all officials. Each local official was granted a leadership position in the MRND, so that the state and the party became one entity in people's daily lives (Prunier 1997, 76). The central government required that residents of each commune register with the local authorities, which in turn reported all births, deaths, and movement in and out of their bailiwick on a monthly basis, a practice that continues today (Des Forges 1999, 42; field notes 2006). Identity cards continued to categorize Rwandans according to their ethnicity. This measure was necessary to implement Habyarimana's policy of "ethnic and regional equilibrium," which reserved seats in educational institutions and in the state apparatus in order to rectify the favoritism shown by the Belgians to Tutsi. On paper, the policy aimed to ensure ethnic equality; in practice, it excluded Tutsi and non-northern Hutu from lucrative government posts. Only 9 percent of positions were reserved for Tutsi, despite the fact than an estimated 15 percent of Rwandans held Tutsi identity cards.

The "hierarchical ethos" and top-down decision-making structures that shaped Habyarimana's regime affected ordinary people (C. Newbury 1992, 199). Mobilizing the population for public work projects such as road repairs, ditch digging, and brush clearing was common practice in most rural communities, harkening back to the colonial practice of *akazi* (or labor conscription by the Europeans) and continuing today with the same practice of *umuganda* (community work). The stated difference in the practice under Habyarimana was that it was voluntary (not mandatory, as it had been under Belgian rule, although naming and shaming were employed to ensure full "voluntary" participation). Such "voluntary" labor was limited to only two days per month (not per week, as it had been). In practice, the government required ordinary people to work on *umuganda* projects on average four days per month, and local officials enforced everyone's full participation. Individuals who did not report for work duty were fined (Des Forges 1999, 42). Some men in their late forties and early fifties who participated in my research reported that the poorest of the poor "had to report for *umuganda* at least one or two days a week or suffer imprisonment or worse" (interviews 2006). They also told me that as the poorest of the poor had to report more frequently in those days because the authorities told them, "Since you don't work for money, you will come work for the state and we will feed your families." Local officials often used this tactic to entice men to participate in *umuganda* projects, as the full participation of the population showed "those at the top" (senior government officials) that the local official was able to control the activities of peasant people in his jurisdiction, just as it does today through *imihigo* local accountability performance contracts (Ingelaere 2011; interviews 2006). When local officials actually delivered food to families as promised, it was "usually rotten or infested" (interviews 2006).

The ordinary peasants I consulted also made it clear that, despite the years of social revolution (1959–62) and Habyarimana's policy of ethnic equilibrium, ethnicity was a tool that elites used to gain and keep power. Burnet notes that many of the women she worked with during her field research "learned who they were when they went to school, obtained their national identity cards (around the age of 16), or applied for jobs. The majority of women I interviewed . . . became aware of their ethnic identity while at school" (Burnet 2005, 68). In 1972 and 1973, before the Habyarimana regime introduced reforms to the education system, teachers forced Tutsi students to stand up in their classrooms and identify their ethnicity, as only Hutu would be allowed to sit for national exams (Burnet 2005, 69).

The highest level of formal education attained among my participants was the equivalent of the third grade in the American system. Most participants had had only a year or two of formal schooling, meaning that none of them had sat for national exams and none had graduated from primary to secondary school. They also all lived in southern Rwanda, where relations between Hutu and Tutsi were more amicable and cooperative than in other regions of the country, particularly the north. For these individuals, ethnic identity had little impact on their daily lives. The ordinary peasants who participated in my research understood that their lives were shaped by their social and class positions and by their daily interactions with local authorities, which in turn were formed by the prevailing regional and class politics at the time. All of the individuals who participated understood themselves to be peasants. As Martin, a Tutsi man who survived the genocide told me,

> I'm a former Tutsi. I had an identity card that said so. But it meant nothing until the genocide. Why do you think they [the government] kept the cards? Even they can't tell who is Tutsi or who is Hutu. They needed cards to tell the killers, just like they needed cards before [under Habyarimana] to determine who would benefit from politics.
>
> But me, and my family, and the others around us, Hutu or Tutsi or what, we are peasants. And the authorities don't care about us. Any of the benefits of being Hutu didn't matter; we [peasants] didn't get anything out of being this ethnicity or that one. We were told what crops to grow and always support the party [MRND]. Coffee was important in those days.[14] But we didn't have land like that. We can hardly feed our families. Some grew coffee instead of food because they were forced. Others grew coffee and stole food from other plots. There were a lot of problems among us [peasants], but they [the authorities] didn't care. We are peasants, and we don't matter for much.
>
> Being Hutu or Tutsi, that was the business of the government and other important people [elites]. We just hoped, like we do now with this government, that we could get some peace. (Interview 2006)

The Habyarimana regime created a strong, centralized, and effective state that served as an instrument of domination and control. In the process, his government sought to contain the regional and ethnic tensions from which Habyarimana's power was born. The system of ethnic equilibrium was unable to contain rivals for state power. Two senior officers in Habyarimana's army made an unsuccessful coup attempt in April 1980 (Gasana 2002, 30). The coup sharpened the divisions within the northern Hutu elite, meaning that those from Habyarimana's home province of Gisenyi were favored over individuals from bordering Ruhengeri province. Habyarimana's most favored individuals were those from the *abahinza* lineage, of which his wife was a member. Habyarimana himself was from an unimportant Hutu lineage; he consequently relied on "his wife's clan . . . to be his ears and eyes" (Prunier 1997, 86). Agathe Habyarimana was nicknamed Kanjogera (the name of King Musinga's prominent and powerful mother) (Barahinyura 1988, 143). Rather than try to enlarge his regional and ethnic power base, Habyarimana limited the fruits of power to those individuals linked or loyal to Mrs. Habyarimana's clan. This inner circle or *akazu* (little hut) became the locus of power from the mid-1980s as Rwanda entered a period of economic decline, which limited its ability to shape the political and social landscape.

In October 1990 the then rebel RPF attacked Rwanda from Uganda. This marked the beginning of a low-intensity civil war and led to negotiations for power sharing among the MRND, the RPF, and other political parties. Habyarimana's regime also suffered under the double pressure of structural adjustment and international pressure to democratize. Because of his willingness to negotiate with the RPF, Habyarimana became a potential enemy of the *akazu*, particularly of its alleged extremist faction, the Zero Network (Réseau zéro). The economic decline, continued elite manipulation of ethnicity, and the civil war all contributed to the disintegration of Rwandan society starting in 1990, which in turn allowed the "self-interested fraction of an elite, not of an ethnic group," to plan and carry out the 1994 genocide (Jefremovas 2000, 304).

Conclusion

The historical record shows that ethnic identities are very much a product of the state and of the various state-building projects that successive regimes have undertaken, demonstrating that the policy of national unity and reconciliation is a product of this historical legacy of administrative domination and regime authority. The policies and actions of the Belgian colonizers and missionaries had a negative impact on the lives of ordinary Rwandans, just as the policy of national unity and reconciliation claims. But ordinary Rwandans also suffered at the hands of their Rwandan overlords under land and clientship arrangements that started under the royal court and that were fully consolidated as oppressive practices of socioeconomic stratification by the end of the colonial period, in 1962. The failure of the Belgians to understand the complexity of Rwanda's political and social organization allowed the king and his chiefs and subchiefs to shape power relations between ordinary Rwandans and the state in strategic ways that consolidated state power at the expense of individual political agency and participation. The intersection of Belgian policy and the practices of local Rwandan authorities transformed power relations, notably through land tenure and distribution patterns. Some individuals, mostly Tutsi but some Hutu, benefited under these changes; others, mostly Hutu but some Tutsi, did not. As state power became more centralized and hierarchical, ordinary people lost their ability to actively shape their everyday realities to suit their daily lived realities. Instead, the relationship of ordinary people to their local authority, not their ethnicity, came to determine their life chances, just as it does today under the policy of national unity and reconciliation. Ethnicity mattered most during periods of acute violence, such as those at the beginning and end of the period of Belgian colonization and again during the 1959–62 Social Revolution. The tactics and practices of control that both Tutsi and Hutu leaders used to justify policies of sociopolitical exclusion to control the state apparatus actually varied little over the years. The supposed historical unity that the policy of national unity and reconciliation of the current government relies upon to justify its policies is not grounded in empirical fact. Instead, it is another example of a strategic version of history designed to protect the grip of political elites on state power.

The historical record also shows that ethnic violence is not an innate aspect of Rwandan society. Quite the opposite; analysis of the historical record illustrates how the manipulation of ethnicity is a tactic used by the elite—whether Hutu or Tutsi—to justify resorting to violence, something in which ordinary peasants are regularly caught. Violence is an everyday part of Rwandans' past and present lives. It is not, however, rooted in ethnic hatred or, as the current government would have us believe, pent-up feelings of genocide ideology among a poor rural population. Violence in Rwanda has been consistently dressed up as ethnic when in fact its organizers and sponsors have merely invoked age-old ethnic animosity to seize, gain, or consolidate power. In this way, the policy of national unity and reconciliation is hardly a new interpretation of history, nor is it representative of an enlightened political elite that claims to "undo the infrastructure and ideology of the past to ensure that genocide never again happens in Rwanda" (Office of the President 1999, 22). Instead, it is a tool that the current government uses to deemphasize the actual causes and consequences of the 1994 genocide while masking its own efforts to mold Rwandan society according to its singular vision of precolonial ethnic unity, a theme that I examine in the next chapter.

3

A Continuum of Violence,
1990–2000

I wanted to go to *ingando* [reeducation camp] but was told I couldn't because I was a Twa in 1994. [The official] said, "You don't need reeducation because you are not part of the genocide. Your people did not kill or get killed." I was so angry with him. I lost my [Twa] mother and sister, and I even hid some Tutsi in my home. I asked my wife to go out during the killing and get food for us. I couldn't go myself. I was too scared. But I knew they wouldn't even look at an old Twa woman. Those Tutsi we saved don't even speak to me when they see me now. And I saved their lives! As soon as he [the official] said that [I don't need reeducation], I slammed my fist on the table like this [*gestures*]. He looked at me, and I knew I had done a wrong thing. He called some people, and I spent the next week in prison. Now I just keep to myself and try not to cause any trouble. (Interview with Théogène, a destitute Twa man, 2006)

Before 1994, I felt proud to be Rwandan. Then there was genocide, and now the new government shames us by saying that we [Hutu] did that. Some of us did. I killed, too. I killed my Tutsi neighbor because we ran when the events started, and we soon understood that only his kind [Tutsi] were getting killed. He said to me over there [*points to the location*], "If the Interahamwe comes, kill me so I can die with respect. I don't want to be thrown away. You can kill me and bury me on my land so my ancestors will know me."

He said this! Imagine how I felt! But I also understood because it was a very difficult time for us. Our [community] was unsettled. Homes were being burned, cows were slaughtered, and many of our women got violenced [raped], although those women don't talk about it, I saw it myself. So when the time came to kill my friend, I did. That is the only Tutsi I killed. For the rest, I just went along in the group. I joined some of the killers so they would think that I supported them. So eventually my government lost, and the Tutsi one came in. I fear a lot now because I know how they [the government] hate Hutu. (Interview with Félicien, an imprisoned Hutu man, 2006)

During the genocide, you cannot imagine how it was. My father was an intellectual and taught at the university. He was amongst the first to be killed when the Interahamwe and the other killers got to Butare. My mother died with him, as did my three sisters and my young brother. They killed them all at the home I grew up in. My father told us when things started in Kigali that the genocide would not reach here [Butare] because of the good relations between Hutu and Tutsi. But he underestimated his colleagues; his Hutu colleagues killed my family. My other brother got killed at a roadblock not far from here. I was alone after that; I am the only survivor in my [immediate] family. The one that killed my brother was a famous Hutu—very powerful since he owned land and had many people working for him. But before things happened [the genocide] he was known to be a moderate.[1] My father was his friend, and he and his wife used to visit us at least once a month. All this and he still killed my brother!

Since my family had been killed, I thought it would be smart to go home and hide there until the killing stopped. When I got there, the Hutu that killed my brother was there. So I panicked. I panicked so badly that I just stood there when I saw him in our kitchen. He saw me and ran out of the house. I knew I was going to die at that moment so I didn't run. I was so tired of hiding and running. . . .

When he came, I hid my face and hoped he would kill me quickly. But instead, he held on to me so tight, and he cried. He wept and wept and asked for my understanding. He said, "It is war. And we are killing all Tutsi. I am doing my duty. I killed many of my friends. You can't stay here. It's not safe because the [death] squads are on their way to loot and then burn this home." I couldn't believe my ears. This Hutu who killed my people was trying to protect me. I told him I was so tired and didn't know what to do to save myself. He said he was tired too. We sat on the ground and rested together for a minute. Then he said, "This is what you will do. You will go to my house. There are other Tutsi there. You cannot stay in the house because we [the killers] are looking for you. The higher-ups have told us to kill you because of your father. You are the only one left in your family, and your name is on our list of people who must be killed. If you go to my home, you will put other Tutsi there in danger. I want you to go to my chicken coop. Hide in there until we can figure out how to care for you. There are too many roadblocks, and the militias are on their way."

> I went to stay under his chickens and stayed there for three weeks until
> the war ended. He brought me food and water. He really saved me. He fled
> into the [internally displaced persons] camps after the French [protection
> force] came here, and I never saw him again. He has never been charged
> with genocide that I know of. All I know is he saved me; maybe he saved
> some others because there were about twenty Tutsi at his house when I
> got there. But he also killed. I don't know what was wrong with his mind,
> but maybe some people do evil things for reasons I don't understand. I
> know that he saved me, but I also know that he killed my brother. (Interview
> with Didier, a salaried poor Tutsi man, 2006)

Each of these individual narratives reveals more than simply different lived
experiences during the 1994 genocide. They also show the nature of local ties in
determining who lived, who died, and how. Individual personal actions and
lived realities are "embedded in local histories, specific circumstances, and
immediate biography" (Nordstrom 2004, 183). Didier, the Tutsi man who hid
in the chicken coop of his Hutu friend, survived because of a known and perhaps
even enthusiastic killer.[2] Félicien, the Hutu man who killed his Tutsi friend, did
so as a favor and then joined the killing squads as a survival strategy to appear
to support the execution of Tutsi in his community. Théogène's narrative shows
how Twa individuals also experienced the genocide through his description of
how he rescued some Tutsi while losing his family members in the genocide.
Implicit in these three excerpts is an appreciation of local power relations.
Those with power, like the killer who spared Didier's life, had different options
available to them (cf. Fujii 2009). Those not in positions of power had more
limited options available to them, but this does not mean that they lacked individual agency. Instead, it was an agency shaped by the complex and shifting
nature of the situation. Didier struggles to understand how an individual respected in the community could kill some Tutsi while saving the lives of others.
Félicien killed as an act of friendship—both he and his Tutsi friend seemed to
understand that options for survival were limited. Théogène understands that
his existence, both during the genocide and now, is shaped by broader historical
patterns that result in his continued sociopolitical marginality as an ethnic Twa.

In order to interpret the ways in which a cross-section of ordinary peasant
Rwandans from different backgrounds understand their own lived experiences
of the 1994 genocide, it is necessary to have an understanding of the broader
social and political context in which the violence occurred. The purpose of this
chapter is to analyze the continuum of violence in Rwanda from 1990, when
the then rebel RPF first invaded Rwanda from Uganda, through 2000, when
the RPF government first began to "talk seriously about national reconciliation" following the defeat of Hutu Power forces in the northwest of the country

and the subsequent consolidation of its political power and territorial control of the country (Waldorf 2006, 38). This exercise is critical since the RPF's near-hegemonic interpretation of the causes and consequences of the 1994 genocide has shaped Rwandans' opportunities to rebuild their lives since. This chapter continues the historical analysis begun in chapter 2 to further situate the broader context of routine physical and structural violence that ordinary peasants experienced before, during, and after the genocide. Before doing so, I first analyze the RPF's official version of the genocide and how it is represented as part of the policy of national unity and reconciliation.

The second section of the chapter analyzes patterns of violence in Rwanda during three distinct periods—the civil war of 1990–94, the 1994 genocide from April to July of that year, and the emergency period from July 1994 to 2000—when the RPF government began to implement the policy of national unity and reconciliation. The emphasis is on the role of the state in fomenting violence to show how the official representation of the genocide is well outside the lived experiences of everyday violence of most Rwandans. This is an important step, as it situates the ways in which Rwandans of different backgrounds experienced violence in the recent past; in particular, the analysis shows that violence was a regular and normal part of everyday life throughout the 1990s. It also shows that the 1994 genocide was not an instance of atavistic ethnic hatred or a spontaneous outburst of tribal violence, as asserted by the version of events found in the policy of national unity and reconciliation. Specifically, the way in which the policy represents the genocide as something that happened only to Tutsi victims whom the RPF eventually saved by taking military control of Rwanda in July 1994 has two main effects: first, it negates the everyday lived experiences of violence that Rwandans of all ethnicities experienced before and after the genocide; second, it privileges the genocide as the only source of violence in the lives of ordinary Rwandans. The remainder of this chapter demonstrates that, in addition to the violence of the 1994 genocide, Rwandans of all ethnicities experienced, to varying degrees of intensity, a continuum of everyday violence before, during, and after the genocide. Instead of acknowledging these differences, the RPF is promoting a policy of national unity and reconciliation that feeds into deep-rooted fear, anger, and despair that many ordinary peasants have felt both before and since the 1994 genocide.

Official Representations of the 1994 Genocide

The policy of national unity and reconciliation relies on two interpretative filters to shape the post-1994 Rwandan sociopolitical order. The first is "history," and the second is "genocide." In this section, I analyze the official representation of "genocide" to show how the policy of national unity and reconciliation collapses the different forms of killing (and the attendant motivations) into a singular representation of genocide as something that happened only to Tutsi. Eltringham and Van Hoyweghen (2000, 106) explain the importance of unpacking the official representation of "genocide": "Official discourse on the 1994 genocide maintains in practice the ethnic division which the RPF-led government denounces in theory: only Tutsi are victims of genocide; moderate Hutu are victims of politicide who died in massacres." Pottier (2002, 126) calls the distinction between Tutsi-survivor and Hutu-perpetrator a "moral hierarchy." Before analyzing the reductionism of the official representation of the 1994 genocide, I first situate the actors and actions of the genocide (April–July 1994) to illustrate the extent to which its official representation does not correspond to individual lived realities.

SITUATING THE GENOCIDE

Between April and July 1994, genocide engulfed Rwanda. Across the hills and in the valleys, in churches and homes, at bus stops and roadblocks, on narrow footpaths and in banana groves, in stadiums and schools, killers slaughtered at least five hundred thousand people, mainly ethnic Tutsi (Des Forges 1999, 15). The genocide was carefully planned by a small elite group of powerful ethnic Hutu extremists who refused to share power under the conditions of the Arusha Accords (discussed later). Through an orchestrated strategy to liquidate Tutsi and any politically moderate Hutu perceived as opposed to the Habyarimana regime, the extremists had one goal in mind: to maintain their monopoly on state power.

The killing started in the capital during the night of April 6–7, 1994, as unknown assailants shot down the plane carrying President Habyarimana as it approached Kigali airport. Militias—the Interahamwe[3] and the Impuzamugambi[4]—led the killing with the help of the Presidential Guard, the army, and local government officials (African Rights 1994; Des Forges 1999; Prunier 1997). Outside Kigali, ordinary Hutu men, often under the direction of militia or government soldiers, committed acts of genocide under the threat of loss of their own life or those of loved ones if they were unwilling to participate (Straus 2006, 122–52). Genocidal violence occurred at different times in different regions of the country (Des Forges 1999, 303–594; Straus 2006, 53–60). In many instances, local political and business elites colluded to enlist ordinary Rwandans to commit genocide (Longman 1995; Wagner 1998). Social ties and local power dynamics often compelled ordinary peasant Hutu to kill. Others resisted participation. Some stood by, while a few rescued instead of killing intended victims (Fujii 2009, 140–47; Straus 2006, 65–94). Not all Hutu participated, and not all participated to the same degree. Some killed enthusiastically; others killed a few (Prunier 1997, 242–50). Some Tutsi men joined in the killing as a means to save themselves and their families (field notes 2006).

The RPF also committed widespread reprisal killings—between ten thousand and fifty thousand Hutu died—while countless others of all ethnicities died as the RPF gave greater priority to military victory than to protecting Tutsi civilians (Des Forges 1999, 16; Kuperman 2004). An estimated ten thousand ethnic Twa were killed during the genocide (IRIN 2001). At least 250,000 women—mostly Tutsi but some Hutu—were raped (Burnet 2012, 16–17; HRW 2004, 7). Some men also admit to having been raped (field notes 2006). Countless others, men and women, young and old, healthy and infirm, were tortured or maimed.

The 1994 genocide is much more than a series of facts and figures about who killed, who died, and who survived. Irrespective of ethnic category, ordinary Rwandans were caught up in the maelstrom. There are countless stories of survival, of friends and family who took extraordinary risks in protecting their Tutsi kith and kin (African Rights 2003f, 2003g; Umutesi 2004). There are stories of Tutsi who put their own lives on the line to protect Hutu family and friends from the coercion and intimidation tactics that the killing squads used to goad ordinary Hutu into killing (African Rights 2003b, 2003c; field notes 2006). Notorious killers protected Tutsi they knew personally, ushering them safely through roadblocks, warning them of the whereabouts of marauding groups, and even hiding them at their homes. Some individuals killed during the day, only to shelter Tutsi friends and relatives at night (field notes 2006). Many Tutsi survived because of the aid and succor of a Hutu family member, friend, colleague, neighbor, or stranger (Jefremovas 1995). There are stories about ethnic Twa and ethnic Hutu who were killed in the genocide because of their stereotypical Tutsi features (field notes 2006).

Instrumentalizing the Genocide

Despite its complexity and reach into the lives of Rwandans, the RPF-led government presents the genocide as a clear-cut affair: Hutu killed Tutsi because of ethnic divisions that were introduced during the colonial period (1890–1962) and hardened to the point of individual action during the postcolonial period (1962–94). According to the policy of national unity and reconciliation, ethnicity is a fiction created by colonial divide-and-rule policies. Ultimate blame for the 1994 genocide therefore lies with Rwanda's colonial powers, which instituted policies that made the Hutu population hate Tutsi. In this telling, divisive politics grounded in decades of bad governance resulted in deep-rooted ethnic hatred of *all* Tutsi by *all* Hutu, causing the 1994 genocide (NURC 2004; Office of the President 1999). This simplistic interpretation of events forms the backbone of the policy of national unity and reconciliation.

Straus (2006), in interviews with accused perpetrators, identifies different motivations for different forms of killing. He writes, "motivation and participation were clearly heterogeneous," with different forms of killing with different motivations occurring simultaneously (Straus 2006, 95). The forms of killing were (1) killing, torture, rape, and mutilation perpetrated against civilians—mainly Tutsi but also politically moderate Hutu—by militias, Forces armées rwandaises (FAR) soldiers, and willing ordinary people; (2) killing, torture, rape, and mutilation perpetrated against Tutsi by ordinary Hutu, typically under duress from local leaders; (3) intended killing of soldiers and collateral killing of civilians (Tutsi, Hutu, and Twa) in the course of the conflict between the RPF and the FAR; (4) killings carried out by the RPF against civilians (Tutsi, Hutu, and Twa); and (5) murder motivated by theft and looting as well as the settling of scores between ordinary people (Straus 2006, 113–18, 135–40, 163–69. On alleged RPF crimes, see Office of the United Nations High Commissioner for Human Rights 2010). Ordinary Rwandans understand that all of these different types of killings took place during the genocide, and they use the phrases "*les événements de 1994*" (the events of 1994) and "*en 1994*" (in 1994) to describe "everything that happened in 1994, not just the genocide" (field notes 2006).

Straus's findings on individual motivations to kill are particularly instructive as they reveal the intentional simplification of the government in grounding its approach to postgenocide justice in the presumed ethnic hatred of all Hutu for all Tutsi (discussed more fully below). His research shows that "preexisting ethnic animosity, widespread prejudice, deeply held ideological beliefs, blind obedience, deprivation, or even greed" did not motivate individual Hutu to kill individual Tutsi (Straus 2006, 96, corroborated by Fujii 2009, 185–86). Instead, Straus finds that "Rwandans' motivations [for killing] were considerably more ordinary and routine than the extraordinary crimes they helped commit" (Straus 2006, 96). Among ordinary Hutu this participation was driven by intra-ethnic pressure from other, usually more socially powerful Hutu, security fears in the context of civil war and genocide, and the opportunity for looting and score settling. Straus concludes that these factors "were salient in a context of national state orders to attack Tutsis, war, dense local institutions, and close-knit settlements" (Straus 2006, 97). As Jean-Claude, a prisoner convicted of genocide crimes, told me, "I killed. I even killed more than ten people. I told [government officials] the names of those I killed, and I told them where and how I killed them. But I didn't kill them because of hatred. I only killed people I didn't know because I feared being killed myself! Even I was told [it is not clear by whom] that my wife would be killed if I did not kill!" (interview 2006).

The available evidence simply does not support Rwandan government claims that ethnic enmity drove the participation of ordinary Rwandans in the 1994 genocide. Officially, this ethnic enmity is called "genocide ideology." Much of the work of the National Unity and Reconciliation Commission is concerned with identifying and eliminating the genocidal thoughts of ordinary Hutu to prepare them to engage in state-led reconciliation activities. In practice, as is further analyzed in the next chapter, an accusation that an individual harbors "genocide ideology" is a tool used against any individual or group that steps outside the accepted boundaries of government policy (Senate of the Republic of Rwanda 2007). As an RPF member and private businessperson said during my reeducation, "we [senior RPF members] would rather be conscious of our enemy [read Hutu] than naively pretend, like you whites, to think we have no enemy out there planning to exterminate us but instead to hopelessly fantasize about a utopian Rwanda" (field notes 2006).[5] Approaching postgenocide justice on the presumption of a criminal (adult male Hutu) population is a useful mechanism that the RPF strategically deploys to control political opponents, deflect criticism of its actions during the genocide, and justify its continued military presence in the eastern Congo (Office of the United Nations High Commissioner for Human Rights 2010; United Nations Group of Experts for the Democratic Republic of the Congo 2012. See Pottier 2002 on the media savoir-faire of the RPF).

The policy of national unity and reconciliation legitimates the moral right of the RPF to rule postgenocide Rwanda. The policy is supported by a historical narrative about Rwanda's past in an effort to shape the collective memory of the genocide, a narrative that eliminates the real socioeconomic inequality and forms of political exclusion faced by most ordinary Rwandans under colonial and postcolonial rule. In particular, it reformulates the violence against Tutsi in 1959, 1962, and 1973 as well as during the 1994 genocide as strictly ethnic in origin, thereby ignoring important class and regional dimensions of those conflicts (see Burnet 2012 on the gender dimensions of these waves of violence). For example, and as analyzed in chapter 2, the policy of national unity and reconciliation ignores the fact that the labels Hutu, Tutsi, and Twa represented status differences that elites sometimes violently enforced in precolonial Rwanda while overlooking the ways in which these labels became politically significant during the colonial period. In addition, it overlooks the ways in which Tutsi elites participated in and benefited from colonial rule (Berger 1981; Des Forges 2011). The policy also depicts the events of 1959 as a "practice geno- cide" when in fact it was a social revolution of Hutu against Tutsi elites, as discussed in chapter 2 (Kinzer 2008, 11; see also C. Newbury 1988 on the cohesion of Hutu oppression). This narrow "official" interpretation of the genocide legitimates the repressive approach of the postgenocide government in three ways. First, it invokes the heroic status of the RPF in liberating Rwandans from "oppressive rulers" (NURC 2004, 9). Second, it provides the RPF with a virtual carte blanche with which it can reconstruct Rwanda and "reconcile" Rwandans according to its own "vision of how things should be done" (MINECOFIN 2000, 12). Third, it allows the RPF to continue to elide the specificity of its own role in the genocide while evoking the genocide guilt card with international audiences (Reyntjens 2004, 2011). The words of a donor representative resident in Kigali illustrate the impact of the genocide guilt card in international circles: "We decided to withdraw from Rwanda at that time [1994] and it is well known that the positions left behind . . . where many Tutsi had gathered around the blue helmets [meaning the United Nations peacekeeping force], they were left there to be killed. We don't feel comfortable with that. This feeling perhaps plays a role too, in our development cooperation programs" (Western diplomat speaking in Kigali in 2009, quoted in Zorbas 2011, 106).

Finally, the policy of national unity and reconciliation does not acknowledge the lived experiences of Rwandans outside the categories of Tutsi survivors and Hutu perpetrators. Conspicuous by their absence are Tutsi and Twa perpetrators, Hutu and Twa rescuers, Tutsi, Hutu, and Twa resisters, and Hutu and Twa survivors. The words of Scholastique, a poor Hutu woman whose husband died during the genocide, sum up the situation well:

> For me, the genocide is what happened after the killing stopped. I lost my [Hutu] husband and four of my children during the events. Now I suffer without hopes and dreams. My brother is in prison, and I have no one to take care of or to take care of me. I feel alone even when I am with other people. And then the government forces us to tell the truth about what we saw. I saw a lot of bodies but never did I see someone getting killed. I heard people dying, but I did not see anything. How can I tell my truth when the government has told me what I have to say? I fear being sent to prison, and I think now that my neighbors do not like that I live in [the same community as before the genocide]. Where can I go, what can I do? The government says Rwanda has been rebuilt, but my life and home are still not repaired. (Interview 2006)

In presenting a particular set of facts about the genocide, the policy of national unity and reconciliation wipes away the specificity of individual acts of genocide, the death after death after death that is the aggregated whole. Such an approach ignores how ordinary Rwandans were enticed into participating or coerced to do so. Each act of violence—a killing, a rape, a threat, a looting—is different and took place within a specific set of circumstances as individuals made their choice to kill, hide, resist, or stand by. This is not to downplay the genocide's magnitude for its Tutsi victims but rather to point out that in assigning collective responsibility to all Hutu, many of whom did not commit acts of genocide, the policy of national unity and reconciliation does more than simply misinterpret the nature of the genocide. It is likely to re-create, given Rwanda's history of ethnic conflict, the same conditions of ethnic inequality, political repression, and socioeconomic exclusion that it claims to undo. The next section illustrates the shortcomings of considering the genocide as an isolated incident rather than as part of a broader continuum of violence that shapes individual lived experiences of fear and insecurity.

Cycles of Violence: The Civil War, Genocide, and Emergency Period in Context

An intense civil war raged from October 1990; this civil war was critical in legitimating and justifying violence that in turn created the context of fear and insecurity that led to the 1994 genocide. In addition to that violence, there were two additional periods in which state-led violence was particularly acute and had varying impacts on the lives of ordinary peasant Rwandans depending on their social location and their ethnic identity as determined by the state. This section analyzes the dynamics of violence during the political transition and civil war (October 1990–April 1994) and the three phases of the "emergency period": the immediate postgenocide period (July 1994–December 1995), the mass return of Hutu refugees from neighboring countries (1996–97), and the rebel insurgency in the northwest (1997–2000). The bulk of the analysis that follows focuses on the civil war period (October 1990–April 1994) to highlight the extent to which RPF military maneuvers and political decisions were part of the broader context of violence that resulted in the 1994 genocide.[6]

Political Transition and Civil War (October 1990–April 1994)

Before the rebel RPF entered Rwanda from Uganda on October 1, 1990, the country was already in crisis and economic decline. The RPF crossed into Rwanda from Gatuna town in Uganda and made its operational base in the Virunga mountain range in northwestern Rwanda between Gisenyi and Ruhengeri towns (see fig. 2, page 33). International donors, including France (President Habyarimana's primary ally), began to pressure Rwanda to liberalize its political system to allow for multiparty politics (Reyntjens 1995, 564). At the same time, the economy faltered as donors tied their funding to political liberalization and the adoption of structural adjustment measures. Record low prices for Rwanda's main sources of foreign income, coffee and tea, compounded an already dire socioeconomic situation (Uvin 1998; Verwimp 2003). Widespread unemployment and famine resulted. Ordinary Rwandans began to express their discontent with the regime by refusing to pay MRND party membership dues or their taxes or even to show deference to local officials (Longman 1995). Joseph U. explained the risks of failing to pay MRND dues: "We [not clear if he means peasants or other Hutu] just felt like our backs were breaking with everything that was going on. Some crops failed. People were hungry. Those who could send their kids to school could no longer do so. So there was pressure on all of us [peasants]. So, to protest, some farmers just agreed to stop paying our dues. We did, and nothing happened [meaning there was no punishment from local officials]. So others in [my community] stopped paying as well. Soon, it seemed like almost no one was paying dues, even though we all knew it was the law" (interview 2006).

In the face of mounting criticisms of his one-party regime, Habyarimana tried to steer the democratization process from the outset. He created a Commission nationale de synthèse (CNS), charged with identifying what democracy meant to ordinary Rwandans, and with drafting a new constitution (Bertrand 2000, 44). Ordinary Rwandans I consulted recalled the consultations and remarked that local officials from the MRND "told us what democracy meant and then offered us alcohol to support their vision at community festivals and [sensitization] meetings" (interview with Thomas, a salaried poor man, 2006). Aurelia, a poor Hutu widow, remarked, "Democracy was and still is something that elites talk about; we just hope their politics don't affect us too much" (interview 2006).

Habyarimana stacked the CNS with members and close allies of his MRND and, having revised the constitution to allow political parties to form, promoted the creation of small parties that were mere satellites to the MRND (Bertrand 2000, 43; Reyntjens 1995, 266).[7] Despite Habyarimana's efforts to control the democratization process, a robust opposition quickly emerged. Several parties that had first been created at the time of independence (1959–62) reemerged, notably the Mouvement démocratique rwandais (MDR), which was a reincarnation of former President Kayibanda's Parti du mouvement de l'émancipation hutu (PARMEHUTU) (discussed in chapter 2). The MDR was founded in March 1991 by disaffected Hutu elites from central Rwanda who seized the opportunity to reenter politics following the coup of 1973 and Habyarimana's subsequent ban on political activity (C. Newbury 1992, 201). Unlike the original PARMEHUTU, which was a party for Hutu, the MDR sought to identify as "a party of the masses" (Bertrand 2000, 94). The party saw itself as the main challenger to the one-party rule of the MRND, which favored Hutu from the north. Its goal was to move beyond the regional and ethnic politics of the MRND in order to bring the issues of all Rwandans to the table.

The MDR leadership saw the civil war as further evidence of the regime's incompetence in dealing with Rwanda's pressing socioeconomic issues, not least of which was the return of Tutsi refugees still living abroad. Other parties emerged in pursuit of a common goal—to overthrow the MRND. The other opposition parties, the Parti social démocrate (PSD), a left-of-center party that drew its membership from the south, and the Parti libéral (PL), a right-of-center party that attracted urbanites, including prominent Tutsi businesspeople, joined forces to press the Habyarimana regime to find a way to end the civil war and solve the economic crisis. In November 1991, the three parties signed a joint memorandum that highlighted the regime's refusal to enact "real" democratic reforms (Prunier 1997, 134). In response, the MRND swore in a new cabinet on December 31, 1991, and appointed one person from the "opposition," a member of the pro-MRND satellite, the Parti chrétien démocrate (PCD) (Reyntjens 1995, 109).

The formal opposition (that actually opposed the MRND) took to the streets in a rare act of mass protest that took place throughout the country (Bertrand 2000, 141–42). In March 1992 the formal opposition forced Habyarimana to accept an agreement with the now united opposition parties to form a new government, with the coveted post of prime minister going to a representative of the MDR. The agreement also required Habyarimana to begin power-sharing peace talks with the RPF (Prunier 1997, 145–50). On the surface, the Habyarimana regime softened its authoritarian control of the state. Behind the scene, members of the MRND's inner circle—the *akazu*—broke away to form their own party, called the Coalition pour la défense de la république (CDR). The CDR not only opposed peace talks with the RPF but also was overtly racist, favoring a Hutu-only Rwanda. Opposition appeals for the RPF and the MRND to fight their battles at the negotiating table fell on deaf ears when the RPF attacked FAR forces stationed near Byumba in February 1993, a blatant violation of a ceasefire agreement that had been negotiated at Arusha (Des Forges 1999, 109). The attack also led the opposition coalition to question its support of the RPF, whose relentless aggression on the battlefield brought into question its willingness to negotiate at the peace table in good faith. The perception among members of the opposition coalition was that the RPF wanted to seize power by any means necessary, not share it (Des Forges 1999, 109–10; Kuperman 2004, 61–63).[8]

Many of the ordinary peasants in southern Rwanda that I consulted felt jostled by elite political machinations. Ephrem's words are emblematic of the fears that rural folks must have felt at the time: "I knew that there was tension

Figure 5. Both before and since the genocide, local government officials are responsible for "sensitizing" citizens to respect the myriad directives and rules issued by central government officials in Kigali. This image was taken in western Rwanda, July 2006. (photo by author)

among the politicians and I feared. My family always fears when the government starts talking about change because it means new rules and regulations. Of course we could not imagine something as dramatic as the genocide, but violence, yes, that is part of our everyday life. Our governments do what they need to keep power. About politics, peasants like me know what we are told [in local sensitization meetings] or what is announced on radio. We knew about this idea of power sharing because it was sometimes discussed by our officials. I don't think anyone knew it would result in genocide!" (interview 2006).

CIVIL WAR AND THE INVASION BY THE RPF

The RPF largely drew its membership from the exiled Tutsi refugee community in Uganda, most of whom had fled Rwanda between 1959 and 1962. Hutu and Twa, as enemies of the Habyarimana regime, members of ethnically mixed families, or those who followed their Tutsi patrons, were also exiled, and some joined the RPF movement (Mamdani 2001, 159–60). Uganda was home to the majority of Rwandans who had fled the political violence during the 1959–62 independence period discussed in chapter 2. There is no agreement on how many refugees lived in Uganda. Van der Meeren (1996, 261) cites a figure of two hundred thousand Tutsi living in registered refugee settlements in Uganda, while Prunier (1997, 62) estimates that there were six hundred thousand Rwandan refugees by 1990. Burundi, Tanzania, and Zaïre also hosted numerous Rwandan refugees. Some individuals fled further afield within Africa, while others went to Europe or North America (van der Meeren 1996, 252). Many Rwandans exiled during the 1959–62 period maintained ties with one another through social and cultural associations (Prunier 1997, 66). These ties proved critical in the financing of the RPF (Kinzer 2008, 81–83).

The ways in which Rwandan exiles got caught up in the national political struggles in Uganda shaped the RPF's decision to invade Rwanda in 1990. Uganda's then president Milton Obote (1962–71 and 1980–85) identified Tutsi from Rwanda as a "public enemy against whom to unite his party" (van der Meeren 1996, 261). In December 1980 Obote branded Rwandan refugees living in Uganda as "alien foreigners" and forced them to live in guarded camps (Scherrer 2002, 49). He later labeled Rwandan Tutsi the "natural allies" of his political foe Yoweri Museveni, leader of the National Resistance Movement (NRM) (Mamdani 2001, 168). This prompted "scores" of young Rwandans to join Museveni's National Resistance Army (NRA) to take up arms with the purpose of overthrowing Obote (Scherrer 2002, 50). Mamdani estimates that approximately a quarter of the NRA membership of sixteen thousand were Rwandan refugees (Mamdami 2001, 170). The participation of Rwandan refugees, several of whom rose to prominence as respected officers in the NRA, would later prove problematic for Museveni once he became Uganda's president, in January 1986 (Mamdani 2001, 174–76).

The large number of Rwandans in senior positions within NRA ranks forced Museveni to respond to public perceptions that Rwandans were taking over Uganda's political leadership. In late 1989 Museveni "released" from military service two high-ranking Rwandan officers—Paul Kagame, the deputy chief of military intelligence, and Fred Rwigema, the deputy minister of defense (Rake 2001, 185). These dismissals provided the impetus for the RPF to organize its invasion, particularly as the joint Rwanda-Uganda ministerial commission set up in 1989 to solve the Rwandan refugee crisis had failed. President Habyarimana refused to accept the mass repatriation of Tutsi refugees from Uganda, allowing only those refugees who would make no land claims to return to Rwanda (Hintjens 1999, 290). In early 1990 Kagame and Rwigema created the military wing of the RPF, the Rwandan Patriotic Army (RPA); the NRA reported more than three thousand deserters to the RPA but took no steps to bring them to barracks (DANIDA 1997, 69). President Museveni provided tacit support, allowing southern Uganda to be used as the RPF's base of operation (Scherrer

2002, 50). Rwandan exiles living in foreign capitals, notably in Washington, DC, and London, lobbied foreign governments to support the RPF's struggle both financially and morally (Kinzer 2008, 56).

The RPF attack on Rwanda from the Ugandan border town of Kagitumba on October 1, 1990, surprised Habyarimana's FAR. The RPF walked to what was then called Gabiro town, some forty miles north of Kigali, without encountering much military resistance. Habyarimana wasted little time in asking for assistance from France, Belgium, and Zaïre (now the Democratic Republic of the Congo), without which the RPF could have easily continued its military advance to Kigali. In order to highlight the need for external assistance, Habyarimana ordered his FAR forces to stage a mock attack on Kigali on October 4, 1990 (Scherrer 2002, 52). French and Belgian paratroopers arrived quickly to support the FAR and to push the RPF back to Uganda. The RPF suffered heavy losses in the withdrawal. Rather than pursue an absolute military victory now that the French were openly supporting the Habyarimana regime, the RPF leadership adopted guerrilla tactics against the cumbersome and undisciplined FAR and its allies (Jones 1999, 57). Local people resident in northern Rwanda felt the chill of the RPF-FAR skirmishes. Marie Claire recounts a sentiment that both captures the mood of the time and reflects the fear felt by peasant Rwandans: "Oh, those days were difficult. Both sides [FAR and RPF] were searching houses and schools, looking for traitors and others who didn't support their program [not clear what she means by this]. We tried to live a normal life. People did their daily things as usual, but no one knew when real war might happen. There were murders and some people disappeared. It was very tense" (interview 2006).

Throughout the civil war, the RPF continued to occupy the northern part of Rwanda. In Kigali and elsewhere across the country, Tutsi civilians, perceived as natural allies of and spies for the RPF "invaders," were victims of arbitrary arrests, political assassinations, and organized massacres (Vandeginste 2003, 253). The civil war with the RPF provided the Habyarimana regime with the necessary pretext to pursue any and all measures needed to protect itself from an enemy that was both external (the RPF and the exiled refugees who supported them) and internal (all Tutsi, elites and nonelites alike, and Hutu political opponents) (Burnet 2005, 82). It also "contributed to the fragmentation of the political landscape and to the introduction of weapons and warriors difficult to control. And, it progressively generated a culture of violence in which political solutions became increasingly difficult" (Reyntjens 1996, 246). It was in this climate that peace negotiations took place in Arusha, Tanzania. Of the ordinary peasants I consulted in the course of my research, very few of them knew of the Arusha process, suggesting that the Habyarimana government did not publicize the negotiations via the usual mechanisms of communicating with ordinary Rwandans—sensitization meetings and radio announcements.

The Arusha Peace Negotiations

The Arusha peace negotiations began in June 1992. Just over a year later, on August 4, 1993, accords were signed by the ruling MRND, the rebel RPF, and the opposition coalition parties—the MDR, PSD, and PL. The agreement included protocols on the union of the FAR and the RPF armies, the repatriation of refugees, and the resettlement of displaced persons (Kroslak 2008, 41–42). It included provisions for power sharing among its signatories, including the creation of a national unity and reconciliation commission and a national summit on unity and reconciliation (Arusha Accords 1993, articles 24 and 88). It also laid out a timetable for installing a broad-based transitional government, which was to be made up of representatives of all Rwanda's political parties, except for the CDR, which the RPF argued was not a political party at all but instead an extremist splinter group of the MRND (Jones 1999, 70–71).

Any optimism that the signing of the Arusha Accords may have generated was short-lived. President Habyarimana resisted their implementation at every step and failed to implement agreed-upon action until international donors pressured him to do so (Uvin 1998, 96). He followed a "two-track policy" of implementing the accords on the one hand while planning the genocide to eliminate the "Tutsi problem" on the other (C. Newbury 1995, 13). The CDR and Hutu Power extremists within the MRND gained the upper hand in October 1993 when Tutsi army officers in Burundi assassinated that country's first democratically elected Hutu president, Melchior Ndadaye. Hutu Power extremists in Rwanda painted his assassination as "undeniable proof" that Tutsi anywhere would do anything to regain power (Turner 2005, 41).[9] The opposition coalition splintered into "extremist" and "moderate" factions. These two factions began to bicker over the assignment of seats within the government set out in the Arusha agreement, which delayed the launch of the transitional government by several months (Jones 1999, 59). The RPF added insult to injury by issuing a bland statement of regret, while praising Ndadaye's assassination among the Rwandan refugees still living in Uganda (Prunier 1997, 201–2). This tipped the balance of power toward Hutu Power extremists as some political moderates looked warily on a continued alliance with the RPF (Jones 2001, 62; Kuperman 2004, 65).

In the wake of Ndadaye's assassination in Burundi, the first battalion of United Nations peacekeepers arrived to monitor the implementation of the Arusha Accords. Habyarimana continued to stall their implementation, notably through the continued use of hate radio and organized violence. From the

opening days of the civil war, the Habyarimana regime understood the importance of using media to rally ordinary Rwandans around the regime. In March
1992 Radio Rwanda was the first to directly encourage the killing of Tutsi in
Bugesera town, south of Kigali (Article 19 1996). Radio-télévision libre des mille
collines (RTLM) began its broadcasts just after the accords were signed, in July
1993. Extremist elements within the MRND and the CDR used the cover of
multipartyism to launch RTLM as a means to complement the message of
state-run Radio Rwanda—that the way to eliminate the RPF "problem" was
to exterminate all Tutsi (Des Forges 1999, 96–105). Far from the usual somber
and serious tones of Radio Rwanda, RTLM programming was informal and
playful and was dedicated to voicing the opinions of ordinary Rwandans: "it
still broadcast official voices often enough to continue to enjoy the authoritative-
ness of national radio, but to that it added the appeal of being the station to
speak for the people" (Des Forges 2007, 29).

RTLM reported Ndadaye's murder "in a highly sensationalized way to
underline supposed Tutsi brutality and heighten Hutu fears of Tutsi" (Des
Forges 2007, 31). RTLM became the voice of Hutu Power, and its extremist
politics and anti-Tutsi vitriol were the order of the day. RTLM broadcasting
also denounced Hutu who were willing to share political power with Tutsi. It
used increasingly violent language, for example saying that Hutu militias would
"rip into little pieces those Hutu who supported the RPF" (Article 19 1996, 56).
RTLM also denounced specific prominent Tutsi and politically moderate Hutu
"as enemies of the nation who should be eliminated one way or another from
the public scene" (Des Forges 2007, 30). The RTLM broadcasts contributed to
the creation of a climate of fear and insecurity among ordinary Rwandans, which
in turn legitimized some ordinary people's decisions to kill when pressured to
do so by Hutu Power militias between April and July 1994. Straus (2007) shows
that ordinary Rwandans exercised considerable agency in deciding whether
and how to participate in the genocide. He concludes that "the evidence
amounts to a persuasive refutation of the commonly held beliefs that radio had
widespread, direct effects and that hate radio was the primary driver of the
genocide and participation in it. . . . Radio emboldened hard-liners and reinforced face-to-face mobilization, which helped those who advocated violence
assert dominance and carry out the genocide" (Straus 2007, 630–31).

Hutu extremists within the MRND and the CDR fed the fear and insecurity
of ordinary Rwandans—educated and peasant folks alike—by making violence
a normal and routine part of everyday life. After the RPF invaded, in October
1990, the Habyarimana government adopted an increasingly explicit policy of
encouraging and planning mass violence among civilians. Local authorities
used false rumors and misinformation to promote ethnic hatred and to incite

the local residents to take part in attacks on Tutsi civilians, who were identified by Hutu Power extremists as either RPF infiltrators (*abacengezi*) or accomplices (*ibyitso*). Local officials instigated violence through awareness-raising campaigns (also known as "sensitization") "to put local peasants 'in the mood,' to drum into them that the people they were to kill are *ibyitso* (accomplices), actual or potential collaborators of the RPF archenemy" (Prunier 1997, 138). The government staged the first event of Hutu violence against Tutsi two weeks after the RPF invasion in Kibilira commune in Gisenyi province near its Virunga base in northwestern Rwanda (Prunier 1997, 109–10). Local officials falsely reported that Tutsi accomplices of the RPF had killed Hutu in their community (Article 19 1996, 14–15). In response, groups of civilians, under the control of Hutu militia leaders, roamed the hills looking for RPF accomplices to kill. Local and regional officials were aware of the violence but chose not to end it until several days later, sending a clear message of tolerance, if not acceptance, of violence against (mainly Tutsi) civilians. The RPF also showed little regard for civilian loss of life during its military campaigns in northern and central Rwanda between October 1990 and April 1994. It was a tactic of both the RPF leadership and the Habyarimana regime to attack civilians and then blame the deaths on the other side (Umutesi 2004, 17–44). Once again, political elites on both sides scapegoated ordinary Rwandans. Joseph M., a poor Tutsi survivor of the genocide, who was visiting family living in northern Rwanda in April 1993, remarked caustically in one of our meetings, "To say it was tense would be about right. It was not clear which neighbors were loyal to the RPF and who were not. Me, I wasn't [loyal] because I try to avoid politics. Even the way the Tutsi got targeted and even killed made it hard to know who was against whom. I returned home [to southern Rwanda] as soon as I raised the money [for bus fare] to do so. The north was too violent for normal life" (interview 2006).

As the civil war continued, the Habyarimana regime moved toward a more explicit policy of promoting ethnic violence among ordinary Rwandans. The regime blamed the Kibilira massacre on the RPF and its Tutsi accomplices, while international media reported it as an instance of "ethnic hatred" (Article 19 1996, 15). Blaming the RPF for violence they had sponsored provided the Hutu Power extremists with the cover they needed to authorize their officials to commit human rights violations against ordinary Rwandans, including mass arrests and imprisonment, disappearances, extrajudicial executions, and, in some cases, death. The civil war also provided the Habyarimana regime with the necessary pretext to train the Hutu Power militias—the Interahamwe and the Impuzamugambi—that would later incite ordinary Hutu to kill Tutsi during the genocide. Members of both militias organized and implemented mass violence, targeting in particular Tutsi civilians and politically moderate

Hutu as accomplices of the RPF. The strengthening of Hutu Power militias added to the normalization of violence and made fear and insecurity a staple of everyday life in pregenocide Rwanda. Throughout 1992 and 1993, Hutu Power extremists ordered political assassinations and large-scale massacres of Tutsi civilians in the central and northern regions of Rwanda. Murders, beatings, disappearances, and imprisonment became a regular and accepted part of daily life (Umutesi 2004, 31). Augustin, a released prisoner, summed up the climate at the time well:

> Oh yes, there was all sorts of violence. They divided us by identity card at the [sensitization] meetings that we had to attend. They would send armed men into the hills to bring us to the meetings. Sometimes we would be sent to training sessions to learn how to kill our neighbors. They told us this was part of our work and not to forget that *umuganda* [collective work] was for the good of the nation. We were told that Tutsi wanted to kill us and to learn to defend ourselves for our own good. Sometimes they gave us food. We usually got [banana] beer.
>
> I never thought about my Tutsi neighbors as evil, but the RPF was in Rwanda and causing headaches for us [Hutu]. They [militia leaders] also told us that we would be rewarded for good behavior when the war was over and peace was restored. They offered things like livestock and *mabati* [roof sheeting]. As things started to heat up [in the months leading up to the 1994 genocide], many of us killed neighbors. We saw how things were going around us. Tutsi were scared, and so were Hutu. We were told that democracy was the problem, that the RPF wanted to take power from Hutu to impose themselves on us again. So yes, I killed, thinking it would be the best thing for me and my family. I did not want to be labeled an accomplice of the RPF. I had a son with a bad illness and had to think about how to get enough money to take care of him. (Interview 2006)

As violence became normalized as part of the everyday realities of ordinary Rwandans, President Habyarimana continued to stall the implementation of the Arusha Accords. In early April 1994 President Ali Hassan Mwinyi of Tanzania convinced Habyarimana to attend a summit in Dar es Salaam, Tanzania, to discuss the regional implications of the crisis in Burundi. On April 6, 1994, Habyarimana returned from Tanzania by private aircraft. The passengers included some of the most powerful members of his government, as well as the new Burundian president, Cyprien Ntaryamira. As the plane was making its landing approach, unknown assailants fired a missile from a nearby hill. The plane crashed; all passengers on board were killed instantly. The crash set off violent responses from both Hutu Power militias and the RPF. Violence broke out immediately in the northern provinces of Ruhengeri and Gisenyi. RPF troops stationed in Kigali took defensive positions around the city (Dallaire 2003, 269). Within twenty-four hours there were no "moderates" left, leaving General Roméo Dallaire, head of the ill-equipped United Nations Assistance Mission to Rwanda (UNAMIR), to negotiate with Hutu extremists to stop killing ethnic Tutsi. Dallaire understood that the political violence in Rwanda was genocide: "In just a few hours the Presidential Guard had conducted an obviously well-organized and well-executed plan—by noon on April 7 the moderate political leadership of Rwanda was dead or in hiding" (Dallaire 2003, 232).

THE POSTGENOCIDE "EMERGENCY" PERIOD
(JULY 1994–DECEMBER 1995)

Across the country, the genocide ended as the RPF took territorial control. It controlled Kigali by July 1, 1994, and had total control of the country by July 18, 1994, when it finally defeated the last remnants of the Hutu Power forces in Gisenyi in the north. In the process of securing territory, the RPF did save Tutsi lives. However, its overarching military goal was to win the war and gain state power. In fact, the RPF "expected their [1990] invasion to trigger a violent backlash against Tutsi civilians in Rwanda" (Kuperman 2004, 61). Kuperman's research also shows that the RPF understood that its efforts to gain state power would provoke genocidal retaliation from Hutu extremists "but viewed this as an acceptable cost of achieving their goal of attaining power in Rwanda" (Kuperman 2004, 63). As the RPF advanced, tens of thousands of ordinary Rwandans of all ethnicities fled, many of them under duress from leaders of the Hutu Power militias. Others fled on the order of local government authorities, which had spread rumors among the refugee population about RPF reprisal killings. Millions fled west into eastern Zaïre; hundreds of thousands remained in the Zone turquoise (which covered parts of Gikongoro, Kibuye, and Cyangugu provinces; see fig. 2, page 33) under the protection of French troops who arrived in June 1994 (Kroslak 2008, 54). The French mission, known as Opération turquoise, has been criticized for its failure to arrest genocidal leaders of the defeated government as they fled into Zaïre either through the Zone turquoise or via the northern withdrawal route through Gisenyi into Goma (Des Forges 1999, 682–84).

A new government was sworn in on July 19, 1994, and faced "seemingly insurmountable" obstacles (UNDP Rwanda 2004, 6). Approximately 10 percent of the population was dead. Another 30 percent had fled into exile (Reyntjens 2004, 178). Many of those who remained inside Rwanda were internally displaced. During the genocide, Rwandans from all walks of life suffered, whether or not they were targeted for killing. Everyone had been exposed to killing in some way or another, and, indeed, all of the Rwandans to whom I spoke,

whether formally in life history interviews or informally via participant observation, reported some form of violent episode that they either experienced or
witnessed. Psychosocial trauma was prevalent. Some studies suggest that as
many as 95 percent of Rwandans witnessed or participated in "extreme acts of
violence" (Ndayambajwe 2001, 46). As the genocidal Hutu Power forces retreated
into Zaïre, they looted or destroyed anything of value. In their wake, they left
razed government offices, schools, hospitals, health clinics, and businesses,
including market stalls and kiosks. Retreating government leaders of the interim
government ordered the looting of the central bank (Prunier 1997, 113). In the
hills, crops rotted in the fields because there was no one to harvest them. In
towns, there was no running water, electricity, or telephone service. Séraphine,
a poor and elderly Twa woman who had lived through political violence in
1959 and 1962 and who did not flee her home in 1994, remarked, "Never has I
seen violence as dramatic as the most recent round [meaning in 1994]. Those
who lived had dead expressions on their faces. No one was whole. It was like
the hills had been ripped out and swallowed us whole [not clear to whom "us"
refers]. It was the worst violence of my life. How all who fled survived at all is a
mystery I will never understand" (interview 2006).

The new government reaffirmed its "commitment to the terms and spirit of
the Arusha Accord" (Reyntjens 2004, 178). A key exception was that the RPF
gave itself all of the posts previously held by the MRND and the CDR. It also
created the new position of vice president, which was filled by Paul Kagame
(Prunier 1997, 300). The cabinet consisted of a Hutu majority (sixteen of
twenty-two posts), including the president (Pasteur Bizimungu, RPF) and the
prime minister (Faustin Twagiramungu, MDR). It seemed as though the RPF
would establish an inclusive government that was committed to national unity
and reconciliation. Politicians, civil servants, judges, and military officials who
had served under the previous regime stayed behind in Kigali and "indicated
their willingness to co-operate with the RPF" (Reyntjens 2004, 180). The RPF
also negotiated with the French military to honor its commitment to withdraw
on August 21, 1994; the French not only had continued to occupy and control
the Zone turquoise but also had provided tacit support to the rump Habyarimana government (Des Forges 1999, 684–90). By the time of the French withdrawal, an additional five hundred thousand Rwandans had left the Zone
(including many of the organizers of the genocide, with the knowledge of French
troops), crossing into Zaïre at Bukavu town into the southern Kivu region of
Zaïre (Prunier 1997, 305).

These political developments indicated to old-caseload refugees (known in
Rwanda simply as "returnees") that it was time to return home.[10] Their unofficial
return to Rwanda (i.e., without being processed by the United Nations High

Commissioner for Refugees [UNHCR]) caused some headaches for the RPF-led government (HRW 2001a, 19–21). Many of the old-caseload returnees had no family or social ties in Rwanda; as a result, they simply occupied homes abandoned during the genocide. As the owners of these homes returned to Rwanda following the genocide, they found their homes either destroyed or occupied by "Anglophone returnees who would not give up their new homes" (field notes 2006). In some cases, attempts by genocide survivors to repossess their homes were met with threats, accusations of being genocide perpetrators, imprisonment, and even assassination instigated by individuals who did not want to give up their property (Burnet 2005, 110). Hutu who returned home faced the possibility of being denounced as genocide perpetrators by virtue of their ethnicity. In some instances, aggrieved genocide survivors took revenge on Hutu, occupying their homes, stealing their livestock and other property, and, in some cases, killing them. Hutu property- and landowners were particularly vulnerable as returnees denounced them as genocide perpetrators, resulting in their arrest and imprisonment.

Some Rwandans, particularly those living near the Zaïrian and Tanzanian borders, remained vulnerable to attacks from members of the Hutu Power forces, the ex-FAR and Interahamwe, who were hiding in the refugee camps. In addition, leaders of the genocide who now occupied positions of authority in the camps threatened to kill anyone who tried to leave (Umutesi 2004, 79). The RPF also committed mass violations of human rights against ordinary Rwandans, notably massacres that took place after the Hutu Power forces had fled. RPF soldiers massacred civilians in eastern, southern, and central Rwanda (Des Forges 1999, 705). The RPF also arbitrarily executed individuals—survivors or returnees, Hutu or Tutsi—if they perceived them to be associated with the former genocidal regime or hostile to the new government (Des Forges 1999, 709). The new RPF-led government distanced itself from these killings by blaming them on undisciplined new RPF soldiers who killed in revenge (Des Forges 1999, 714). In April 1995 the RPF killed eight thousand civilians, many of whom were perceived to be ethnic Hutu, at the Kibeho internally displaced persons camp in southwestern Rwanda. The RPF blamed the massacre on Interahamwe militia members living in the camps. As the truth came to light through humanitarian aid workers and human rights activists, the government eventually recanted, justifying the massacre by saying it had attacked Kibeho to eliminate Interahamwe living in the camp (Pottier 2002, 76).

The human rights abuses perpetrated by the RPF led many Rwandans to question its commitment to a government of national unity and reconciliation. It became increasingly clear that Hutu members of the government had little, if any, decision-making power and that they could hold public office only as long as they did not challenge the RPF's actions. In particular, prominent Hutu politicians and long-time allies of the RPF resigned in August 1995, among them Interior Minister Seth Sendashonga (RPF), Justice Minister Alphonse Nkubito (PSD), and Prime Minister Twagiramungu (MDR) (Reyntjens 2004, 180). More than forty prominent figures—both Hutu and Tutsi—fled into exile between 1995 and 2010, while several others were assassinated or imprisoned or disappeared (HRW 2003a, 8–9; ICG 2002, 28–29; Reyntjens 2011, 28). The 1995 resignations meant that new cabinet members had to be appointed. The RPF appointed new Hutu to cabinet posts while at the same time installing its loyalists as deputies within Hutu-led ministries. This gave the appearance of an ethnically balanced government when in fact the real power within ministries lay with the RPF appointees (Reyntjens 2004, 187–90). Political power was concentrated in the hands of a small group of individuals closely associated with Vice President Kagame, who claimed that ethnicity was a fictional hangover from Belgian colonial rule while boasting that Hutu were well represented in his government (Gourevitch 1996, 164). Kagame further boasted that his commitment to sharing power with Hutu politicians was "sincere" since, if he wanted to, he could have "taken over everything but the fact is that we did it differently [in opting for a government based on power sharing]" (Gourevitch 1996, 168–69).[11] From October to December 1995, the RPF continued its pattern of human rights abuses. Hutu were particularly subject to arbitrary arrest on suspicion of having committed acts of genocide. Many remained jailed for years without formal charge. The RPF explained these arrests as "necessary," given the continued incursions of Interahamwe and other forces intent on destabilizing Rwanda from the refugee camps in Zaïre (Vandeginste 2003, 254).

REPATRIATION OF REFUGEES
(1996–97)

By the end of 1996, UNHCR estimated that there were almost 1.2 million refugees living in eastern Zaïre and another six hundred thousand in western Tanzania (UNHCR 1997). Another 270,000 Rwandans were registered as refugees in Burundi. UNHCR reported ninety thousand Rwandan refugees under its care in Uganda (UNHCR 1997). The sheer number of refugees, along with the complexity of the situation, meant that humanitarian organizations opted immediately following the genocide to organize the camps on the basis of Rwandan geographic regions and administrative structures to distribute relief (Minear and Guillot 1996, 99). This had the unintended effect of reinforcing the authority and power of political and military leaders from the Habyarimana regime who had fled into neighboring countries, some of whom were guilty of acts of genocide. These leaders also used their positions of authority to spread misinformation about security and living conditions in Rwanda (Umutesi 2004,

89–102). Many Rwandan refugees received death threats if they tried to return; leaders in the camps wanted to maintain high numbers of refugees to justify the continued food and medical relief provided by international organizations (Minear and Guillot 1996, 107). The former Rwandan authorities who controlled the refugee camps in Zaïre hoarded international relief assistance; ordinary Rwandan refugees received very little medical or food aid, existing on "a little oil, some sugar and biscuits" (interviews 2006). In the immediate postgenocide period (1994–96), the RPF-led government in Kigali did not want these refugees to return home and made it difficult for them to do so. The government's attitude had shifted by mid-1996 when it began to forcibly return the Rwandan refugees living in camps along the border with Zaïre. The regime saw the refugee camps, particularly those in Zaïre, as sites where Hutu Power forces could regroup and rearm, since these men were hiding among the general refugee population (UNHCR 1997).

Just as domestic politics in Uganda forced the RPF decision to invade Rwanda in October 1990, domestic politics in the Kivu regions of western Zaïre facilitated the forcible repatriation of Rwandan refugees. The mass influx of refugees from Rwanda in late 1994 reignited tensions between the Banyamulenge and the Banyarwanda living in the Congo. The Congolese Banyarwanda (meaning those from Rwanda) have lived in the Kivus for several hundred years. Hutu live mainly in northern Kivu, while Tutsi live in the south. But the distinctions between them were regional, not ethnic. It was not until the 1990s, when political tensions again emerged in Rwanda, that the identity of the Banyarwanda as Kinyarwanda speakers of a particular locale shifted to an ethnic one of being either Hutu or Tutsi. The Banyarwanda of the Congo comprise three distinct groups: (1) nationals who were resident in the Congo before the Belgian colonizers arrived, (2) migrants who crossed into the Congo during the colonial era under compulsion or in search of a livelihood, and (3) refugees who arrived in the postcolonial periods as a result of political instability in their home countries (Burundi, Rwanda, and Uganda). Before the arrival of mainly Hutu refugees in 1994, nationals and migrants outnumbered refugees.

When the RPF was organizing to invade Rwanda in 1990, it reached out to Tutsi in the diaspora and connected with the Banyamulenge of southern Kivu, not the Banyarwanda community in the Congo more generally (Vlassenroot 2002, 502). The term Banyamulenge (those who live in Mulenge) gained political meaning after Rwandan Tutsi arrived between 1959 and 1962 as a way to distinguish them from the newly arrived Banyarwanda. This had the effect of changing the identities of Banyamulenge from territorial and class-based ones to a predominantly ethnic one, as Tutsi from Rwanda and Burundi arrived following political upheaval at home. When the Hutu power extremists arrived among the 1994 refugees, they militarized the camps and "made life hell for Tutsi in North and South Kivu" (Mamdani 2001, 255). Soon, Banyamulenge became a generic term for all Kinyarwanda-speaking individuals living in the Congo, whether they were Congolese Tutsi or Hutu refugees who arrived in 1994 (Willame 1997, 78–83). This is in contrast to the original use of the term Banyamulenge, which referred to the fifty thousand or so inhabitants of the Mulenge plateau, south of Bukavu in the eastern part of the Congo, who were considered to be Tutsi. During the war that began in 1996, the Banyamulenge expanded the meaning of the term to include other Tutsi from other areas of the eastern Congo, including north Kivu, increasing their number to about four hundred thousand. In January 1972 Zaïrian president Mobutu Sese Seko signed a decree giving Zaïrian citizenship to all natives of Rwanda and Burundi who had settled in Zaïre before 1950. Mobutu reversed this decision in 1981, meaning that only those Banyarwanda who had obtained legal naturalization actually held Zaïrian citizenship (Nzongola-Ntalaja 1996, 2).

Hutu Power elements living in the refugee camps incited attacks on Tutsi living in the Kivus. Local and regional Zaïrian authorities did not intervene to stop these attacks; in fact, they silently encouraged them in hopes that the Rwandan refugees would return home on their own (Makombo 1998, 53). In September 1996 the deputy governor of South Kivu announced on local radio that if the Banyamulenge (now meaning all Rwandans in the eastern Congo, not just those from South Kivu) did not leave Zaïre within a week, they would be imprisoned in the camps and killed (Nzongola-Ntalaja 1996, 2). Perhaps ironically, this announcement provided the necessary pretext for the RPF to attack and dismantle the refugee camps. The RPF again asked the international community to disarm the Hutu Power forces and their Zaïrian counterparts. When the request went unheeded, the RPF and local Banyamulenge took matters into their own hands in attacking their attackers. Throughout August and September 1996, the Banyamulenge rebels attacked Interahamwe and Zaïrian army forces stationed in the refugee camps. Indeed, seventeen of the thirty-seven Rwandans who participated in my research reported directly experiencing either forced displacement or physical violence at the hand of the RPF in the camps in late 1996. Joseph B., a destitute Hutu man, was just sixteen years old in 1996. He reports that the RPF targeted "young men like me [resident in the camps]. Anyone who was young got harassed, beat up and even killed when questioned by RPF officials. There was no authority in the camps and the RPF killed, but then so did Interahamwe. When I saw someone in a uniform or with a weapon, I really feared for my life" (interview, 2006).

By November 1996 the Banyamulenge rebellion had acquired a name, Alliance des forces démocratiques pour la libération du Congo/Zaïre (AFDL), and a leader, Laurent-Desiré Kabila, handpicked by the RPF to give a Zaïrian face to it all. Tens of thousands of refugees—ordinary Rwandan Hutu and Tutsi—were caught up in the melee; many lost their lives (Umutesi 2004, 138–63). Orchestrated and assisted by the RPF regime in Kigali, the AFDL rebels quickly moved from south to north, gaining control of the three hundred miles of Zaïre's eastern frontier in a series of attacks between October 1996 and May 1997 (HRW 1997, 16). In February 1997 AFDL rebels and their allies attacked the makeshift camps of fleeing refugees at Tingi-Tingi and Amisi. Tens of thousands of ordinary Rwandans and Congolese died (Umutesi 2004, 164–94). The international community stood by and watched as RPF-aided AFDL rebels repatriated most of the refugees to Rwanda in 1997 (Chaulia 2002). Some six hundred thousand refugees began to make the dangerous and arduous trek back into Rwanda. Approximately four hundred thousand refugees went in the opposite direction and fled deeper into Zaïre. AFDL rebels massacred thousands of civilian rebels in the process; tens of thousands of deaths were caused by inhumane camp conditions and diseases such as cholera, dysentery, and malaria. The AFDL blocked international humanitarian assistance to the refugees (IRIN 1998).

In an unfortunate turn of events, the Tanzanian government announced shortly after the forcible closures of the camps in Zaïre that all Rwandan refugees in Tanzania must leave by the end of December 1996 (Human Rights First 2002; UNHCR 1997). Tanzanian security forces began to forcibly remove refugees, ignoring their right to return to Rwanda voluntarily. Nearly three hundred thousand of the five hundred thousand Rwandans resident in Ngara camp fled western Tanzania to avoid being sent home (USCRI 2004). For many, the flight was in vain as Tanzanian forces intercepted them and channeled them toward the Rwandan border where UNHCR struggled to register and process them. Instead, these refugees walked back to their home communities "under the direction of Rwandan Patriotic Army soldiers," many of them to find that their fields had been planted and their homes occupied or destroyed by genocide survivors or Tutsi returnees (Pottier 1997, 405). Tanzanian soldiers arrested thousands of these refugees on suspicion of genocide. Genocide survivors and returnees often made false accusations of participation in genocide against Hutu who returned from Tanzania in order to prevent these new returnees from reclaiming their homes and other property (field notes 2006).

THE REBEL INSURGENCY IN THE NORTHWEST
(1997–2000)

The flood of refugees returning from both Zaïre and Tanzania led to a dramatic decline in Rwanda's internal security situation. By mid-1997, the UN and international NGOs stopped all of their activities in the northwest—emergency reconstruction projects and human rights monitoring alike. The internal political situation in Rwanda was simply too unstable for these organizations to safely and productively carry out their work. Most of the northwest region of the country (Kibuye, Ruhengeri, and Gisenyi provinces) was off limits to foreigners because of the UN's stringent security controls for internationals living in Rwanda (field notes 2006). The RPF forbade internationals working in Rwanda to travel to the northwest, citing the "obvious" security concerns associated with the unregistered return of Hutu refugees who "participated in the genocide. Why else would they flee then resist returning home?" (interview with senior RPF official 2006). Reyntjens contextualizes this quotation in his analysis of Rwandan politics in 1997–98: "Convinced of its 'due right,' the regime implements its security policy in a unilateral, aggressive and arrogant manner: it presents itself as a victim of the genocide which the world would not or could not stop and thus has no obligations to the international community, which has no moral authority to teach lessons in the field of human rights or any other field" (1999, 26). Giving credibility to such strong statements among international donors and aid workers alike was the fact that some ex-FAR, Interahamwe militia, and other Hutu Power elements did indeed use the cover of mass refugee flows to return to Rwanda to attack civilians in an effort to destabilize the RPF-led government.

The RPF identified the Hutu Power forces as *abacengezi* (infiltrators), just as the Habyarimana regime had done with the RPF incursions into the country in 1990–94. Ordinary people were once again caught in the crossfire both in Rwanda and in camps in neighboring Zaïre as the RPF countered to eliminate the Hutu Power insurgency that "threatened Rwanda's present and future peace and security" (interview with senior RPF official 2006). In suppressing this insurgency, RPF troops killed tens of thousands of unarmed civilians, a slaughter that the government justified by citing its need for security (HRW 2001a, 2). Joseph N., a Tutsi survivor of the genocide who returned to southern Rwanda in December 1996, shared that by the summer of 1997 indiscriminate killings were commonplace. He said, "The Rwandan Patriotic Army had its boys [soldiers] everywhere. Even small children were unable to move around without fearing for their lives. They would kill anyone who disobeyed them. But we [the population] did not know how they expected us to behave. Me? I hid most of the time, not even going out to cultivate. My sisters went because the RPF did not kill women as easily [presumably meaning as readily as it did men]" (interview 2006).

Both sides adopted a "deliberate strategy of confusion so as to be able to blame attacks on each other" (Amnesty International 1997). Ordinary Rwandans became targets of arbitrary violence by one side or the other. Ordinary Hutu and Tutsi perceived by the RPF as sympathetic to the *abacengezi* were subject to arbitrary arrest, ill treatment, and prolonged detention in life-threatening conditions, as well as death. Tactics used by the RPF to control its population included routine searching of peasants' homes to identify those who were hiding or feeding *abacengezi* infiltrators—the same tactics that FAR forces had used to identify those who were hiding RPF rebels during the civil war of the early 1990s. Hutu Power insurgents targeted ordinary people, burning their houses, slaughtering their livestock, and killing those who did not help them fight the RPF (Amnesty International 1997). Fierce fighting raged between the two sides for much of 1997 and 1998. Crops went unplanted, and famine affected hundreds of thousands of civilians in both eastern Zaïre and northern Rwanda (FAO 1998).

In late 1998 the tide turned toward the RPF, which had invaded the eastern Congo, ostensibly to oust Laurent Kabila following a souring of relations between the RPF and Kabila's AFDL. The RPF's presence in the eastern Congo disrupted the ability of the Hutu Power infiltrators to organize and invade Rwanda and eliminated their supply routes. The RPF urged ordinary Rwandans to move from their homesteads into displacement camps to protect them from the insurgent raids. Individuals suspected by the RPF of aiding the Hutu infiltrators were imprisoned on suspicion of genocide, forcibly located to the displacement camps, or killed by RPF soldiers. Many ordinary Rwandans felt that their greatest risk now was not from insurgents but from local authorities charged with protecting them (HRW 2001b). Marie Claire, the sole participant in my research who lived in the northwest during the insurgency, highlights the extent of the insecurity among ordinary Rwandans:

> Boys were particularly vulnerable since the RPF would round them up and make them soldiers. Girls got to stay with their families, then the infiltrators would come and violence [rape] that girl. Maybe they heard that the RPF visited that family. It was almost like both sides knew who was supporting which side and how to violence them. Orphans had it the worst because they had no choice but to go to the [displacement] camps. Every boy orphan that I know, even single orphans [having lost one parent], got recruited to the RPF once those camps opened. For the rest of us, we lost our crops and our homes and everything really. They called it the post-genocide period, but really it felt like the genocide continued right up until the *abacengezi* got chased back. My young sister lives in [community], so I left as soon as I was able to live with her. I don't go back up north because I am a Hutu. I might get accused of something just for visiting! (Interview 2006)

In the rest of the country, ordinary Rwandans lived in fear that the RPF's rule was just the reverse image of Habyarimana's oppressive and exclusionary dictatorship. Ordinary Hutu were particularly vulnerable as the RPF, under the newly passed Organic Law for punishing genocide and crimes against humanity, continued to target them, particularly adult Hutu men, for their presumed participation in the genocide. In October 1996 there were an estimated ninety thousand detainees incarcerated on suspicion of genocide, of whom two thousand were identified as Category 1 accused (LIPRODHOR 2001). When the law was passed, human rights organizations noted a dramatic increase in arbitrary arrests (IRIN 1997, 4). Those Hutu not under suspicion of participating in the genocide were sent to *ingando* (reeducation camps) to "learn how to live as neighbors with Tutsi" (interview with senior RPF official 2006). The RPF saw the mass corralling of Hutu as necessary to plant the seeds of reconciliation while providing a structured environment in which to disseminate its ideology through political indoctrination (Mgbako 2005, 202). During my own *ingando* experience with released prisoners in 2006, "the men around me said that they found the structure of the [reeducation] to be 'no different than being in prison'" (Thomson 2011d, 335).

The RPF continued its drift toward authoritarian rule, the concentration and abuse of power in the hands of RPF loyalists, and continued human rights abuses (Reyntjens 2004, 2006, 2011). Throughout 1999 and into 2000, the RPF neutralized its political opposition, weakened the human rights community, silenced journalists, and marginalized the independent civil society that had emerged before the genocide. The RPF continued to engage in assassinations and arrests of political rivals. The most notable exile of the time is Joseph Sebarenzi of the Parti libéral, Speaker of the National Assembly, and a genocide survivor who "suddenly resigned [in January 2000] under pressure from groups within the RPF" (Reyntjens 2004, 181; Sebarenzi 2009). Simmering tensions between Tutsi returnees, notably those from Uganda, and Tutsi survivors emerged. Returnees were often suspicious of Tutsi and Hutu who grew up inside the country, assuming they must have collaborated with the killing squads to have survived the genocide (interviews 2006; see also Burnet 2009). Conflict among returnees was common, as differing experiences of exile shaped their interactions. Returnees from Uganda, where the RPF was founded, saw it as "their army," as many of them had organized fund-raisers to fund the rebel movement (field notes 2006). These returnees saw themselves as having more of a right to return to Rwanda than others, particularly those who "decided" to flee to Burundi or the Congo (interviews 2006). Conflict along language lines was also common, with Anglophones dominating public life to the exclusion of Francophones. Many returnees from Uganda felt that their experience of exile was "worse" than the experience of those who had fled to other countries in the Great Lakes region because of the hardships they experienced in exile in Uganda; they felt justified in enjoying the spoils of their loyalty to the RPF now that they had control of the government (field notes 2006).

Two events combined to mark the consolidation of RPF political and social power in postgenocide Rwanda. First, the RPF unilaterally extended the so-called transitional period from genocide to democratic rule by four years (to July 2003); second, Paul Kagame ascended to the presidency in March 2000. Skeptics saw the extension of the transition period as a strategic move by the RPF to continue to consolidate its grip on state power in advance of Rwanda's first postgenocide elections, in March 2001. Vice-President Paul Kagame acceded to the presidency when RPF loyalist (and ethnic Hutu) Pasteur Bizimungu resigned "for personal reasons" (Reyntjens 2004, 181). This is not to suggest that a Tutsi regime governed Rwanda by the end of 2000. Rather, the RPF sought to gain and maintain physical and psychological control of the political and social landscape in postgenocide Rwanda by populating the administrative machinery of government and by granting positions of power and prestige to its loyalists, who were, in the main, ethnic Tutsi. The RPF hardly speaks for all Tutsi, as evidenced in its continued marginalization of genocide survivors while favoring Anglophone returnees. Genocide survivors clashed with the RPF-led government on several issues, most notably the integration of suspected genocide perpetrators into the government and military (Kinzer 2008, 216–18). Tutsi survivor organizations were also outraged by the government's policy of publicly displaying skulls, bones, and mummified corpses at memorial sites across the country in violation of Rwandan cultural and religious codes (Burnet 2012, 99–101). In addition, survivors' organizations were openly opposed to the RPF's strategy to commemorate and memorialize the genocide. The elimination of the insurgency in the northwest combined with the marginalization of genocide survivors and other political opponents to give the RPF the political room it needed to declare national unity and reconciliation as "a policy objective" once it was in a position to control the process (Reyntjens and Vandeginste 2005, 103).

Conclusion

Deconstructing the official version of the genocide and contrasting it with the broader sociopolitical context in Rwanda before and after the genocide serves a dual analytical role. First, it shows how the policy of national unity and reconciliation seeks to both simplify and shroud the individual acts that, in the aggregate, made up the 1994 genocide in ways that allow the RPF to silence its opposition by painting a specific version of events around an event that defies easy description or definition. Second, it shows how the simplistic official version of the 1994 genocide is far removed from the multiplicity of individual experiences of violence that ordinary Rwandans lived through during genocide in particular and throughout the 1990s more generally. This is a critical aspect of the policy of national unity and reconciliation, which approaches ethnic unity through the maximal prosecution of adult Hutu as the sole perpetrators of acts of genocide with the purpose of "eradicating the ideology of genocide living inside them" (interview with NURC official 2006). Far from being a criminal population, Hutu (along with some Tutsi and Twa) killed their family, friends, and neighbors for a variety of reasons, as the excerpts that opened this chapter illustrate. Many individuals took part in the genocide "because of direct state-backed pressure and because they were scared," not necessarily because they held deep-rooted ethnic hatred, as the policy of national unity and reconciliation contends (Straus 2006, 245).

The chapter also showed that the policy of national unity and reconciliation is silent on other forms of violence perpetrated against ordinary Rwandans of all ethnicities throughout the 1990s by competing parties seeking to seize or maintain state power. Ethnic identities structured which individuals were the targets of violence, how they were targeted, when, and by whom. Ethnic Tutsi were the targets of the Hutu Power forces during the 1994 genocide. Ordinary Rwandans of all ethnicities were caught in the crossfire between the RPF and Habyarimana's FAR during the civil war. The RPF also killed ordinary Rwandans during and after the genocide. The RPF specifically targeted ordinary Hutu during the operation to eliminate the insurgency in the northwest. Everyday violence differed in intensity and scope throughout the 1990s; there is, however, one constant—people were caught up in the maelstrom on the basis of their ethnic identity as determined by the state or those seeking to gain state power. Indeed, a survey of the different forms of everyday violence carried out during the 1990s highlights the need for the postgenocide policy of national unity to take into account the everyday lived experiences of violence of ordinary Rwandans throughout the decade, not just during the 1994 genocide. Rather than acknowledge how Rwandans from different backgrounds recall and make sense of the violence they experienced or witnessed, the RPF regime opts to take a top-down, centralized approach to national unity and reconciliation that seeks to control who can say what and when about their individual experiences of violence. The next chapter continues this analysis in identifying the practices of national unity and reconciliation that the RPF regime employs to maintain control of the postgenocide sociopolitical landscape.

4

Practices of National Unity and Reconciliation

Our main priorities after the genocide were to restore peace and security. We successfully did that, and now the focus is on long-term development and the continued promotion of national unity. Rwanda will become the economic hub of the region under our policies. As a nation we cannot afford to continue the violence that has shaped Rwandan history all these many years. Good governance and a capable state are necessary to shape a positive future for all Rwandans. (Interview with senior RPF official 2006)[1]

For me, the state means those with power, and with power you protect your own people. None of my people have power. They are dead or are in jail. If I thought these strategies of reconciliation were really designed to keep us together and living in peace, I would support it. But this government holds power through officials that don't even speak Kinyarwanda! How are we to negotiate our daily needs with officials that are strangers to us? The state is just something that I try to avoid. (Interview with Gaston, a destitute released prisoner, 2006)

These two quotations reveal the gap between the elite version of postgenocide Rwanda and that of the many ordinary peasant Rwandans who participated in my research on the role of the state in promoting national unity and reconciliation. For the government, a "capable state" will "shape a positive future for all Rwandans" and allow for the "continued promotion of national unity," whereas Gaston feels the state is best avoided and is wary of its strategies of reconciliation. For the RPF-led government, "Rwanda is a nation rehabilitated, whose past is truly the past, whose present is peaceful and stable, and whose future beckons ever more brightly with each passing year" (ORTPN 2004, 4). Behind this idealized image of Rwanda as a nation rehabilitated are the daily realities of ordinary Rwandan men and women who lived through the 1994 genocide. Their daily struggles to reestablish livelihoods, reconstitute social and economic networks, and reconcile with neighbors, friends, and, in some cases, family are subject to the top-down and state-led practices of national unity and reconciliation that are the subject matter of this chapter. Everyday forms of resistance to the demands of the policy of national unity and reconciliation cannot be analyzed without an understanding of the broader framework of power that the policy represents in the lives of ordinary peasants. The various practices and mechanisms of national unity operate within the dense apparatus of the Rwandan state and are a central element of the RPF's unity-building activities, which are, in turn, the foundation of its Vision 2020 development program (Purdeková 2012a, 192; Straus and Waldorf 2011, 8–10).

An analytical focus on the interaction of thirty-seven ordinary peasant Rwandans resident in the south with the constituent elements of the policy of national unity and reconciliation reveals a reality very different from the government's idealized version of Rwanda as a "nation rehabilitated." For the rural Rwandans who participated in my research, the future is hardly bright, as the past continues to shape their daily present. The policy of national unity and reconciliation has outlawed public discussion of or even reference to one's ethnicity—speaking of being Tutsi, Hutu, or Twa. Individuals can speak only of being "Rwandan" in state-sanctioned settings—for example, in *ingando* re-education camps, at *gacaca* justice trials, during genocide mourning week, and through their membership in civil society organizations. There has been no frank or open discussion of how ethnic categories shaped the violence of the genocide, nor has there been any official recognition of different lived experiences of the 1994 genocide beyond the fact that only Tutsi were victims of violence during the genocide and that only Hutu killed. The RPF also does not allow for public discussion of physical violence that individual Rwandans experienced before and after the genocide, particularly the violence they experienced at the hands of its soldiers. Instead, the postgenocide government uses its power to ensure that ordinary Rwandans respect the rules promulgated through its policy of national unity and reconciliation about which Rwandans can speak about their experiences of the genocide and how. As Olive, a destitute Hutu woman, said, "When the state organizes reconciliation, I go because I have no choice" (interview 2006).

The opening quotations also allude to the vexed relationship between some ordinary Rwandans and the practices instituted by the postgenocide state in the pursuit of national unity and reconciliation. From the perspective of the peasant Rwandans who participated in my research, the policy represents an oppressive force in their daily lives. The postgenocide state "organizes everything," and it "makes decisions" in the name of national unity and reconciliation that ordinary people are then left to interpret and implement according to the official narrative (interviews 2006). The purpose of this chapter is to dissect the institutional practices and mechanisms of the policy of national unity and reconciliation to show how the RPF and its agents use the apparatus and authority of the state to enforce the policy. Deconstruction of the various practices and mechanisms of the postgenocide state helps to illuminate the social and political differences that the policy masks while showing the extent to which it represents an oppressive and structural form of social control in the everyday lives of ordinary Rwandans.

Understanding the Apparatus of National Unity and Reconciliation

An understanding of the requirements of the policy of national unity and reconciliation allows for subsequent analysis that enables us to understand the everyday acts of resistance of ordinary Rwandans as purposeful reactions to the power of the postgenocide state as exercised through the policy of national unity and reconciliation. The practical, everyday effects of power are determined by the relationship of domination and resistance between the powerful and the so-called powerless. By "powerless" I mean individuals "over whom power is exercised without their exercising it; the powerless are situated so that they must take orders and rarely have a right to give them" (Young 2004, 52). From this perspective, the dominance of state power is not simply an attribute of the apparatus of the state but rather a product of the relations between the state's ruling regime of elites and its citizens and of the resultant distribution of power among them. This approach allows for an analysis that looks beyond who has power (i.e., state elites) to focus on what kind of power is being exercised and by whom (Foucault 1977, 1980). The apparatus of the state influences the circulation of power insofar as it affects the social and political distribution of knowledge, something that RPF elites do very well (Pottier 2002, 151–78; Purdeková 2012a, 193–96). Analysis of these relational aspects of power reveals that political and social change rely on more than the institutional practices of the ruling elite; they also depend on the nature of the social and political relations between individuals and the state—in this case between ordinary Rwandans and agents of the RPF regime.

A focus on power relations at the level of the individual allows for an analysis of the broader social, institutional, and structural contexts that shape individual interactions with state power such as those of the thirty-seven ordinary Rwandans from the south who participated in my research. Young (1990, 89) concludes that power exists only in action and must therefore be analyzed as something that is "widely dispersed and diffused." Young's critique points us to a specific understanding of the power relationship as one that is unjust and oppressive to those over whom power is exercised, one that is conceptually understood as domination (Young 1990, 2004). For ordinary peasant Rwandans, the policy of national unity and reconciliation is a source of sociopolitical exclusion, economic inequality, and individual humiliation as they struggle to comply with its many demands.

The Policy of National Unity and Reconciliation

The policy of national unity and reconciliation is an ambitious social engineering project that the RPF believes will forge a unified Rwandan identity while fostering reconciliation between survivors of the genocide and its perpetrators. The official narrative of national unity and reconciliation argues that the combination of a docile and obedient population, a legacy of authoritarian government, and colonial policies of ethnic divisionism caused the 1994 genocide. The official narrative is that "Rwanda cannot recover from the effects of the genocide until national unity is restored" (interview with senior RPF official 2006). Ethnic unity is a "traditional value which must be reasserted, reinforced and taught to all Rwandans" and is considered to be "the basis of future peace and security" (Office of the President 1999, 16).

The policy further posits that a democratic political culture and respect for the human rights of all Rwandans are also necessary as they provide the foundation from which "those accused of genocide can take responsibility for their actions" and which "those who survived can participate in judging them [during *gacaca* court proceedings]" (interview with Ministry of Justice [MINIJUST] official 2006). The policy also encourages Rwandans to hold their local officials to account for decisions that are not in the best interests of the community and to resist reckless leaders who might manipulate them to behave "wickedly," that is, to engage in corruption (interviews 2006; NURC 2007b; Office of the President 1999a, 63–64). The need for local officials to be accountable for how they serve the communities to which they have been assigned by the central government has since been codified in the form of *imihigo* (performance) contracts that appointed officials sign directly with President Kagame and in which they vow "to execute their tasks with bravery and zeal" (Ingelaere 2011, 71).[2]

For local officials and ordinary Rwandans alike, stepping outside the prescribed roles of national unity and reconciliation brings a reaction from the government and its agents that is quick and relentless: imprisonment without charge, disappearance, intimidation, even death (Amnesty International 2010; Cooke 2011; *Frontline* 2005; Himbara 2012; HRW 2008, 2010, 2011; LGDL 2004; Maina and Kibalama 2006; MSF 2006c; Reyntjens 2011). The cost at the community level among ordinary folks is just as steep but is of a different scale: gossip, character assassination, denunciation, shunning, and outcasting serve to isolate, ostracize, and demonize individuals on the basis of where they were during the genocide and whether they experienced, witnessed, resisted, or acted the bystander to the violence. Denunciation is by far the most serious of these techniques, as it usually results in a prison sentence at best or in disappearance or death at worst. Both sets of actors—local officials and ordinary people alike—are constrained by overbearing administrative structures and information networks, resulting in the ubiquitous presence of the state and its agents in daily life through "surveillance and indirect control, the display and use of informants, formal and informal police, the dominance and strength of the military" (Purdeková 2012a, 205).

This near constant surveillance, by local authorities and neighbors alike, means that the essentialist categories of survivors (read Tutsi) and perpetrators (read Hutu) are made real by the policy of national unity and reconciliation despite the various and multiple forms of violence that Rwandans experienced before, during, and after the 1994 genocide (as discussed in chapter 3). For example, the policy officially substitutes "perpetrator" for "Hutu" and is thus able to exclude from public life those Hutu who do not toe the line on the basis that they are all perpetrators (*génocidaires*).[3] The policy of national unity and reconciliation appears to be inclusive and conciliatory when in fact Hutu can participate only as perpetrators. The policy also successfully denies the presence of "Hutu moderates" in postgenocide Rwanda; its logic is that if the "moderates" are dead or have fled, then those Hutu who remain in country must by definition be "extremists." The official position is that reconciliation between these two groups is ongoing and successful—Rwanda is both peaceful and safe. Survivors can speak of their experiences in sanctioned settings, such as during the April mourning period or at *gacaca* trials. Perpetrators can hang their head in shame and ask for forgiveness once they have told the truth about what they did. It is these two narrow and essentialist categories of "survivor" and "perpetrator" that are the protagonist of national unity and reconciliation, to the exclusion of other actors and experiences of violence.

For the ordinary Rwandans who participated in my research, the penalties of falling afoul of the accepted but unscripted boundaries of the policy of national unity and reconciliation are too high to be openly risked. The most marginal seek to avoid contact with the government and its agents, while the government works to make sure everyone participates according to the official narrative. For example, Judith, a destitute Hutu woman, was put in *cachot* (detention) by the appointed local government official in her community because she failed to attend *gacaca* in mid-May 2006. She says:

> He put me in prison because I disrespected the rule about attending *gacaca*. I already told my truth [last week], and it was rejected by the judges. They said in front of everyone that my evidence was no good; some laughed. Some [Tutsi] survivors have said I should be kicked out of [the women's cooperative to which she belongs] because I am not respecting the rules of reconciliation. What is the point of going if I am going to be ridiculed, to be told my truth is not good enough? They tell us to tell our truth, they then say it's no good; this is how this government operates? Of course I know I have to attend, but I have mouths to feed. I need to plant my fields. There is no one to help me with this; so I decided to miss *gacaca*.
>
> I even left home very early in the morning, thinking that they [the judges] would not miss my presence. When [the local official] noticed I wasn't there, he sent a military to come and get me. Now I am more than humiliated; I now have problems with my neighbors and survivors. And my kids, too. I had to leave them alone for five nights while I rotted in prison. No one fed me or even my kids during those days . . . this is reconciliation? I am more fearful than ever since I spent those nights in *cachot*. What is next? I don't know, but I do know it is best to avoid contact with government officials who push me to reconcile in ways that I don't understand. (Interview 2006)

This excerpt also shows that ordinary Rwandans need to understand their role as determined by the policy of national unity and reconciliation so that individuals can offer the requisite performance in its name. In order to guarantee that national unity and reconciliation are carried out as envisaged in the official narrative, the RPF has instituted a variety of mechanisms to ensure that Rwandans, elites and peasant folk alike, reconcile according to script.

Practices of National Unity and Reconciliation

I have already examined some of the RPF's practices of national unity and reconciliation in earlier chapters: (1) the exploitation of the perceived ethnic unity of precolonial Rwanda (chapter 2); (2) government control of public information, including the RPF's reinterpretation of its role in stopping the genocide as well as its misrepresentation of the levels of peace and reconciliation among ordinary Rwandans (chapter 3); and (3) the constitutional illegality of public references to ethnic divisionism or trivializing the genocide (chapter 3). Twelve additional practices can be identified.[1]

First, the repression of political dissent: the RPF does not tolerate any form of political dissent. Instead, it works to maintain "total control over the political landscape" (Reyntjens 2006, 1107). Functional opposition political parties exist as part of a RPF-led coalition that was formed in advance of Rwanda's 2003 and 2010 national elections (Meierhenrich 2006; Reyntjens 2011). The RPF has carefully eliminated the possibility of an organized internal political opposition, including by dissolving the Mouvement démocratique républicain (MDR) on the basis of allegations of ethnic divisionism and by harassing and eventually imprisoning the leader of United Democratic Front–Inkingi in January 2010 (Rafti 2004; Reyntjens 2004, 2011). The RPF beats up or imprisons political moderates, elite Tutsi and Hutu alike, as well as prominent members of civil society who speak out against the postgenocide policies. Persecuted individuals who can arrange it flee into exile (Amnesty International 2005; Reyntjens 2006, 2011; Sebarenzi 2011). The RPF accuses elite Hutu critics of harboring genocide ideology, while elite Tutsi, including formerly prominent members of the RPF, are accused of corruption (Amnesty International 2011; Global Integrity 2011).[5] By the end of 2006, many ordinary Rwandans understood that accusing some- one of corruption was a tactic of the government to eliminate its opponents: "the perception remains that many government officials have engaged in cor- ruption but are protected as long as they remain in good stead with the *akazu* [President Kagame's inner circle]" (Burnet 2007, 22; Global Integrity 2011).

The RPF also maintains a tight rein on the media. The RPF accuses journal- ists who speak out against its policies of ethnic divisionism or of preaching genocide ideology under the 2001 "divisionism" law. Only those media outlets that express views in line with those of the government are able to speak out; as a result, many self-censor (Uvin 2003, 1). Instances of "courageous journalism" have in turn been followed by "crackdowns on the media" (Burnet 2007, 5). Media independence and freedom of expression have declined considerably since 2000. For example, the RPF accused the editor of *Umuseso*, said to be Rwanda's "last remaining independent newspaper," of ethnic divisionism in 2003 and again in 2010 (Reyntjens 2006, 1107; RSF 2010). The RPF continues to harass and detain without charge journalists who criticize government policies. Several journalists have fled the country; others have been beaten up (RSF 2002, 2012; field notes 2006).

Second, elimination of references to ethnicity from public discourse: the RPF justifies its intolerance of political dissent in the name of eliminating the ideology of genocide and ethnic divisionism. The central idea of the policy of national unity and reconciliation is the slogan of "one Rwanda for all Rwan- dans." Since the RPF believes that ethnic disunity caused the genocide, then the creation of an inclusive Rwandan citizenship, of a monolithic identity, is the "obvious solution to overcome our legacy of ethnic hatred and violence. We are no longer Tutsi, Hutu or Twa—we are Rwandans!" (interview with NURC official 2006). The RPF invokes its vision of "Rwandan-ness," that is, the promise of a unified national identity, as a strategic tool with which to silence its critics and opponents with allegations that they are "un-Rwandan." Individuals, elite and ordinary folk alike, who question the role of the RPF in stopping the 1994 genocide or who make public references to war crimes or other human rights abuses that it committed before, during, or after the genocide are beaten up or imprisoned or disappear; some are killed in mysterious circumstances (Beswick 2010; field notes 2006; HRW 2007, 2011). The RPF limits public speech to acceptable topics, namely the hero status of the RPF for liberating Tutsi from "the noose of Hutu power" and the resilience and ability of Tutsi survivors to forgive "the wrong-doings of Hutu who killed" (interview with senior RPF official 2006).

In government discourse, the second component of the official narrative of "national unity and reconciliation" is broadly understood to mean that survivors (read Tutsi) forgive while perpetrators (read Hutu) tell the truth about what they did during the genocide. As one senior RPF official in the Ministry of Culture explained:

> In Rwanda's parlance, reconciliation is short for national unity and national reconciliation. Rwandans are just simple peasant people, and they need us to make decisions for them. We have given them peace, but they don't know what to do with it. Survivors are traumatized because of what happened to them. That is why we brought back *gacaca* and *ingando* camps. Hutu will tell the truth about what they did during the genocide, and justice will come. They will get reconciled because that is how it used to be between Hutu and Tutsi. Once we teach them, they will learn. . . . National unity and reconciliation is within reach. (Interview 2006)

The ordinary Rwandans who participated in my research are more than just skeptical about the government's commitment to national unity and reconciliation; they also recognize it as a form of social control. The words of Joseph M., a poor Tutsi survivor, are emblematic of the widely held perception among survivors I interviewed:

> We [survivors] need to know the truth about what happened to our loved ones. We need to have the right to bury them where they belong [at home], not in public memorials. We need to know how they died and who killed them. They talk about national unity and reconciliation. But they don't know what unity or reconciliation means. I know I am a Tutsi, how

can I not? I ran and hid because of being a Tutsi. Now I have to forget that in the name of unity and reconciliation. Unity for whom? Reconciliation for whom? It is a political game that is the responsibility of local officials. Reconciliation is not an administrative matter; it is an affair of the heart, of accepting the wrong and then forgiving the ones who harmed you. (Interview 2006)

The words of this prisoner are representative of the sentiments of former Hutu that I consulted:

We [prisoners] are in here for different reasons. I killed, but some did not. They got caught up in politics when they came back [from Zaïre]. I confessed to get a reduced sentence.[6] But they changed the rules, and some who confessed got between twenty and twenty-five years at *gacaca*. They said I would get out after ten years if I confessed. Part of confessing was reeducation. Reeducation to learn how to live with my Tutsi neighbors. I didn't actually know what that meant because I have always lived with Tutsi. The Tutsi I know are poor like my family, and we struggled together sometimes. But the new government says that we must learn national unity and reconciliation. So I got reeducated in 1999. There I learned about national unity and reconciliation. But I told my truth. It was even acknowledged by the authorities because they reduced my sentence! But then at *gacaca* [in 2005] my truth was denounced as a lie and [I] got another twenty-five years! National unity and reconciliation is just a way for this government to eliminate Hutu. It's like the new authorities are trying to kill former Hutu through excessive punishment. (Interview with Jean-Claude, a convicted prisoner, 2006)

Third, the collectivization of Hutu guilt for the 1994 genocide: in labeling all Hutu as perpetrators of the genocide (*génocidaires*), the RPF has effectively chosen a strategy of maximum persecution. The RPF arrested anyone who took part in the genocide without regard to individual motivations for participating in the killing. Interahamwe militias and other state agents of the previous regime forced many ordinary Hutu men to participate. By 2000 the RPF had detained more than one hundred thousand individuals for acts of genocide (PRI 2007, 12). In assigning collective guilt to the Hutu population, the policy of national unity and reconciliation makes no distinction among different types of participation in the 1994 genocide. The Ministry of Local Government estimates that there were at least three million perpetrators (MINALOC 2002). Academic research does not support the government's practice of collective guilt, finding instead that between 175,000 and 200,000 individuals participated—hardly the numbers needed to justify the assignment of collective guilt to Hutu (Straus 2004).

Collective guilt also limits the participation of individual Hutu in community life. Opportunities for paid employment are scarce at best, and the difficulties Hutus face in finding work are compounded by the suspicion that "those who fled [into neighboring countries] must be by definition guilty of genocide" (field notes 2006; Tertsakian 2008). Full participation in community life is also limited because the perception that all Hutu are guilty of genocide shapes individual opportunities to reintegrate into one's hill. Many Hutu men told me that it is better not to participate in community life rather than to be regarded with suspicion (corroborated by Tertsakian 2011). For example,

> When we go to *umuganda* [community work], everyone knows which of us [Hutu] is a released prisoner. Tutsi neighbors tell the [local official] that they are too afraid to work next to us [Hutu], particularly when we work with *pangas* [machetes]. Then you see them later and they laugh because we had to do their *umuganda* labor. I was released for lack of evidence, but that does not matter. I am Hutu, so I must be guilty. (Interview with Thomas, a salaried poor man, 2006)

Fourth, politicization of Tutsi victimhood: under the policy of national unity and reconciliation, only Tutsi are able to call themselves "survivors." This has the effect of negating the lived experiences of the genocide of Hutu and Twa men and women who also risked death in Rwanda in 1994. It also silences the experiences of individuals from ethnically mixed families who lost some family members but not others on the basis of ethnicity before, during, and after the genocide. According to one RPF official, "Hutu cannot be survivors because they were not targeted for dying" (interview with Ministry of Culture official 2006). While this interpretation accords with the legal definition of genocide, it is also an effective technique for silencing non-Tutsi about the violence they suffered before, during, and after the genocide at the hands of the RPF. As Joseph N., a destitute Tutsi survivor of the genocide, said, "In April, we mourn as we are told [by our local officials]. If we mourn too much or not enough, there can be trouble. One time, my son showed sympathy for a former Hutu who is our pastor and neighbor. This is illegal so he went to prison until I could raise enough money to get him released."

Fifth, politicization of individual mourning: individual mourning is politicized in that the government officially recognizes it only during the annual mourning period during the month of April. Only official survivors are recognized, and the RPF represents only their trauma symbolically through the image of the lonely, wounded survivor as the personification of the genocide. The government invokes this image of the traumatized survivor to silence criticism, particularly from the international community. Especially powerful is the image of the wailing survivor, usually a woman, head in hands, and in a spasm of trauma that has come to reflect Rwanda's mourning week, which is dedicated to remembering and memorializing Tutsi lives lost. Lives lost—Hutu, Tutsi, and Twa—in the violence before and after the genocide are not memorialized. Instead, the government uses the mourning period to assert its official version of what happened during the genocide and to "keep the genocide alive" (Rwandan ombudsman, quoted in Meierhenrich 2011, 292). The government requires that Rwandans of all ethnicities attend mourning events throughout the month of April, notably the exhumation of mass graves and the reburial of bodies, and listen to the speeches of government officials that remind the population of the need to "never again" allow genocide in Rwanda.

Many ordinary Rwandans that I spoke with in 2006, both in formal interviews and through participant observation, said that they felt the RPF was manipulating the way the genocide is remembered to maintain its position of power and wealth rather than truly seeking to unify the country (field notes 2006, corroborated by Meierhenrich 2011, 287–93). For example, "We dig up bodies for reburial at the national ceremony but how do we know those remains are even Tutsi bodies? We [Hutu] died as well, but nothing is mentioned about how we suffered during the genocide. Not all of us killed. Instead we go because our new government says we must; we were told this very clearly at *ingando*" (interview with Gaston, a destitute released Hutu prisoner, 2006). Others, particularly Tutsi survivors, acknowledged the reburials as "a little bit necessary for national healing" but would prefer to do it in private, "away from the spotlight" (field notes 2006). Rwandan culture frowns upon public displays of emotion, and most of the Tutsi survivors that I spoke with found mourning week "offensive," "upsetting," and "humiliating" (field notes 2006). This was particularly so for Tutsi widows who had lost their Hutu fathers, husbands, sons, or brothers during the genocide, as there is no official outlet for their grief. In homogenizing the diverse individual lived experiences of victims of the genocide—Hutu, Tutsi, and Twa—as well as those of individuals who lived through the violence of the 1990–94 civil war and the emergency period after the genocide (1994–2000), the RPF is stage-managing and politicizing individual mourning.

In May 2008 the RPF amended the 2003 constitution to require that the genocide be known officially as the "genocide committed on Tutsi" (AFROL 2008; IRDP 2008). This move further excluded the possibility of non-Tutsi survivors while allowing the government to continue to reify its role in stopping the genocide, as the amendment makes a powerful distinction between those who were the perpetrators of the genocide (Hutu) and those who stopped it (the RPF). It also eliminated the possibility that "Hutu men made fateful choices to participate in violence against their Tutsi neighbors because they were afraid and because they felt pressure from other Hutus to do so" (Straus 2006, 231). Instead, the constitutional amendment was yet another tactic that the RPF-led government used to affirm its contention that the deep-rooted but latent ethnic enmity of all Hutu for all Tutsi was a root cause of the genocide. Similarly, the government created the National Commission for the Fight against Genocide (known by its French-language acronym, CNLG) in September 2007 in an effort to further legitimize its official version of history. Part of the commission's mandate was to research the causes and consequences of the genocide and "to elaborate and put in place strategies that are meant to fight revisionism, negationism and trivialization" (MINIJUST 2007b, art. 1[7]; CNLG 2013).

Sixth, new national symbols: in 2001, the RPF adopted a new flag, national anthem, and national seal, since "the old ones are stained with Tutsi blood. We need a fresh start with new symbols to represent Rwanda as it is: peaceful and prosperous" (interview with Ministry of Culture official 2006). The flag, the official said, needed to be changed because of its "association with Hutu domination over Tutsi." The old flag was based on the Belgian flag and was made up of three vertical bands, one each of red, yellow, and green, with the letter "R" in the middle. The new postgenocide flag is made up of three horizontal stripes, green on the bottom, yellow in the middle, and light blue on top, with a beaming sun on the right side. The green represents "the promise of prosperity" through the "modern and rational use of the country's resources"; the yellow band of the sun's rays represents the hope of economic development and the "awakening" of the Rwandan people from "old tendencies of hatred"; and the blue represents "peace and stability for all" (interview with Ministry of Culture official 2006).

The RPF adopted a new national anthem on October 25, 2001, with the official justification that the old song encouraged the Hutu to throw off the "chains of Tutsi oppression." It replaced the old anthem with new lyrics that "promote the idea of one Rwanda for all Rwandans" (interview with Ministry of Culture official 2006). Ordinary Rwandans who participated in my research, Tutsi and Hutu alike, were baffled by the introduction of new national symbols, noting that the new symbols "seemed to be designed for those who returned after the war" rather than "designed to facilitate peace and security" (interview with Emmanuel, a poor Tutsi survivor of the genocide, 2006). Another individual recognized that the new symbols were an effort to "remind those like me [a released prisoner] that Rwanda no longer belongs to us [Hutu]" (interview with Tharcisse, a destitute released Hutu prisoner, 2006). Burnet found similar sentiments among Rwandans she spoke with at the time the new flag and anthem were introduced: "The majority of Rwandans that I asked about the new flag and anthem smiled wanly or made a comment to the effect that the state does as the state sees fit and the citizens wait to see what will happen next. The few Rwandans willing to speak more openly wondered why, if the country was the same, the people needed a new flag and a new national anthem. They viewed the new symbols as representing RPF dominance in the New Rwanda" (Burnet 2012, 166). A majority of the Rwandans I consulted told me that for them, the new national anthem is actually an RPF war song that warns Tutsi to protect themselves against Hutu.[7]

Seventh, the National Unity and Reconciliation Commission (NURC): in 1999, the RPF created the NURC. The NURC is managed on a daily basis by the executive secretary, who is responsible to its deputy chairperson.[8] The deputy in turn reports to the chairperson of the NURC, who is accountable to Parliament for all its activities and publications (interview with NURC official 2006; NURC 2007a). There is also a Council of Commissioners, which acts as an advisory body under the guidance of the chairperson (NURC n.d.). There are twelve commissioners, all of whom "are directly appointed by President Kagame" (interview with NURC official 2006). There are two substantive NURC programs—Civic Education and Conflict Management and Peace Building—both of which are staffed by young Anglophone returnees (NURC 2007c, 2007d). All NURC staff "must be members of the RPF" (interview with NURC official 2006). All staff are based in Kigali and travel to the "hills [rural areas] to check in on how unity and reconciliation activities are faring once every month" since it is "a non-negotiable option for Rwandese" (interview with NURC official 2006).

The NURC is tasked with "emphasizing the unifying aspects of Rwandan history, such as our shared culture and language and deemphasizing divisive ones like the legacy of colonial rule and divisive politics" in all activities in the public sphere, including government, the private sector, civil society, and the media (interview with senior NURC official 2006). Its primary task is to sensitize "Rwandans on the importance of national unity," propose "measures that can eradicate divisions among Rwandans and . . . reinforce national unity and reconciliation," and denounce and fight "against acts, writings and utterances which are intended to promote any kind of discrimination or intolerance" (NURC 2007b). It also holds regular consultative meetings, including a national summit (held biannually, usually in August) to ensure that all government agencies, political parties, local officials, and Rwandans "from all walks of life respect and observe the policy of national unity and reconciliation" (NURC 2000, 21, 2007g). It organizes the *ingando* reeducation camps, holds community festivals to promote unity and reconciliation "among the grassroots" (NURC 2007h), provides funds to students' clubs (NURC 2007i), and consults with other government bodies on key aspects of their mandate to ensure across-the-board compliance with the policy of national unity and reconciliation (NURC 2007b). For example, in 2006 the NURC approved the secondary school curriculum produced by the Ministry of Education, following careful review to ensure strict adherence to the "proper version of Rwandan history and our historical unity before the colonizers arrived" (interview with NURC official 2006).[9]

Eighth, the *ingando* reeducation camps: another mechanism of national unity and reconciliation is the "reeducation" of certain segments of the population through solidarity camps. The RPF encourages some Rwandans—government ministers, church leaders, university lecturers—and requires others—ex-soldiers, ex-combatants, released prisoners, *gacaca* judges, and incoming university students—to attend *ingando* for periods ranging from several days to several months to study government programs and Rwandan history, and to learn about how to unify and reconcile (NURC 2006a, 2006b, 2006c).[10] The format differs according to the profile of the participants. Those individuals required to attend *ingando* do so for an average of twelve weeks, and participants live together in close barrack-style quarters (field notes 2006; Thomson 2011d). There is a significant military presence, with armed soldiers monitoring the activities of participants. The setting is formal, and information is delivered lecture-style; there is little "downtime" as participants follow a structured program of "reeducation," with a focus on their socioeconomic reintegration into Rwandan society. *Ingando* are held in all five provinces, although most individuals receive their reeducation in a locale other than their home community (World Bank 2002, 17). The version of history taught at the *ingando* camps is offensive to many ordinary Rwandans who have participated, notably Hutu who experienced the events of 1959–62. *Ingando* camps also teach participants, the majority of whom are ethnic Hutu, that reconciliation means to remain silent and not question the RPF's vision of national unity and reconciliation (Thomson 2011d). As Joseph B., a destitute Hutu who graduated from *ingando* in 2002, said: "I am a former Hutu. This means I am a source of shame for this government. They think that only Hutu killed. *Ingando* is just a way for them [the government] to make sure we don't think for ourselves. The message is that we are not full citizens."

Ninth, mandatory participation at the now closed *gacaca* trials (discussed in detail in chapter 6): the RPF created the *gacaca* courts in 2001 as a response to the backlog of more than one hundred thousand genocide suspects and to establish a truthful record of what happened during the genocide as a means to promote unity and reconciliation among Rwandans. The government portrayed the *gacaca* courts as a "traditional" community-based and participatory process that "clear[ed] the backlog of cases" while "promoting national unity and reconciliation" (interview with Ministry of Justice official 2006). The purpose was to bring together local communities to witness, identify, corroborate, and prosecute perpetrators. There were almost ten thousand *gacaca* jurisdictions, meaning one for each cell and sector. Perpetrators "told their truth," while survivors were, once the truth had been established, to forgive. Participation in *gacaca* was mandatory, and individuals were sometimes fined and/or imprisoned for failure to participate (MINIJUST 2004, 8). In practice, the *gacaca* courts increased the number of accused because of new denunciations, which means that the *gacaca* process has increased the prison population, not reduced it as the government envisaged.

Tenth, administrative presence and control at the local level: the RPF tries to control the flow of information, particularly any dissent from government policy, through a highly devolved administrative structure that has to be "felt" in a localized and intimate fashion. The lowest unit in the Rwandan administrative structure, according to the government, is the family, while the highest is the central government (NURC 2000, 14; 2004, 9). Rwanda is governed by "two layers of government (central and local) and one of six administrative entities: the Province (*Intara*), the District (*Akarere*), the Sector (*Umurenge*), the Cell (*Akagari*) and the Village (*Umudugudu*)" (MINALOC 2007, 8). The sixth and lowest level of government (one that is left out of this list) is the *nyumbakumi* (meaning "responsible for ten households"). Since 2006 there have been 5 provinces (North, South, East, West, and Kigali), 30 districts, 416 sectors, and 9,165 cells (see fig. 3 in chapter 1 for a map of the post-2006 administrative boundaries). Most decisions are made at the lower levels of government, with committee structures at the sector and cell levels in place to oversee the individual and group activities of all Rwandans. During my reeducation interviews with senior government officials, I asked how many villages and *nyumbakumi* there were, but no one was able to answer. A representative of MINALOC stated prosaically, "There are as many as the population requires to meet the development needs of their locale" (field notes 2006).

The sector-level office is the most important in terms of both its physical presence and its political authority as the place where ordinary Rwandans experience "the state" (see fig. 6). Sector-level officials, the most important of whom is the RPF-appointed executive secretary, are responsible for ensuring that the national unity and reconciliation, development, and service delivery policies of the central government are implemented at the local level (Ansoms 2009, 307; Ingelaere 2011, 69). Sector-level officials take few, if any, decisions on their own. Instead, their primary task is to implement decisions made in Kigali, making local governance "paralysed and ineffective because it waits for vital information to make it down the tree-like 'plumbing' of the state" (Purdeková 2011, 479). As Ingelaere notes (2011, 69), "there is a clear hierarchy between

Figure 6. Rural residents shelter from the rain at their local sector-level office, April 2002. (photo by anonymous, © 2002)

Figure 7. In 2006 the RPF was the only political party allowed to have office locations in district capitals across the country. Since then, RPF-satellite parties are able to operate at the sector and cell levels. This image is of an RPF provincial office building in Butare (now Huye) town, May 2006. (photo by author)

appointed and elected postholders, with only those in appointed positions receiving a regular salary from the central/district administration."

In the sectors in southern Rwanda where I worked, the relationship between appointed and elected officials was clear, with each appointed official having the power to make decisions about the national unity and development of his constituency in line with the national vision. There is little room for creativity or problem-solving as local leaders are expected to unify and develop those in their bailiwick quickly and in accordance with their *imihigo* (performance) contract. Many executive secretaries receive military training before taking up their appointed posts (field notes 2006, corroborated by Ingelaere 2011, 75n2). In addition, the majority of appointed local officials I met were members of the RPF, highlighting the overlap between the apparatus of the state and the political party. Only RPF members are government administrators throughout the seven layers of the bureaucracy, and indeed the RPF is the only political party in Rwanda with a defined presence at the village, cell, and sector levels (field notes 2006, corroborated by Purdeková 2011, 480–82) (see fig. 7).

All of the officials at the cell level that I met also looked to Kigali for their policy instructions. The unpaid but elected coordinator is responsible for the daily administration of the people in his or her jurisdiction, working as the head of (also volunteer and unpaid) cell committees. Taken together, the sector and the cell represent the immediate source of state power at the level of the individual. It is at these levels that the control and authority of government play out in daily life. Reports on individual behavior, as well as requests for government assistance, start at the local level. As a member of one my local research partner organizations said, "There is no one level [of bureaucracy] that is more important than the other. Each has its purpose and a specific task and that is something Rwandans know how to respect. But at the lowest levels, it can really feel heavy. If you are having an affair, they [local administrators] know. If you are drunk or if your house is in disrepair, they know. If you fail to attend sensitization meetings, they know. If you want to join a cooperative, you must get a signature from the [cell] coordinator who might ask for the signature of your village coordinator who might also ask for the signature of your *nyumbakumi*. So there are a lot of people watching you, checking on your actions and the people you are with. Without signatures, nothing happens. If you are not a good citizen who supports national unity and reconciliation, you will rot [at home]" (field notes 2006).

Eleventh, social surveillance: the policy of national unity and reconciliation provides incentives to local security and administrative personnel to remain vigilant against criminal elements, those who hold genocidal ideologies, or anyone who fails to promote unity in accordance with the dictates of the policy. The government provides livestock (cattle, goats, sheep, and rabbits), as well as radios and refrigerators, to local security forces as incentives to control the population. Local political and military authorities who fail to control those within their jurisdiction are subject to a variety of sanctions, including dismissal, imprisonment, and naming and shaming for "poor work ethic," "corruption," "sexual immorality," or "having HIV/AIDS" (interviews 2006).

Dense networks of spies are known to exist throughout Rwanda (and abroad), and the Department of Military Intelligence is rumored to pay for valid information (field notes 2006). The low-level bureaucrats report the activities of individuals in their bailiwick to the immediate superior at the next level of government, who then decides whether the information warrants transmission to the next level up, and so on. Ordinary Rwandans all know of state surveillance; most shrug their shoulders, acknowledging prosaically that "we are monitored to make sure we do what we are told; we did it before the genocide [under Habyarimana] in the name of national development and now we do it in the name of national unity and reconciliation" (interviews 2006, corroborated by Verwimp 2003; Desrosiers and Thomson 2011).

Twelfth, government cooptation of associational life: the RPF maintains tight control of civil society organizations and other forms of associational life. In 2001 the RPF passed the Law on Non-Profit Associations, which provided it with the power to control projects, budgets, and the hiring of new staff; it also required all organizations to obtain a renewable certificate of registration from MINALOC. The certificate is granted on the basis of the organization's mission statement and annual report and must be renewed biannually. The registration process allows government authorities to monitor the activities of civil society and to control its publications.

In 2001, and again in 2004, LIPRODHOR, one of the few remaining local independent human rights organizations in Rwanda, was summoned by the National Unity and Reconciliation Commission and MINALOC to respond to allegations that its representatives were acting against national unity and reconciliation (Amnesty International 2004). Nine LIPRODHOR employees fled into exile, and the organization was shut down in December 2004 on unsubstantiated charges that the policies and practices of the organization were "divisionist" and that its representatives were promoting "genocide ideology" among ordinary Rwandans (Amnesty International 2005). The "new" LIPRODHOR, which is managed by individuals who are "closely connected with the authorities," was reopened after an internal investigation to root out those individuals "having the genocide ideology" (Maina and Kabilama 2006, 47).

Between July 2004 and January 2005, several domestic human rights NGOs that openly criticized the RPF and documented human rights abuses by government authorities were closed (field notes 2006). As a result, many civil society organizations practice self-censorship (HRW 2007); at the time of writing, civil society organizations in Rwanda are not free of government oversight (Gready 2011). Most such organizations play an important role in filling the social void in the lives of many Rwandans in the aftermath of the genocide. In particular, women's organizations work to meet the basic needs of their members while providing much-needed social support to individuals who lost their families and social support networks during the genocide (Newbury and Baldwin 2001, 23). As a result of their social role, the RPF sees women's organizations "as the real civil society" (interview with Ministry of Culture official 2006).

Women-focused organizations in civil society have been instrumental in creating legal mechanisms designed to protect Rwandan women, such as the inheritance law of 1998. Burnet notes that there are other "unifying issues" for government and women's organizations to rally around, notably land tenure and land use, since women "are most vulnerable to losing access to land," but "women's NGOs and MIGEPROF [the Ministry of Gender and Women in Development] have refused to define land as a women's issue" given its political "volatility" (Burnet 2008a, 379–80). In addition, the RPF advises civil society organizations on what development issues they may work on, who is allowed to join, and how the rules and conditions of participation are set (field notes 2006). Most organizations, particularly those in Kigali, are dedicated to servicing so-called survivor issues, including psychosocial trauma counseling, HIV/AIDS support, and the provision of micro-credit. Membership in civil society organizations is officially open to both Tutsi and Hutu survivors. Many Hutu "survivors" do marginally benefit from their membership in organizations that support survivors, although specific privileges such as access to subsidized health care and the waiver of school fees for children are available only to Tutsi women in their recognized status as "real survivors" (field notes 2006). Tutsi and Hutu women who remarry sometimes lose access to these privileges, not on the basis of their ethnicity but rather because they have been able to reconstitute their families (field notes 2006).

Conclusion

This chapter analyzed the mechanisms of the policy of national unity and reconciliation to illustrate the extent to which it structures the daily lives of ordinary Rwandans. Identification of the myriad practices of power that the RPF uses to promote its policy of national unity and reconciliation demonstrates the extent of RPF control of the political and social landscape through the policy of national unity and reconciliation. A focus on the practices of national unity and reconciliation allows for analysis of the social and political differences that the policy masks. In particular, the chapter described the structural bed-rock of the policy of national unity and reconciliation to illustrate its myriad forms at all levels of society, notably at the local level, where "the state" is most acutely experienced. Such an approach is necessary to set the stage for the next two chapters so that we may understand the everyday acts of resistance of some ordinary Rwandans to the dictates of the policy of national unity and reconcilia-tion as purposeful responses.

5

Everyday Resistance to National Unity and Reconciliation

Jolie and I used to meet almost every Tuesday afternoon. We would bump into one another at the kiosk near my residence. She sometimes stopped to buy cooking oil or matches there on her way home from the market. Sometimes I would walk home with her so we could spend some private time together, sharing stories about our children in particular and family lineages more broadly. She was fascinated that someone like me would choose to live in Rwanda, given its "problems" and my "freedom to live anywhere." My explanation that I was in Rwanda as a long-term visitor because of my interest in reconciliation processes in the country was met with some confusion. Jolie was one of the few Rwandans I met who did not lose any immediate family members during the genocide, and she often shared stories with me about how her "good luck" translated into social shunning and economic hardship afterward. Her Tutsi husband joined in the killing in May 1994 as a "way to stay alive. They thought he was one of them and so he survived. He killed at least three people, but we never talk about it because we can't." She is unable to join any of the associations set up for "survivors" of the genocide since she does not "qualify as a Hutu woman. I mean they say 'good luck,' but they just use that as an excuse to keep me out of their association."

When I asked whom she meant when she spoke of "they," Jolie explained:

> "They" are Tutsi survivors. We [survivors] are many, but only a few get benefits. It is hardest for me because some of them know that my husband killed to stay alive. They seemed to understand just after the genocide, but

then the government brought *gacaca* and some of them participate fully. What if they speak against him and I have to raise these kids alone? People like me stay on the sidelines to avoid too much trouble. My husband once wanted to admit to his crimes [to the authorities], but I begged him not to. I am a former Hutu married to a former Tutsi. Am I not a survivor? Did I live through the genocide? Did I lose relatives? Is my husband half crazed because of what he did? I survived the events, and even I could say that my husband is lost to me now. He feels a lot of guilt and shame for his actions [during the genocide]. We have not discussed his actions since a long time. It is not really possible now. There are too many people that could denounce him [to the authorities] and make our lives very hard.

It is much harder to live together with my husband and my neighbors since the genocide because of what happened. Everyone killing everyone and others stealing; some just hid. Many died, many killed, many lost their belongings. Just coping is what I think about most. Really. It is just getting to the next day. What those survivors who won't let me join their group fail to understand is that I am suffering as well. Coping is a task; it takes a lot of my energy. My family has many needs. I have two other kids [orphans] that live with us now that need feeding. One has malaria, and I have no money for his medicine. When I give to that kid, I take away from my own kids. My husband is only of little comfort. He hardly works at all. He has no ideas of his own since *gacaca* started. He works only to avoid contact with other people. He is isolating me as well. What else can I do but just keep going? My problems are many, and the solutions are few. I could speak out like some of my foolish [*abasazi*] neighbors. Instead, I will continue to try to get support from the survivors association, even though they say I am not a survivor. What other solution is there? How can you seriously ask me who "they" are when you know full well the answer? (Interview 2006)

Jolie and I had spent enough time together over the preceding few months for me to know that what she had just told me was difficult for her to say; I apologized for my insensitivity. I knew quite well how hard her life was since the genocide. She had shared some of her "inner secrets" with me before but always reminded me to say nothing to anyone lest "it attract the attention of the authorities." The need to avoid the attention of the authorities, particularly appointed local government officials and members of the local security forces, is an everyday lament for many ordinary Rwandans. Ordinary Rwandans like Jolie live under close surveillance from the government (as well as each other), as analyzed in chapter 4. The threat of retaliation is constant and runs the gamut of sanctions—from losing access to social benefits, to social shunning and outcasting, to imprisonment and, in extreme cases, disappearance and even death. This chapter examines the everyday acts of resistance of ordinary Rwandans to the policy of national unity and reconciliation, the precise forms of which depend on the unique combination of dangers and opportunities that exist in any given situation. By necessity, Rwandans' everyday acts of resistance are tactical since government officials and other agents of the state suppress any perceived challenge to the requirements of the policy, sometimes with a ferocity that dramatically exceeds the original violation.

About a week after Jolie's outburst, we found each other at our regular meeting point, the kiosk; she greeted me warmly and said, "Did you tell anyone about what I told you last time? You know, about how I would continue to fight to get [membership in] the survivors' organization?" I reassured her that I had not uttered a word to anyone about our private conversations. She sparkled with delight as she pulled a government-issued health card out of her handkerchief, which she kept carefully folded and tucked underneath the head wrap she usually wore. "Do you see this? Do you know what this is?" I nodded yes. She continued,

> You see what can be done with some persistence? I finally got the signature I needed from the FARG official, and here is proof that I am now a full member.[1] Even my husband did not believe what I accomplished. But I did. I really did it. I got some protection from this government for my children. She said "no" many times before now, but finally, I am a member! This is my first step to getting more support and to getting it as a survivor. Maybe next they will accept me as one of them!

Jolie's experience exemplifies a number of qualities of everyday resistance, which are subtle, indirect, and nonconfrontational acts that those subject to power enact to show their anger, opposition, or indignation vis-à-vis what they perceive as unfair or unjust actions against them. Many ordinary Rwandans understand that the policy of national unity and reconciliation represents wrongs against them and are unable or unwilling to openly risk direct action to remedy their situation. In Jolie's case, as a former Hutu, she is not officially recognized as a "survivor" of the 1994 genocide, which in turn shapes her interactions with local officials and other agents of the state. The FARG representative in her community had not provided the necessary signatures to allow Jolie to join the local chapter of her survivors' organization.

Jolie did not share with me the specifics of how she was finally able to get the necessary signature that allowed her to get medical insurance, but she told me she persisted, which is but one quality of everyday acts of resistance, given the attendant risks of "pushing too hard even though [the right to benefits] is mine." Given the extent to which Hutu peasant women have been marginalized in postgenocide Rwanda, I assume she also showed another quality of everyday resistance—prudence—in pursing the necessary signatures first from the local FARG representative and then from the responsible local officials at both the cell and the sector levels who must also sign before the request can be approved and the medical card issued. Her persistence and prudence in gaining medical coverage from FARG also show that she did not have an expectation of immediate success, evidenced in her remark to me that "just coping is what I think about most." This points to a third quality of everyday resistance—an effort to accomplish a stated goal that will benefit the resister, however bleak the prospects for success.

Jolie's act of resistance is not one that is tied to the overthrow of the Rwandan state. Instead, it is a form of everyday resistance that is in effect an act of individual subversion that does more than make her life more sustainable. It also opens up the possibility of understanding and explaining the extent to which the policy of national unity and reconciliation operates as the dominant form of social control in the daily lives of ordinary Rwandans. In this sense, the everyday acts of resistance of ordinary Rwandans act as a diagnostic of state power as they indicate sites of struggle between individuals and the practices and mechanisms of the policy of national unity and reconciliation. Identifying acts of everyday resistance allows for an analysis of the forms of power that ordinary Rwandans are caught up in and of the complex processes of the policy of national unity and reconciliation from their perspective, not that of government elites.

On the surface, Jolie's success in securing benefits as a survivor of the 1994 genocide may not appear to be an act of resistance. On closer examination, however, her experience reveals the multilayered negotiations of power in which she is enmeshed—directly with her husband and her local FARG representative; indirectly with other women survivors who could testify against her husband at *gacaca*. In securing membership in her local FARG chapter, Jolie gained more than the medical coverage that she and her family so desperately needed. She may have also regained her dignity, which will in turn buoy her spirit for the inevitable next struggle that she will encounter in her life as a destitute peasant Hutu woman in postgenocide Rwanda. Jolie strategically engaged with the authorities to get medical benefits, and her experience is representative of the spirit and quality of many forms of everyday resistance as subtle, indirect, and microlevel actions. Indeed, in highly politicized environments that are characterized by intense government surveillance and scrutiny of individual behavior, the routine business of just living one's life and the normal tools of everyday communication are important devices for the expression of resistance. Jolie's experience illustrates that everyday acts of resistance are often subtle, sometimes imperceptible; they are nonconfrontational yet determined actions, despite the associated risks. As such, we can begin to understand and analyze the everyday forms of resistance that individuals render in the name of national unity and reconciliation as forms of resistance rather than as survival strategies or as forms of obedient compliance.[2]

In focusing on the everyday acts of resistance of ordinary Rwandans to the multiple and intersecting structures of state power, the chapter argues that the policy of national unity and reconciliation cannot be understood in isolation from the interactions of ordinary Rwandans with its mechanisms; it is the dialectic between the individual and the policy that determines individual opportunities to exercise agency, in which negotiating, maneuvering, and muddling through are all essential aspects of individual efforts to resist its demands.

The argument is developed in three sections. The first sets out the analytical framework employed to understand the everyday acts of resistance of ordinary Rwandans. The second section situates the broader socioeconomic climate in postgenocide Rwanda to illustrate the conditions in which Rwandans live their lives. In particular, the section focuses on the socioeconomic hierarchy that shapes their interactions with both local authorities and one another. These two sections combine to set the stage for the third section of this chapter, as well as for chapter 6, which examines the everyday resistance of ordinary Rwandans to the *gacaca* trials. This final section examines a cross-section of such acts of resistance and selects mechanisms of the policy of national unity and reconciliation to illustrate the system of state power in which ordinary Rwandans at the lowest levels of the social hierarchy have been caught up since the 1994 genocide.

Conceptualizing Everyday Resistance

If the outcome of the exercise of power is to serve the interests of the power holders, then everyday resistance, when effectively executed, is intended to serve the interests of the powerless (Scott 1985, 1–27). Resistance as an analytical concept acts "as a chemical catalyst so as to bring to light power relations, to locate their position, find out their application and the methods used" (Foucault 1969 [2002], 329). Traditionally, resistance is identified when four criteria are met: (1) the action is collective and organized, (2) the action is principled and selfless, (3) the action has revolutionary impact, and (4) the action negates the bases of domination (Scott 1985, 241–303). As a nation, Rwanda has only one historical case that fits these criteria, the Social Revolution of 1959, in which ethnic Hutu rebelled against the dominance of ethnic Tutsi in state institutions and positions of social privilege (C. Newbury 1988).

The early resistance literature and its critics fail to delineate in any fruitful way what constitutes an everyday act of resistance, focusing instead on organized and group action. For instance, Issacman and Issacman (1977, 47) identified the withholding of labor for cotton production by Mozambican peasants as an act of resistance. Others, however, interpret the same event as peasant inaction, stealth, or mutedness in the face of power (Crummey 1986; Scott 1985, 1990). Vail and White (1986, 195) broadened the concept even further to include "everything from footdragging and dissimulation to social banditry, arson, poaching, theft, avoidance of conscription, desertion, migration, and riot." This is a different definition from that put forth by James Scott, the grandfather of the concept of everyday resistance, who argued that peasant politics are basically concerned with "bread-and-butter issues" and can be fruitfully employed to understand and explain confrontational forms of class struggle, rather than state power, as I am doing in this case (Scott 1985, 296).

As Jolie's story illustrates, I conceptualize everyday resistance to include any subtle, indirect, and nonconfrontational act that makes daily life more sustainable in light of the strong and centralized power of the policy of national unity and reconciliation. Everyday acts of resistance involve some combination of persistence, prudence, and individual effort to accomplish a specific goal. Two additional qualities can also be identified. The first is lack of awareness on the part of the target—the government official or other agent of the state. For example, the ordinary peasant who gets up early to avoid being available to participate in a *gacaca* court knows she is vulnerable and does not dare risk an open confrontation with her local government officials. Everyday resisters choose to counteract or frustrate the mechanisms of the policy of national unity and reconciliation; attempting to defeat or overthrow it is not their purpose. In getting up early to go to her field, the everyday resister makes it harder for the government official to exercise his authority because she is not home to receive the order to attend the *gacaca* trial. In other words, "everyday resistance emphasizes a constant strategic alertness on the part of those involved that places a lot of weight on agency and calculation" (Sivaramakrishnan 2005, 350–51).

The second additional quality is benefit to the resister. On occasion, a long-term benefit will be the result, as was the case with Jolie, who received medical coverage for herself and her family. More common is short-term benefit. In my example of the woman who gets up early to tend her fields, she will be successful in avoiding *gacaca* only every so often, because the local official will inevitably find ways to force her to participate in future sessions. At least with regard to those *gacaca* sessions in which she successfully avoids forced participation, she has practiced everyday resistance. The local authorities might not even notice her absence, particularly if she is expected not to testify but merely to attend. If too many individuals practice everyday resistance in the same way, the local official will likely notice that many ordinary Rwandans are not participating as expected. Having raised the attention of the local official, the act is no longer one of everyday resistance but instead becomes one of confrontational resistance where individuals collude—knowingly or not—to avoid participation in *gacaca* sessions. If too many people undertake acts that also allow them to avoid *gacaca* sessions, harm can befall the resisters, thereby invalidating the strategy of everyday resistance.

The five qualities of everyday resistance operate on a continuum. Specific acts of everyday resistance include one or more of these qualities. There is no "pure" form of everyday resistance. Instead, such acts are "largely implicit" (Comaroff 1985, 261). Given the forces arrayed against ordinary Rwandans in the promotion of national unity and reconciliation, simply holding the line is interpreted as an act of everyday resistance. If the individual does no more than maintain his or her resources—land holdings or access to school fees, for example—in the face of attempts by local authorities to take them away for any reason, then the individual is practicing everyday resistance. Where survival depends on acquiescence or quiescence, the individual may do just one or the other or both, depending on the context and circumstances on that particular day and contingent on the stated goal (Gaventa 1980, 20–25). For example, everyday resistance can include ignoring the demands of a local government official in nonobvious ways or refusing to be bullied by a member of the security forces. Acts of everyday resistance allow for examination of the actions of individual Rwandans that may appear innocuous or meaningless to show that their actions are strategic and purposeful rather than an indication of their presumed obedience to government directives or their willingness to "forgive and forget" or "tell their truth" in the name of national unity and reconciliation.

An analytical focus on the everyday acts of resistance of ordinary Rwandans runs the risk of exaggerating their ability to make choices and act on them. It also runs the risk of overemphasizing individuals' ability to counter or mitigate sociopolitical structures of domination such as the policy of national unity and reconciliation. Within the anthropological literature, analysts tend to romanticize resistance "to read all forms of resistance as signs of ineffectiveness of systems of power and of the resilience and creativity of the human spirit" (Abu-Lughod 1990, 42). To avoid this trap, I emphasize individual agency to understand the power relations in which individuals are enmeshed and the resultant social and political inequalities and hierarchies. Agency is not exclusively tied to one individual actor but is instead bound up with the power hierarchies that structural forms of inequality ultimately produce (Emirbayer and Mische 1998). In delinking agency from structure, we learn how individual actors are able to evaluate critically the conditions of their lives to illustrate how individuals are not only enmeshed but also positioned differently in relation to a particular system of power. This chapter and chapter 6 demonstrate how ordinary

Rwandans practice everyday acts of resistance to minimize the effects of the policy of national unity and reconciliation in their daily lives. The emphasis is not on acts of everyday resistance per se but rather what the chosen forms of resistance say about the policy as a system of state power.

Daily Hardships: The Socioeconomic Context

In order to situate the everyday acts of resistance of some ordinary Rwandans to the mechanisms of the policy of national unity and reconciliation, it is first necessary to situate the broader socioeconomic context in which they live their lives. For foreign visitors who base their stay in Rwanda's capital city, Kigali, and take day trips along the paved main roads to visit the national museum in the south, to see the mountain gorillas in the north, to visit Lake Kivu in the west, and to safari to Akagera National Park in the east, the deep poverty and daily hardships that confront ordinary Rwandans are difficult to imagine. The Office Rwandaise du tourisme et des parcs nationaux (ORTPN), Rwanda's national tourist agency, encourages international visitors to "experience" Rwanda by day tripping from Kigali (ORTPN 2004, 5). Kigali boasts a modern airport, several international hotels, a modern information and communications technology (ICT) infrastructure that includes numerous wireless hot spots, and countless new residential and commercial properties. Numerous cafés and nightclubs have opened to cater to Kigali's growing middle class of bureaucrats and businesspeople, as well as expatriates. Kigali also has a "low crime rate, clean streets and civic order" that "outsiders appreciate" (Kinzer 2008, 239).

Behind this pristine image is the daily reality of crushing poverty that shapes the everyday lives of most Rwandans. For example, the government decreed in July 2006 that only covered shoes must be worn in Kigali and other town centers such as Butare (Huye), Gikongoro (Nyamagabe), and Gitarama (Muhanga). Many ordinary Rwandans, most of whom wear rubber flip-flops because of their low cost, are now unable to enter town to sell their wares at market. The regulation states that covered footwear is necessary "for cleanliness as well as food safety" (interview with MINALOC official 2006). A MINALOC official told me in September 2006 that Kigali "only had 12 percent of its citizens suffer urban poverty" and bragged "that is the lowest urban poverty rate in Africa!" When I suggested that the low rate of urban poverty was probably the result of the government razing residents' properties in the interests of "cleanliness" and "forcing" people back into the countryside, the official agreed that was possible but urged me to think about how clean and safe Kigali is: "Without those poor running around threatening our resources, we can think of ways to develop Kigali even further!" (field notes 2006). The International Monetary Fund (IMF) reports an urban poverty rate of 20 percent. Southern province, where most of my participants live, has the highest rate of poverty in the country, with 65–67

Figure 8. Children in the midst of their morning chores, June 2006. (photo by Isabella Flüeler, © 2006)

Figure 9. Evening falls on the informal neighborhood known as "Kiyovu des pauvres" located in central Kigali, May 2006. By 2010 the government had razed informal urban neighborhoods across the country to make way for "modern" housing in the name of modernization and economic development. (photo by author)

percent of the population living below the poverty line (IMF 2008, 162; National Institute of Statistics 2012, 11).

An estimated 87 percent of Rwandans are subsistence farmers (National Institute of Statistics 2006, 27). In 2006 the official poverty line was a daily income per adult of 175 Rwandan francs (Frw) (or US$0.48), while the extreme poverty line was a daily income per adult of 120 Frw (or US$0.26) (MINICOFIN 2001, 9). Among the ordinary Rwandans who participated in my research, the average income per household was 50 Frw (US$0.09) per day or 20,000 Frw per year (US$40). Justino and Verwimp (2008, 15) found that households whose home was destroyed during the genocide or that lost land after the genocide through squatting or forced migration into villages (*imidugudu*) lived in greater poverty than their also poor relatives and neighbors. Southern Rwanda, where most of the Rwandans who participated in my research live, remains among Rwanda's poorest provinces, despite positive economic growth since the end of the genocide, because of the high levels of Tutsi loss of life during the genocide combined with low levels of resettlement of returnees in this region of the country.

Only three of my thirty-seven participants said that they had actually seen paper money, even though the lowest available denomination is 100 Frw (US$0.21). With rare exception, the ordinary Rwandans I met were thin, barefoot, and dressed in ragged clothes, which in many cases was the extent of their full wardrobe. Few owned shoes, making trips to market an additional burden as they had to rely on family and neighbors to be able to afford a single pair of shoes. Several women I knew shared a pair of covered shoes, carrying them in a bag just in case they were stopped by a police officer to show that they owned covered shoes (field notes 2006). Their hands and faces were weathered and gave the women the appearance of an age older than their biological years. People's eyes were lackluster from continued hunger; some had orange hair, a telltale sign of malnutrition. In 2003 the UN Food and Agriculture Organization (FAO) estimated that the per capita consumption of calories in Rwanda was 2,070 kilocalories (kcal), of which a mere 54 calories were protein (FAO 2004, 2). This average daily caloric intake may seem acceptable by American standards, where the average daily caloric requirement for a sedentary or lightly active adult is between 1,290 kcal per day (women) and 1,975 kcal per day (men), of which at least 40 percent are protein based. For peasant Rwandans, who earn their livelihood through manual labor, both the basic caloric and the protein intake are too low to allow them to sustain normal levels of activity, and the quality of the food fails to meet basic nutritional guidelines (FAO 2001, 35–52). I regularly saw evidence of starvation. Several of my research participants as well as their children exhibited symptoms of kwashiorkor and marasmus (forms of malnutrition caused by lack of protein in the diet). Several of the women who participated in my research told me that they sometimes eat dirt or swallow pebbles to ward off hunger pangs; two women had lost children to starvation since the genocide. Men told me that they drank banana beer "to fill the void of days without food" (field notes 2006). Their wives scoffed at the idea that drinking beer is a suitable solution to deal with chronic hunger. One woman told me, "When we have nothing I mix *haricots* [green beans] with dirt to make a mixture that would keep us until the next meal. If my husband would stop drinking beer, we might have a little left over to buy some rice or bread" (interview with Olive, a destitute Hutu woman, 2006).

Women suffer the additional indignity of struggling with the men in their lives for resources and personal power at the household level. More than one-third of Rwandan women reported having experienced spousal violence — physical, emotional, or sexual (UNDP Rwanda 2007, 33). The legacy of the genocide means that women head more than a third of Rwandan households, 56 percent of which are widows of the genocide (UNDP Rwanda 2007, 33). There is no way to know whether these figures include women other than Tutsi survivors of the genocide, as the government of Rwanda does not allow the disaggregation of statistical data on the basis of ethnic identity. Presumably, the figure of 56 percent is composed of Tutsi widows of the genocide, as they are the only accepted category of "survivors." Of the sixteen women that participated in my research, all but two considered themselves widows of the genocide (even those that had remarried). One woman said, "Oh yes, I remarried for survival. I need a husband to help with everything, especially to help with the fields. I loved my real husband but this one? Really, it was a matter of survival" (interview with Marie Claire, a destitute Hutu widow, 2006).

Female-headed households have a "higher and deeper incidence of poverty" than other households (UNDP Rwanda 2007, 3). The average life expectancy for Rwandans is 45.2 years; half of the children born in Rwanda since the genocide will not live past their fortieth birthday (UNDP 2008). For all of the thirty-seven ordinary Rwandans who participated in my research, the lack of food, clean water, and affordable and proximate health services was a constant lament. Many of the women who participated in my research had the additional burden of child care, including the care of orphaned relatives whose parents had died before, during, or after the genocide. Most Rwandans also live with untreated posttraumatic stress disorder (PTSD). Psychosocial trauma is prevalent; some studies suggest that as many as 95 percent of Rwandans witnessed or participated in "extreme acts of violence" (Ndayambaje 2001, 46). Three-quarters of my participants told me that they had symptoms suggestive of psychological trauma. Only a third of these individuals were in treatment for their PTSD. Those who were not in treatment cited the lack of counselors as a barrier to treatment; a bigger issue was their concern for privacy. One woman said it best: "Of course I have trauma. Why do you think I agreed to speak with you? I can talk to you and feel safe that my secrets will not be shared with other Rwandese. I don't have this feeling with the counselors [who live] here [in my community]" (interview with Béatha, a destitute Hutu widow, 2006).

The division of labor in rural areas runs rigidly along gender lines. Peasant women work from before the sun rises until after it has set every day of the year. In the home, they cook all meals, wash dishes, clean, do laundry, sew and mend clothing, and ferry water. Most try to earn a productive income, which many do through petty trade of surplus produce that they grow themselves. Peasant men engage in animal husbandry and may also work in the fields, although among the men who participated in my research, tending to crops (as well as children) is seen as a task for women. Men told me of the shame they felt at having to work in the fields alongside their women relatives, as well as of the additional burden of not having access to income-generating work, such as carpentry or driving a taxi-moto. Hutu men who have completed their *ingando* reeducation feel this most acutely, as they expected to find gainful employment following their return to their home community (field notes 2006). In the communities where I interviewed ordinary peasant Rwandans, I rarely saw men in the fields. When they did work the fields, it was before the full heat of the day. By 11:00 a.m. or so, men could be seen lounging in the tall grass or near the banana groves, chatting with other men, while women, many of them with infants strapped to their backs, continued to tend to their fields. Ephrem, a poor Hutu man, explained their absence: "We do the very heavy work, like preparing the beds and preparing the irrigation. We also help if necessary with the planting and the harvesting. But tending to weeds? That is work for women" (interview 2006).

Compounding the challenges faced by ordinary Rwandan men and women is the perception on the part of government officials, both at the local level and in Kigali, that peasants are but a homogeneous mass to be governed. The words of one local official working in a location near Gitarama town are emblematic: ordinary Rwandans are "a mass of poor peasants that we are responsible to re-educate and then govern. Tutsi are survivors, and we urge them to forgive. Hutu are suspects, and we urge them to tell their truth" (interview with Ministry of Community Development official 2006). Within this "mass" of poor ordinary Rwandans are the socioeconomic categories and the inequalities they engender, which in turn shape individual life chances as well as opportunities for moving up or falling down the social ladder. All of the ordinary Rwandans who participated in my research understand that only elites can hold political power (i.e., it is both acknowledged and accepted that politics is the domain of the elite, whether political, business, or religious). Social mobility, moving up to the ranks of the powerful, or, as one of my research participants put it, "becoming an important person," is rare and is not something that the ordinary Rwandans who participated in my research expect to happen. Instead, their efforts are aimed at maintaining their meager socioeconomic location.

This lack of opportunity for social mobility exists where hierarchy is the societal standard, inequality is anticipated, less powerful people expect to be dependent on more powerful people, centralization of state institutions is popular and unquestioned, subordinates envision being told what to do, and privileges and social status are expected for elite members of society (Archer 2003, 136–37). In resource-scarce environments like postgenocide Rwanda, where the social structure is firmly entrenched and individual options and opportunities are structured by one's location in the social hierarchy, it is important to understand where individuals are situated economically. This matters because one's socioeconomic class shapes one's life chances. It also determines how and when other Rwandans, notably elites, engage and interact with the destitute, poor, and salaried poor individuals like those who participated in my research, as well as how they interact with others in their socioeconomic class. An appreciation of the socioeconomic categories that stratify Rwandan society is also important because this stratification shapes individuals' options to practice everyday resistance. Knowing one's place in the social hierarchy ensures that the resister is aware of the risks inherent in choosing which strategy of everyday resistance is most appropriate and when to deploy it.

The boundaries of the six socioeconomic categories that stratify Rwandan society are relatively fixed (MINECOFIN 2001; see table 1 in the introduction). There are differences between Rwandans who occupy the three lowest categories—the most vulnerable, the destitute, and the poor—but these are muted by the fact that many of these peasants have little to no access to cash, leaving them most susceptible to climatic shock. Members of these socioeconomic categories also have little formal education, which means that individuals in higher social categories write them off as "needing us to decide what to do for them" since they have no "ideas of their own and so can't move up in life" (interview with MINALOC official 2006). The lowest category are the *abatindi nyakujya* (the most vulnerable or those living in abject poverty; sing. *umutindi nyakujya*), individuals who have no social standing whatsoever. Most beg to survive; some resort to prostitution or theft, which in turn isolates them from other categories of peasants. They are considered by many, including other most vulnerable individuals, to be "without hope" (field notes 2006). They have "poor personal hygiene and live in garbage cans or in barns," which means "they cannot be taught, so there is no use in trying" (interview with

Ministry of Culture official 2006). For ordinary Rwandans, reaching out to help a most vulnerable person often elicits scorn from other peasants, which "makes it hard to help them. Even when it is clear that they are suffering, few reach out to them because it can cause problems with family and friends who ask, 'Why do you help that goat [lost soul]?'" (interview with Espérance, a poor Tutsi widow, 2006).

The individuals who participated in my research come from the next three categories on the social ladder—*abatindi* (destitute), *abakene* (poor), and *abakene bifashije* (salaried poor). Composing the second lowest category in the social strata are the *abatindi* (destitute; sing. *umutindi*), who sometimes own land but who are unable to work it successfully, either through personal inability or because the field is fallow. They eat only when they are able to share in the harvest of others. They often have some form of makeshift shelter. Any economic gains that a destitute *umutindi* peasant might make come through the forging of alliances with other destitute Rwandans, usually to buy a goat or a sheep or to share in each other's harvest to ensure that all members of the family get enough to eat on a regular basis. Joseph N., a destitute Tutsi widower, told me, "We eat when we can, and we share, knowing it is good insurance if our own crops fail. Those we share with share with us, and we all eat a little instead of nothing" (interview 2006).

The next highest socioeconomic category is the *abakene* (poor; sing. *umukene*), all of whom hold land, which, however, is rarely sufficiently productive. They own small livestock such as chickens, goats, or sheep. As a group, *abakene* are most likely to be called on by members of higher socioeconomic classes to work their fields in exchange for cash. Some have excess harvest, which they take to market to sell. Access to microcredit is also a possibility, but this comes through alliances within their social network of relatives and friends, not through formal credit facilities. The *abakene bifashije* (the salaried poor; sing. *umukene wifashije*) constitute the last, and highest, category of the peasantry. These individuals have both a one-room house and some land. They often own more than one cow, along with several goats, sheep, and chickens. Some own motorcycles. Most own no-speed bicycles. They rarely work for others, as their production makes them self-sufficient. It "can be a great shame" if a salaried poor individual has to work for others, as he can usually sell some livestock to weather climatic or economic downturns (interview with Didier, a salaried poor Tutsi man, 2006).

If the individual is educated beyond the eighth grade, he might have access to formal credit facilities and might even qualify for a credit card, although for many salaried poor cash flow is a concern. These families usually live off the means of production, which can include ownership of a kiosk shop. The salaried poor often act as appointed local officials within communities, even though they receive no salary for their work. Many are also elected *gacaca* judges. The prestige of being asked to serve can open up opportunities to become an *umukungu* (rich without money; pl. *abakungu*), the socioeconomic category of many appointed local officials (field notes 2006). *Abakungu* have more than one plot of land and often own several heads of cattle. They often have development-related jobs and earn salaries as appointed local officials or as project officers or managers of a civil society organization. Many have house staff (servants) from among the poor and vulnerable categories. These servants rarely receive a wage, working instead in exchange for room and board. The rich without money are so called because there is little left over for productive means once school fees and health costs have been paid. They often have access to a vehicle and housing through formal employment.[3]

The highest socioeconomic category is that of the *abakire* (the rich; sing. *umukire*), which is the category of most urban elites. They have land, excess production, several heads of cattle, and other livestock, as well as paid employment, either as civil servants or in private business. Peasant Rwandans told me that the rich are easy to identify "because they are always dressed up, they have cell phones, and they never walk anywhere" (field notes 2006). They own at least one car and always have servants to prepare their meals and keep their homes presentable for entertaining and other social activities, notably weddings and funerals.

It is within this structured socioeconomic hierarchy that ordinary Rwandans battle daily to ensure their own and their family's survival; to do so they must continually protect themselves against the apparatus of the state—the RPF and its agents, who vigorously promote the policy of national unity and reconciliation. A recurrent theme in my conversations with ordinary Rwandans was the omnipresence of local officials, notably those who "came after the genocide to find themselves in a position of authority even though they have never even lived in the community before" (field notes 2006). As noted in chapter 4, the implementation of the requirements of the policy of national unity and reconciliation is the top priority for appointed and elected local officials alike. At the lower levels of Rwanda's administrative structure—the sector and the cell—there is a distinction between the power and prestige of the appointed and salaried executive secretary and those of elected, nonsalaried officials. The executive secretary is the most important person at the local level and is usually an individual who comes from outside the sector (and, in many cases, grew up outside Rwanda). Of the forty-six elected and returnee local officials I met during my fieldwork, all but three were known members of the RPF. One said, "You must be a member of the RPF if you are to gain a good [government] position.

I joined to provide for my family and have not regretted my decision" (field notes 2006).

The National Unity and Reconciliation Commission (NURC) is responsible for providing training to local officials to ensure that their actions accord with national policy. This puts undue stress on the ordinary people, as executive secretaries at both the cell and the sector levels are personally accountable to President Kagame, not to local populations. It can also be taxing for local officials, many of whom are young and inexperienced managers who have little sense of how best to interpret their responsibilities to both the central authorities and the local population. For local officials who grew up abroad and whose life experiences have been shaped by conditions of exile rather than by having lived through violence before and during the 1994 genocide, responding to the needs of ordinary Rwandans at the bottom of the social hierarchy is a challenge. In addition to having a different cultural worldview, many returnees see ordinary Rwandans solely in terms of their ethnicity. For most ordinary Rwandans, economic survival is their main priority; ethnicity is only a minor factor in everyday life and matters most when one encounters state power, most notably the various practices and mechanisms of the policy of national unity and reconciliation.

The thirty-seven ordinary Rwandans who participated in my research occupy the lower levels of the social hierarchy and struggle to meet their basic needs and those of their families under the watchful eye of local officials, who have little sense of how the violence of the genocide has shaped their poverty. For example, Tutsi survivors living in southern Rwanda told me that they were financially poorer since the genocide because they had lost so many of their family members, particularly children, who could husband livestock or tend fields. Hutu men living in southwest Rwanda who fled to the refugee camps in Zaïre also reported increased poverty, combined with loss of social status as probable *génocidaires*, as their land holdings were reduced or eliminated on their return home.

Of the forty-six local officials on whom I relied to conduct my research in southwest Rwanda, thirty-three were Anglophone returnees who held salaried positions at the sector level, while another seven Anglophone returnees held salaried posts at the cell level, meaning that only six officials (fewer than 10 percent) were potentially resident in their bailiwick before the genocide. That so many local officials come from outside the community raised concerns among the many ordinary peasant Rwandans I consulted, who were worried about officials' ability to understand and appreciate their everyday needs. Under Habyarimana, local officials were residents of the communities they served and maintained network ties and social alliances with the rural community of their childhood (de Lame 2005a, 62–63). Since 2000 local officials have been appointed by President Kagame directly, and since 2006 they have been contractually obligated to develop the area under their supervision in line with national policy objectives (i.e., through *imihigo* contracts). Ordinary peasants I consulted spoke of the disdain that local officials had for them, as well as of the difficulties they faced in trying to "modernize" in accordance with new measures of "progress and development" introduced since 2000 (field notes 2006, corroborated by Purdeková 2012a).

A good example of the drive to modernize without due regard to the needs of peasant Rwandans is the national land policy, which the RPF introduced in 2000. It has increased the vulnerability of peasant families as it seeks to "modernize agriculture" and encourage the "rational use of land" (MINITERRE 2004, 9). Rwanda's mountainous terrain, combined with variations in soil quality, means that few ordinary Rwandans have sufficient arable land to provide for the basic nutritional needs of their families. The average land holding is just 0.65 hectares (Huggins 2012). Dispersed plots, often shared in alliances with other families, serve as a form of insurance for peasant families to ensure that enough crops are harvested to provide sufficient food for basic survival. The RFP's land policy considers usage for basic survival irrational and makes it illegal for peasants to work together to tend their fields as local growing and climatic conditions allow (field notes 2006). The RPF ordered local officials to appropriate irrationally used land and gave large plots to "senior government and military officials and important businessmen" who now use the land for commercial purposes (Burnet 2007, 19; Huggins 2012). Displaced ordinary Rwandans experienced the double insult of not being compensated for their expropriated land and not being hired to work for a daily wage for the new rich *abakire* landowners. Many complained that individuals were brought in from outside their communities to work the fields. Joseph B., a destitute Hutu man, said, "We don't even benefit from their employment. How are we supposed to eat without land?" (interview 2006). Janvier, a poor Tutsi man, said, "The new landowners have brought their own people to work their land; they live here now and have changed everything. First they take our land, then they bring their own people to cultivate it? How can we eat? How can we exist? We cannot afford most things; it is very hard" (interview 2006). Academic studies verify these hardships, arguing that the top-down and state-led implementation of the land law could result in growing inequality, increased landlessness, and socioeconomic tensions (Ansoms 2008, 2009, 2011; Des Forges 2006; Huggins 2011, 2012; Pottier 2006).

The efforts of many ordinary Rwandans to accommodate the additional burden imposed on their already strained lives through postgenocide policies

Figure 10. Shaping the poverty of rural Rwandans are small plot sizes and poor soil quality. This image is of a hill in western Rwanda, March 2006. (photo by author)

like the new land policy have resulted in subtle changes in the ways that they interact with their local officials, as agents of the state, in their everyday lives. Rwandan culture has strict codes about who can speak out against such injustices and when. Indeed, there is no strong historical record of individuals speaking out against the oppressive actions of others who are more socially or economically powerful than they are. Individual facility in the art of disguising and concealing one's real feelings or opinions on a given matter is self-taught and culturally sanctioned; dissimulation and acquiescence are both common. This leads outsiders, as well as RPF elites, to conclude that ordinary Rwandans are obedient and comply without any reflection to their demands.

Instead, ordinary Rwandans have a variety of everyday strategies of resistance available to them as they navigate the difficult terrain of daily survival in postgenocide Rwanda. Despite continuing hardships, they reveal strong wills, fierce pride, and creativity in making their lives more sustainable. For example, among the thirty-seven ordinary Rwandans I consulted, one destitute Twa woman refused to remove from her land the makeshift grave marker she had constructed to remember the friends and family lost during the genocide. A poor Hutu woman spoke out against the local representative of the Survivors' Fund, recounting his mismanagement of funds intended for the poorest of the poor. A destitute Tutsi man challenged an armed member of the Local Defense Forces when he tried to take the family's only goat back to barracks. The next section examines the strategies of everyday resistance that ordinary Rwandans subtly and tactically employ to voice dissatisfaction with the government and its policy of national unity and reconciliation while trying to make their daily lives more dignified.

The Everyday Acts of Resistance of Ordinary Rwandans

A focus on the everyday acts of resistance of ordinary peasant Rwandans resident in the south allows for a fuller picture of the reach of state power and its felt effects in their everyday lives. This section is divided into three parts and illustrates the specific tactics that some ordinary Rwandans enact in their efforts to minimize the impact of the policy in their everyday lives, to show how they resist state-led, top-down unity and reconciliation initiatives.

Before examining three specific everyday actions of resistance to the policy of national unity and reconciliation, I wish to note that the analysis focuses on specific actions rather than on mental tactics, such as imaginary conversations with local officials or other Rwandans in which individuals express anger, rehearse devastating retorts, or deliver clever rebuttals. Rwandans told me of their arsenal of mental tactics of everyday resistance on numerous occasions, and I learned that they have a tradition of speaking their truth to government officials or other agents of the state, a fact that directly challenges government notions that ordinary people "do what they are told" or "don't know what to do until we tell them to do it" (interview with NURC official 2006). The mental tactic most frequently relied on by some ordinary Rwandans to limit their interactions with local officials and with each other is the practice of *ceceka* (literally, "be quiet" or "shut up"), meaning that many individuals remain silent in the presence of the local authorities (and sometimes one another).

Some analysts have focused on how ordinary Hutu use *ceceka* to frustrate the functioning of the *gacaca* courts, where Hutu accused of acts of genocide are expected to tell their truth (Chakravarty 2006; Rettig 2008). Chakravarty identifies *ceceka* as the name of an underground organization of Hutu that is spreading the word not to testify at *gacaca* tribunals. There is no available information on its leadership or membership (Chakravarty 2006, 12; Rettig 2008). Instead, some Hutu choose not to testify against other Hutu, placing the evidentiary burden on Tutsi survivors, a theme that I examine further in chapter 6.[4] All of the ordinary Rwandans who participated in my research understood well the risks of speaking out against the mechanisms of the policy of national unity and reconciliation, which is what makes their everyday acts of resistance to its dictates even more revealing.

There are three categories of individual who are willing to speak out against government policy or openly defy the directives of government officials. Two of these are relevant when we think about the everyday acts of resistance of ordinary Rwandans to the policy of national unity and reconciliation. The first group is known among their peers as *abasazi* ("foolish"; sing. *umusazi*). They use their "madness" to give the impression that they are mentally unstable, to justify their willingness to say what others will not or cannot attempt because the penalties for falling afoul of the government directives are simply too much to bear (interviews 2006). Second are the individuals known as *ibyihebe* ("fearless"; sing. *icyihebe*). Most of the individuals who participated in my research understood the risks of sharing their experiences of life before, during, and after the 1994 genocide and no longer feared speaking out because of the hardships they endured. This concept applies mainly to Tutsi survivors of the genocide, many of whom consider themselves "the walking dead." The third category of individuals who are able and willing to speak out is the *ibipinga* ("those with deep-rooted principles"; sing. *igipinga*).[5] This name is applied to journalists, human rights activists, and other intellectuals who take the risk to speak out against the government because of their deep-rooted principles, knowing full well that the consequences can be grave.

As we saw in chapter 4, the relationship between ordinary Rwandans at the bottom of the socioeconomic hierarchy and the postgenocide state is a vexed one. To illustrate the extent to which the policy is an oppressive force in their daily lives, specifically to explain its restrictions and hardships, I have chosen three specific types of everyday resistance: (1) staying on the sidelines, (2) irreverent compliance, and (3) withdrawn muteness. I analyze these three actions, chosen from the myriad tactics that ordinary Rwandans shared with me, to show that different forms of everyday resistance can be situated on a continuum. At one end of the continuum are isolated actions that do not change one's lot in life but nonetheless evince the simple, though crucial, awareness that one has been treated disrespectfully in the name of national unity and reconciliation. At the other end are reflexive acts of resistance through which individuals refuse, in creative and conscious ways, to submit to the demands of the policy of national unity and reconciliation. In thinking about the everyday acts of resistance of ordinary Rwandans as existing along a continuum, we learn about more than the hardships that individuals have experienced in their daily lives since the genocide. We also see what their chosen forms of resistance say about the policy of national unity and reconciliation.

Staying on the Sidelines

The first form of everyday resistance involving individual efforts to avoid participating in the policy of national unity and reconciliation is the practice of "staying on the sidelines," that is, finding ways to avoid having to participate fully by using a variety of avoidance tactics. For example, many ordinary peasants—Hutu, Tutsi, and Twa—told me that they try as much as possible to stay on the sidelines to avoid too much trouble with the local authorities. Prosper, a destitute ethnic Twa, tries to stay on the sidelines as a "way to protect my soul. My [local official] doesn't understand that my people [the Twa] died because of the events [of 1994] and that I have new problems that need solutions since they say peace and unity have been restored. It is better to avoid contact than to be forced to reject your ancestry" (interview 2006). Ethnic Twa in pre- and postgenocide Rwanda endure worse socioeconomic conditions than the national population (CAURWA 2004). Since 2001, when the ethnic divisionism laws came into force, organizations working for Twa people have had to change their names as well as their substantive focus to comply with the new regulations. This puts organizations that work for the rights of Twa people in the difficult position of having to justify their work with a segment of the population that has not been adequately reached by the existing programs and policies of the postgenocide government. It also makes it difficult for foreign donors to continue to sponsor programs and activities that directly support Twa organizations, as their presence is against national unity and reconciliation. CAURWA (Communauté des autochtones rwandais) is the primary civil society organization in Rwanda that represents Twa interests, and its representatives have not escaped the harassment and intimidation tactics that the postgenocide government employs to control the social and political landscape. In 2005 the Ministry of Justice ordered CAURWA to change its name to the Communauté des potiers rwandais (COPORWA) or risk closure on the charge of ethnic divisionism. COPORWA no longer represents Twa interests but instead represents those who work as potters, the majority of whom are ethnic Twa (Beswick 2011; Thomson 2009b).

Aurelia, a poor ethnic Hutu widow, told me that she actively tries to avoid her local official:

> The best strategy is to avoid the authorities. When you see them, they make demands for reconciliation. [My official] knows that I lost all of my people [immediate family members] during the events. He knows I am weakened and therefore pushes me to tell my truth. But my people are dead. What is there to tell? Because I am a former Hutu, all I can do is try to get recognition as a survivor of the genocide so I can get some [financial]

support. Of course that is Tutsi business, but still, it is a matter of survival. It is hard to ask for help when I prefer not to speak with my local official because I fear his demands. (Interview 2006)

Vianney, a poor ethnic Tutsi man, also seeks to stay on the sidelines:

Because of the hardships, I lost my whole family. What is the point of forgiveness anyway? The Hutu who killed, they know who they are, but are they able to tell their truth? No, and I understand why not. If they say anything, they go straight to prison. I understand their problems; I blame this government for its lack of fairness. If we could all just get along, I know we could find some way to coexist. Reconciliation is never going to happen. At least not for me; I am alone because of genocide. It is better to remain distant than to get mixed up with the ideas and plans of this [post-genocide] government. (Interview 2006)

Avoiding interaction with local officials is a constant preoccupation and is a tactic that some ordinary Rwandans employ to avoid participation in elements of the policy of national unity and reconciliation that they deem unfair or disrespectful of their lived experiences of violence before, during, and after the 1994 genocide. Several women told me how they do laundry in creeks and rivulets side by side for extended periods, often very early in the morning, to avoid having to meet their local authorities or even other women. Florence beamed with pride when she shared her everyday tactic of choice: "Getting up early is a very good defense. It only becomes a problem when too many of us decide to miss *gacaca* or to be absent when the *ingando* graduates come back to our hill. When that happens, I act like I have malaria or explain to the official that I have 'women's problems.' He never asks. Instead he runs the other way. Indeed, I am too old for those [women's] problems, but he leaves me alone every time!" (interview with Florence, a poor Hutu widow, 2006).

Ordinary men, particularly released prisoners, shared how they used the marketplace as a domain where they could whisper news of political developments. They shared information about who had been arrested, denounced, or put in prison since the previous market day and news of how *gacaca* trials were progressing in different communities and of how *ingando* graduates were coping with the return home following extended prison stays. Secretive ingenuity facilitates the flow of political information among ordinary Hutu men. Gaston, a poor released prisoner, explained it best:

We [Hutu] have few options. Going to the bars is no longer an option. We are viewed with suspicion; few of us do that anymore. If the authorities see a group of former Hutu at a bar, then we can all get interrogated. They think we are plotting genocide or something. Instead of facing charges of genocide ideology, we communicate when we go to market to sell. The authorities are right there, even the LDF soldiers, and sometimes military men come to shop. We pass information by scribbling on gourds [yellow squash]. When we pass vegetables, the officials think we are just sharing our produce. But with a pencil, we can share information so our brothers know what is happening and when. This helps us avoid contact with the authorities who need us to participate at *gacaca* because we know what each other is experiencing. It is also empowering because, while they try to get our produce for as little money as possible, we are disrespecting them! (Interview 2006)

In addition to staying on the sidelines of the various practices of national unity and reconciliation for political reasons, most ordinary Rwandans struggle in their daily lives to ensure their economic survival. It is the struggle to eat and to find ways to send their children to school that shapes their everyday acts of resistance and drives them to stay on the sidelines. Avoiding contact with local officials and other agents of the state is more than just a tactic of protecting themselves from the demands of the policy of national unity and reconciliation. It is the daily struggle for economic survival that in part shapes the politics of ordinary Rwandans. Indeed, the level of political acumen that they exhibit when determining how and when to engage their local officials so that they can appear to be "cooperative, interested in peace and reconciliation, and ready to tell our truth" belies elite perceptions that ordinary folk are, in the words of one NURC official, "just mere peasants who need us to tell them what to do. Really, they are like infants. We need to parent them so they know about peace and reconciliation" (field notes 2006). Many ordinary Rwandans actually rely on the condescension of elites to maneuver, as they understand that their efforts to survive are political: "Everything in the country is political. I am hungry. I have seen people die during war and starve during so-called times of peace. If you can't feed your family, then your thoughts are about survival, not about much else. Of course we need peace. But peace as this government explains it is actually a form of violence against us [survivors]. Avoiding local officials who want us to reconcile is politics. There can be no peace in the heart if there is no peace in the stomach" (interview with Jeanne, a poor Tutsi widow, 2006).

Economic survival is a necessity for many ordinary Rwandans, particularly those at the bottom of the socioeconomic hierarchy. This is especially the case for mandatory activities that ordinary Rwandans must attend in the name of national unity and reconciliation (e.g., government speeches, *umuganda* community work days, *gacaca* trials) instead of tending to their fields, as the postgenocide government does not provide basic social services, despite almost a decade of economic growth. Any economic gains in the country have accrued to elites in Kigali as the government seeks to streamline and modernize the Rwandan economy. Several individuals shared with me the difficulties of meeting their basic needs and those of their families, for example when bridges and roads that link rural communities to the market centers are washed away. Joseph M., a destitute Hutu released prisoner, told me,

> There is the fact that this government does not provide the basic items needed for us to be successful. How can I earn to care for my kids if I cannot get to market? The bridge [to town] went out last year, and there is no sign that they [the government] will repair it. What are we to do but do it ourselves? We are not going to ask [the local authorities] to help us with rebuilding it. It is best to keep distant. Instead of standing up to tell them we need a bridge, some of us work hard to repair it.
>
> This is not an official means of reconciliation, but I have worked side by side with men who also want to provide for their families. We understand that the bridge is important to us all, and we try to work together. It is risky, particularly for men like me, because when they see us working together, they think we are plotting genocide. Some might be doing that; I don't know what is in the hearts of others. What I know is that this government won't help us, so we have to help ourselves. We don't ask for permission; we just do it and hope that our efforts won't be noticed until the work is done. Of course if there is any backlash, some or all of us go to *cachot* [detention]. If there is praise for our efforts from the central authorities, it is the local official who benefits. (Interview 2006)

The everyday acts of resistance of ordinary Rwandans who "stay on the sidelines" are subtle, indirect, and nonconfrontational. Implicit acts of everyday resistance, like washing laundry or building a bridge, may appear on the surface to be survival strategies. What these everyday acts of resistance reveal is that some ordinary Rwandans not only understand that the policy of national unity and reconciliation is an oppressive form of power but also believe that it makes their daily struggle to provide for their basic needs more complicated. Rather than blindly or willingly accept state-led directives to reconcile with one another, ordinary Rwandans recognize that the policy is yet another form of social control that they strategically avoid so that they can get on with more pressing matters—the daily realities of economic survival.

Irreverent Compliance

A second form of everyday resistance that many ordinary Rwandans exhibit is the practice of irreverent compliance, meaning that they follow the rules and regulations of the policy of national unity and reconciliation in ways that respect their position of inferiority to the authority of local officials. Irreverent compliance is a response of ordinary peasants to the various assaults on their dignity, notably the expectation that they will participate earnestly and readily in prescribed activities of national unity and reconciliation. Some ordinary Rwandans have devised a number of ways to subvert the expectations of some aspects of the policy of national unity and reconciliation, particularly around the return ceremonies for *ingando* graduates following their release from prison and the pressures of forced participation in national mourning activities every April. For instance, Tutsi survivors who are forced to attend the return ceremony of a Hutu individual who they believe should not have been released from prison will laugh outlandishly at the remarks of local authorities during their "welcome home" speeches. In this way, they practice irreverent compliance; individuals attend the mandatory meetings but let the official know in subtle ways of their contempt or disrespect. For example, Esther told me about how she is able to "disrespect the system" while avoiding punishment for expressing her discontent with government policy at the frequent sensitization speeches that local officials make on all aspects of the policy of national unity and reconciliation:

> Oh yes, when [the local official] says [at a speech] that [the graduate] has been reeducated through *ingando* training, I laugh out loud, or, if that is not possible, I glare at him, to let him know that I do not believe for even one minute that *ingando* is a good idea for peace and unity. Because we gather [in groups of thirty or more people] at the [local government] offices, it is hard for the official to know it is me who laughed. Sometimes, he stops and stares into the crowd. In those moments, there is a risk that a neighbor will point me out as the one who disrespected the official. When he doesn't, I sometimes move to the other side of the crowd so he can't find [and punish] me. (Interview with Esther, a poor Tutsi widow, 2006)

Esther's act of irreverent compliance may appear to accomplish very little, but on closer examination it is clear that her tactics exploit one of the most vexing insecurities faced by appointed and volunteer local government officials in postgenocide Rwanda (and other authoritarian settings). As individuals who exercise their authority through fear, local officials expect a certain measure of deference and compliance with their demands. Indeed, the power and authority of local officials are reinforced through a strong central government, which makes acts of vocal disrespect like Esther's all the more revealing, precisely because compliance is expected; any refusal to attend the *ingando* "welcome home" ceremony would constitute an affront, if not a challenge, to the authority of the local official. Esther's action of laughing or glaring at an event in which she is forced to participate provides the official with little more than evidence that someone in the crowd is expressing disrespect. In giving the appearance of consent and approval by attending the *ingando* ceremony, Esther has found a way to express her contempt while at the same time maintaining her subordinate position.

Inconsequential acts such as laughing at the words of a local official during a perfunctory speech can provide a foundation for more effective action, as evidenced in the irreverent compliance of Tutsi survivors like Esther, as well as of those individuals—Hutu and Twa—who are not officially recognized as survivors of the 1994 genocide. For these individuals, mourning week represents a sphere of defiance in which individuals seek to protect their dignity as well as that of their loved ones whose lives were lost during the 1994 genocide, as well as during, before, and after the violence. Janvier, a poor Tutsi survivor, explained to me how he resists mourning week despite the requirement that he attend and "show solidarity for Tutsi lives lost" (interview with NURC official 2006):

> Mourning week is a joke. How stupid does this government think we [Tutsi] survivors are? We [Tutsi] talk about the ways this government disrespects our lives. I mean, we were targeted because we were Tutsi; now we have to forget about that in the name of national unity and reconciliation. Me, I cannot. Tutsi is what I am. So the officials make speeches, and we have to mourn in "official" ways. This means nothing. Many of my people are really dead; many around me are alive, but they act like they are dead. Seriously, this idea that I am survivor is too much to bear. This government says they saved us and saved Rwanda. This is just not true. So when they [government officials] make speeches on radio, I just turn it off, which can get me in trouble [with the authorities] if a neighbor who is an enemy passes by and learns that I am not listening. Of course, I am a former Tutsi, so maybe that wouldn't happen, but anything is possible these days.
>
> Local authorities make public speeches we must attend. Now, I have benefits as a [cooperative] member. There is no way I am going to risk losing those funds. I need them to live. So it was first in 1999, once I had some strength and could think about regaining some balance in my head, I made a big decision to reject my local official. We were standing in the crowd after the speech. A very disappointing speech, which is what shaped my decision. So I was standing quite close to him [the speechmaker], and I stuck my tongue out at him. He did not see me, but other [Tutsi survivors] did. Some of them squirmed, and others covered their mouths to stop their laughter. One woman, she gasped, which made the official look around to understand why our mood had changed. He saw me with a stone face and did nothing. After that, some of us stand up to officials who force us to

mourn our dead and our lives in ways that are offensive to us. One was caught mocking [the official], and she spent the night in *cachot* [detention]. She still mocks when she can, and so do I. If I can't mourn in my own way, at least I can show disrespect in private ways that other survivors understand. (Interview 2006)

Several ordinary Rwandans defy the demand that they officially mourn lost loved ones. In 2006 the government decreed that the remains of individuals who were buried in mass graves during the 1994 genocide would be moved to local authority offices, where "official grave markers" would provide "the appropriate respect and officially honor to those who perished during the genocide" (interview with Ministry of Culture official 2006). For survivors of all ethnicities, the official mass graves are an affront for two reasons. First, the graves are locked and can be opened only with the written permission of the local cell coordinator, something that many ordinary Rwandans avoid seeking given their preference to avoid contact with local officials. Second, mass graves do not respect the wish of survivors and their families—Tutsi, Hutu, and

Figure 11. Since 2006, genocide memorials like this one in at the St. Jean Catholic Church have been kept under lock and key. This image was taken in Kibuye (now Karongi) town, August 2006. (photo by author)

Twa—to have the remains of their lost relatives buried on their own land so that they can care for the grave and honor their dead according to Rwandan custom. The directive is particularly offensive to Hutu and Twa survivors who participated in my research, as most of them lost family members and friends after the official end of the genocide in July 1994, at Kibeho camp or the refugee camps in Zaïre, or through disease or starvation. One Tutsi survivor told me that that her local official offered to give her "some bones that might be those of your relatives" if she paid him FRw 100,000 (US$221), an obvious form of corruption (interview with Espérance, a poor Tutsi widow, 2006).

Séraphine, an elderly Twa survivor of the political violence of 1959 and of the 1994 genocide, defied the directive to mourn her lost relatives in sanctioned mass graves:

> Sneaking a bone. A big bone, like my husband had. The official looked away, and I grabbed it and hid it in my skirt. My friend helped me because we knew that I could go to prison or worse for grabbing a bone. She distracted him, and I grabbed it.
>
> The government rule is that you must mourn at public ceremonies. Mourning means being respectful to those who died. This means Tutsi. It also means showing upset and even weeping or sobbing. I want nothing to do with that as my people [ethnic Twa] are not recognized there. And the national memorial centers like the one at Gikongoro [now Nyamagabe], we have to pay a fee to enter. I have no money to eat. How can I possibly travel and then pay to enter? Of course, when you enter [the memorial], I am told you have to sign a book so then the government knows you have visited. No. I am unable to mourn in ways that are more than shameful of the way my people died. My husband died at Kibeho camp, and the RPF did it. We all know that [not clear who "we" refers to]. To say that only Tutsi are the survivors of the genocide is just false. But I am an old woman, so what can I really do? I just appear to be mourning for them.
>
> So I go to the [mourning] events. I hang my head. I act ashamed of what we Rwandans did to Tutsi. Basically, I do everything this government says we have to do to respect the lives of Tutsi that fell during the genocide. But in my heart, I am remembering my people. After [the ceremony], I go home and sit under my banana tree and pour some sorghum [beer] on my husband's grave so I can share with him like we used to.
>
> Everyone knows that others died too. Maybe not because of genocide but because of other forms of violence. It was like that in 1959 and in 1994. Killing, killing, killing. It is everyone's business, not just the business of Tutsi and Hutu like the government says now and like it did in 1959.
>
> So I took a bone, knowing I could go to prison or worse. I don't think he [the local official] will ever find out because I am an old woman and

old women don't challenge our officials. But since the genocide and the
rules of this new government, I have to do something to find ways to live
my life in peace. (Interview 2006)

Séraphine proudly pointed to where the femur was buried on her own
property, where she had created a shrine to her friends and family lost during
the genocide, a crime that most ordinary Rwandans believe is punishable by
law (it is not actual law). That the recovered bone is unlikely to be that of her
husband does not matter; as Séraphine pointed out her makeshift grave to me,
she said, "The government won't let me heal in my own time, in my own way.
So I had to do what was right for my heart. I need to see the tombstone even if
the bone is not truly that of [my husband]. I want to care for it and honor his
memory. I planted this banana tree so the official won't know from his car that
it is a tomb for a survivor like me [an ethnic Twa]" (interview 2006).

The compliance of many ordinary Rwandans is an indicator of the systemic
forms of structural violence to which local officials subject ordinary Rwandans
in the name of national unity and reconciliation. Acts of irreverent compliance
are indeed one of the more disguised forms of everyday resistance; they are the
desperate acts of persons living in extreme poverty, emotional pain, continual
fear, and constant isolation. Laughing, glaring, and defying government orders
on how to mourn the lives of loved ones are ways that some ordinary Rwandans
continue to resist the demands of the policy of national unity and reconciliation
prudently, creatively, and with determination, even in the presence of local officials, in ways that restore their dignity. In a context of social control like postgenocide Rwanda, many ordinary peasants recognize that the policy of national
unity and reconciliation is a form of violence against them. They also understand that even the smallest act can be met with brutal reprisals from local officials and other agents of the state. Irreverent compliance as a form of everyday
resistance is a useful indicator of the extent to which ordinary Rwandans consider the directives of national unity and reconciliation an illegitimate burden
in their daily efforts to rebuild their lives and livelihoods.

Withdrawn Muteness

A third form of everyday resistance that some ordinary Rwandans practice as
they perform national unity and reconciliation is "withdrawn muteness." This
term refers to purposeful and strategic moments of silence that ordinary Rwandans employ to defy the expectations of the policy in ways that either protect
their meager resources or ensure their dignity in their interactions with local
officials. Withdrawn muteness is enacted through the ways in which the body
and face are held and are a standard response of many ordinary Rwandans to

local authorities or other agents of the state. This leads elites to conclude wrongly that ordinary Rwandans are not political beings, since they lack "the necessary education and consciousness to understand politics. It is because they are not modern that we have to educate them on becoming Rwandans" (interview with NURC official 2006). Among the ordinary Rwandans I met, far from any primary road, electric line, or other modern convenience, I encountered individuals who possessed levels of political awareness that energize and shape everyday acts of resistance as subtle and indirect as withdrawn muteness. Trésor, a destitute Tutsi teenager, describes withdrawn muteness as a tactic that sabotages the efforts of local officials to promote reconciliation among ordinary Rwandans:

> Remaining silent is very rewarding because it angers local officials. They ask if we are stupid. They ask if we understand. They ask why we are so difficult. That is the point. When he [the local official] gets mad, I smile inside because I know he is frustrated and annoyed. The officials work to make us get reconciled while people like me [orphans and other survivors] just want to be left alone. I mean, life is enough of a struggle without the burden of reconciling with people who may or may not have killed. Being silent is a good way to appreciate the difficulties of life since the genocide. We have all been hurt in some way, but we recognize the pain and continue on. Silence helps us do that in ways that make sense to us, not to local officials. (Interview 2006)

Withdrawn muteness is also the tactic of choice for the imprisoned Hutu, who have even fewer options to resist. Of the six such individuals to whom I spoke, three had confessed to their crimes of acts of genocide and the remaining three swore their innocence. Prisoners use withdrawn muteness as a way to avoid cooperating with prison authorities, as well as with the soldiers assigned to guard them during the days on which prisoners fulfill their *travaux d'intérêt général* (works in the general interest, TIG) obligations. *Tigistes* (those who perform TIG) are prisoners who serve part of their sentence by carrying out works in the general interest; they dig ditches, build roads, and terrace hillside plots of land to prevent soil erosion and maximize crop yields. They also build homes for Tutsi survivors of the genocide (interview with prison official 2006). Officially, *tigistes* are allowed to return to their home communities and spend part of the day (7:00 a.m. to 2:00 p.m.) in service to TIG projects. The *tigistes* I interviewed worked on TIG projects during the day but spent their evenings in the local prison. It is also designed to promote reconciliation "because [Tutsi] survivors get used to seeing prisoners in their communities" (interview with prison official 2006). When asked why the prisoners I spoke to were not allowed back into their communities as part of their TIG sentence, the official told me that this is because "[Tutsi] survivors are not yet ready to welcome them back [to their communities]."

The words of one prisoner sum up the perspective of confessed prisoners: "We have never been allowed back [home]. They say it is because survivors don't want us. That may be because some of us did terrible things, but we have never been given the chance to reintegrate. What is the point of *ingando* and TIG if we never get a chance to try to reconcile? We are slaves to this government like our ancestors were slaves during colonial times" (interview with Félicien, a prisoner who confessed to acts of genocide, 2006). Jean-Bosco shared that playing dumb is a useful tactic. He says:

> When I was nominated for TIG, I jumped at the opportunity because I heard it was a way to get back home much sooner than rotting here in prison. So we go with soldiers or *gendarmes* [policemen] to do work. Hard work, manual work. So the boys [soldiers] all know that I am a medical doctor, so I act like I don't know how to terrace or dig. I have never done this work before, but it is not very hard. It is just degrading and not something that I will do without the ability to go home at night. Now of course they [prison officials] exaggerated about the right to live at home while performing TIG. I shouldn't have been surprised, as this government just wants to keep educated Hutu out of the public system. This is why I am in prison even though I am 100 percent innocent. I saved lives during the genocide and even did not run [to Zaïre] afterwards. I stayed in Butare and worked at the hospital, patching up everyone—Tutsi or Hutu. Some died on my [operating] table. Others survived. I am guilty for the death of those that died. It is clear that locked up in prison is where this government wants educated Hutu like me. False allegations of committing genocide are just a form of genocide that this government practices against [educated] Hutu like me.
>
> So with these young boys that are responsible for prisoners when we are out on TIG, I just play stupid. I look at my feet, I look at the sky. I stare at them as they speak to me about how to work the shovel. I act completely ignorant and say nothing. I did this every time for months and months. I think it was almost one year before the soldiers began to tell one another that I was useless and could not be counted on to do manual work. It is a risky strategy as I will never fulfill the TIG requirements of my sentence. But I also know from being outside in the community that someone like me will never get out of prison. There is no justice in this Rwanda since the genocide. So I do what I can to limit my responsibilities. (Interview with Jean-Bosco, an imprisoned Hutu, 2006)

Jean-Bosco plays dumb and remains silent as a strategy to make his life in prison more bearable. He also says nothing and feigns ignorance to maintain his sense of self as someone who is above manual labor; his actions guarantee him (at least in his eyes) his dominant position as a medical doctor with the "young boys [soldiers] who are responsible for prisoners." Indeed, Jean-Bosco understands that, as an "educated Hutu," he is likely to spend the rest of his life in prison. This, in turn, shapes his decision to feign ignorance. His subtle and nonconfrontational action of everyday resistance also reveals the forms of power in which Jean-Bosco is enmeshed. As a Hutu prisoner with few, if any, options to receive justice and return to his community, Jean-Bosco undertakes actions that show the analytical usefulness of the concept of everyday resistance. While his action is limited, individual, and bordering on resignation, it reveals a poignant and meaningful element of the concept of everyday resistance — awareness of the oppressive elements of TIG activities that are upheld by local officials. Jean-Bosco recognizes the structural violence that TIG represents in his daily life. Withdrawn muteness shows that he will not submit entirely to the discipline of the soldiers and other agents of the state charged with overseeing and controlling his participation in TIG projects. It also indicates the oppressive nature of state power that Jean-Bosco is up against as a member of one of post-genocide Rwanda's most marginal categories and illustrates how individuals resist the demands of the policy of national unity and reconciliation in minute and nonobvious ways.

Conclusion

A focus on the everyday acts of resistance of ordinary Rwandan men and women allows for a fuller picture of what these resistance practices indicate about the system of power they are up against. Indeed, a careful look at what may appear on the surface to be trivial acts—for example, remaining silent or mocking local officials—provides insight into the kinds of power relations ordinary Rwandans are caught up in. These acts are also contingent on the relationships between the ordinary individual, as persons subject to the power of the state, and the various mechanisms of national unity and reconciliation. More than simply restoring the agency of ordinary Rwandans as political beings who possess intimate knowledge of the exercise of power in postgenocide Rwanda, they make clear the various and multiple strands of social and political power as local officials work to promote the policy of national unity and reconciliation.

This chapter also showed how subtle, indirect, and nonconfrontational acts of everyday resistance reflect individual understandings of the operation and function of state power in postgenocide Rwanda. Indeed, the strongest evidence for the existence and importance of identifying and analyzing acts of everyday resistance is their ability to identify sites of opposition and struggle within the policy. Speaking of everyday resistance does more than show the creativity, ingenuity, and resourcefulness of the many ordinary Rwandans who are subject to the dictates of the policy of national unity and reconciliation; it also reveals the marginal sociopolitical position of ordinary peasants in identifying the places of resistance where the oppressive power of the state is enacted in their daily lives. A focus on the everyday acts of resistance of ordinary Rwandans also illustrates the overlapping and intersecting forms of social control embodied in the policy of national unity and reconciliation, while revealing the structural limitations it places on ordinary Rwandans whose lived experiences of violence are outside the dictates of the many practices and mechanisms of state power found in the policy.

6

Everyday Resistance
to the *Gacaca* Process

This chapter examines one specific mechanism of the policy of national unity and reconciliation, the *gacaca* (ga-cha-cha) courts. The courts are an open-air local-level retributive mechanism that the government instituted to prosecute individuals for crimes of genocide. The "modern" postgenocide version of *gacaca* is loosely based on a traditional dispute-resolution mechanism of the same name (Waldorf 2006, 48–55). The postgenocide government prioritized legal proceedings as the primary means of national unity and reconciliation. It opted for a variety of judicial processes—the International Criminal Tribunal for Rwanda (ICTR), the national courts, and the *gacaca* courts—to fight the culture of impunity and to foster respect for the rule of law (Office of the President 1999). The *gacaca* courts are a central part of the government's national unity and reconciliation "toolkit" and emphasize legal retribution over social reconciliation (Zorbas 2004, 29). For the government, *gacaca* is a "truth and reconciliation strategy" that accomplished the following: (1) it established a truthful record of what really happened during the 1994 genocide, (2) it accelerated the release of more than 120,000 individuals accused of acts of genocide so that they could return home and "help re-build Rwanda rather than just sitting in jail," (3) it eradicated the culture of impunity, and (4) it promoted national unity and reconciliation (interview with MINIJUST official 2006; Rusagara 2005).[1] For many ordinary Rwandans, the *gacaca* courts represented a form of state control in their lives, whose demands they tried to resist subtly and strategically.

This chapter focuses on the government's efforts to promote national unity and reconciliation through the *gacaca* courts. It argues that the *gacaca* courts are another mechanism of the postgenocide government that reinforces state power and promotes the image of Rwanda as a "nation rehabilitated" in the name of national unity and reconciliation and at the expense of individual well-being (ORTPN 2004, 4). Specifically, the chapter focuses mainly on the everyday acts of resistance of Tutsi survivors, as key actors in the performance of *gacaca*, to illustrate how the courts limit individual agency and to demonstrate the subtle and creative ways survivors expressed their discontent with government policy before the *gacaca* courts. The argument is developed in three sections. The first section brings together the analysis of chapters 3 and 4 to illustrate the extent to which the *gacaca* courts act as a part of the system of state power. This chapter takes the analysis further in examining the everyday acts of resistance of some ordinary Rwandans to the *gacaca* courts to show that, instead of promoting national unity and reconciliation, the courts are a mechanism where individuals subtly expressed their discontent with the postgenocide policies of the RPF. The *gacaca* courts represent to them an illegitimate site of everyday resistance to the policies of the RPF-led government, not one of national unity or reconciliation.

The second section illustrates the nature of state involvement in and control of the *gacaca* process. Specifically, this section examines the extent to which state agents (local officials and military police alike) seek to control the *gacaca* process to emphasize the many constraints that the policy of national unity and reconciliation imposes on individuals. It also demonstrates how the policy forces individuals to participate at *gacaca* in ways that promote a sense of fear and insecurity in ordinary Rwandans. This section sets the stage for the final section of the chapter—the acts of everyday resistance of Tutsi survivors. This final section focuses on Tutsi survivors as key actors in the *gacaca* process because it is their ability and willingness to testify about who did what to whom, where, and when that is, according to the government, critical to its efforts to promote national unity and reconciliation.

The Power of State and the *Gacaca* Process

Žižek suggests that it is not the civilized public appearance of the state apparatus but rather the underworld of written codes of conduct and ritual that is the actual life-world of citizens—in other words, it is these behind-the-scenes lived realities that reveal how individuals subject to state power feel its force in their daily lives. This underworld is able to operate only because the image of a fair and impartial "state" and the obedient citizen creates the sense of conceptual distance necessary for the regime to create an image of itself as one that tries to treat its citizens fairly in pursuit of the goals of the regime (Žižek 1996, 101). The *gacaca* process represents such an underworld, as the postgenocide government promotes its policy of national unity and reconciliation as a project that will result in an ethnically unified "one Rwanda for all Rwandans." The *gacaca* law requires ordinary Rwandans to participate, and individuals are cast into the following prescripted roles: (1) citizen spectators, (2) judges, (3) witnesses, (4) prisoners who have confessed to acts of genocide, (5) prisoners who have not confessed to their crimes, or (6) survivors (NURC 2003, 8).[2] Individuals who do not perform according to the assigned script fall afoul of the postgenocide state and its agents and are subject to a variety of sanctions. For example, Tutsi survivors can lose their membership in civil society organizations that provide free health care or subsidized school fees. Prisoners who confess in hopes of receiving a reduced sentence can find themselves with full sentences of life in prison. Community spectators and witnesses can run into trouble with government officials if they speak out of turn or off topic. Judges must oversee and implement the *gacaca* process in accordance with government standards; those who do not can be imprisoned and/or denounced, which often means a loss of social and economic status.

The constant threat of sanction means that some ordinary Rwandans were tactical when making their performance before the *gacaca* courts, as local officials and military police actively work to suppress any challenge to the policy of national unity and reconciliation. In order to get an official rendering of justice via the *gacaca* courts, local officials constantly reminded ordinary Rwandans to "watch themselves" lest the veil of fair and impartial state be pulled back (interview with RPF official 2006). Self-sanctioning behavior is the result of this surveillance and, in turn, narrows the ability and willingness of survivors and perpetrators to reconcile outside the official mechanism of *gacaca*. Following Žižek, the policy of national unity and reconciliation maintains the civilized appearance of peace and security in ways that do not match individual lived experiences of the genocide. National unity and reconciliation are products of the postgenocide regime and do not necessarily exist in people's everyday lives.

That individuals are unable to explore the possibility of reconciliation outside the glare of state power requires an approach that takes into consideration three different dimensions of state power: the idea of the state, the practices of the state, and its culture. The state-idea is "an ideological artifact attributing unity, morality, and independence to the disunited, amoral, and dependent workings of the practice of government" (Abrams 1988, 81). This belief in the state "conceals the workings of relations of rule and forms of discipline in day-to-day life" (Alonso 1994, 381). This has important implications for the *gacaca* process, which is overseen by a number of local power brokers, including the sector- and cell-appointed local government officials, military police, and the *gacaca* judges (*inyangamugayo*, literally "those who detest disgrace"). In cases where individual compliance with the rituals of *gacaca* was low, plain-clothed security agents were assigned by the central government to monitor the process (field notes 2006). State agents in uniform were often armed with AK-47s or other instruments of force, including truncheons. Plain-clothed agents of the state were omnipresent but played no official role in *gacaca* proceedings. These individuals made no attempt to hide their presence, and, in my experience, everyone in attendance knew well who the state agents were and why they were there. Alice said it well: "Of course we all see them. And we all know why they come. To get justice the way it is supposed to be done. They talk only to those [appointed] officials, and they have covered shoes and sunglasses. It is very obvious they come from outside [our cell]. One who came to witness [*gacaca*] proceedings didn't actually speak enough of our language [Kinyarwanda] to observe properly and had to get help from one of the *inyangamugayo* who he knows. We never saw him again. The [current] observer always sits there, away from the other observers" (interview with Alice, a poor Tutsi widow, 2006).

At the level of the ordinary individual, local officials who are willing to uphold the idea of the state make it real in everyday life. As analyzed in chapter 4, both appointed and elected local officials are chosen for their ability and willingness to effectively and efficiently promote national unity and reconciliation or risk sanction from their bosses in Kigali.[3] If a local official is unable to force individuals resident in his bailiwick to perform the demands of the policy of national unity and reconciliation, the official is likely to be replaced from the center with someone who is more able to do so. Actions such as replacing local officials are an indication of the extent to which the postgenocide government recognizes that its policy of national unity and reconciliation relies on coercive actions; it is hardly something that many Rwandans deem legitimate or just.

The practices of the Rwandan state in pursuit of national unity and reconciliation, such as the *gacaca* courts, take place in articulated "state spaces" (Scott 1998, 186). In the process of controlling the spaces where unity and reconciliation can officially occur, the Rwandan state has neutralized or eliminated non-state spaces, thereby rendering these spaces suspect, which in turn constrains the ability of many ordinary Rwandans to resist practices of national unity and reconciliation. Such acts that occur outside the gaze of the state do not officially count, as there is no official present there to register and legitimate the encounter. Reconciliation must be legible to all—the *gacaca* courts reiterate the power of the postgenocide state to produce the image of lasting peace in the form of a unified "Rwandan" identity. Projects such as the policy of national unity and

Figure 12. A survivor of the 1994 genocide provides evidence before her local *gacaca* court while members of her community look on. The individuals seated at the desk, wearing sashes, are judges. Those seated at the desk without sashes are government observers. (photo by Anne Aghion, *My Neighbor, My Killer*, © 2009)

reconciliation "reveal both the power and the limitations of the regime's project by announcing the gap between enforcing participation and commanding belief" (Wedeen 1999, 22).

The "culture of state" refers to the practices of representation and interpretation that characterize the relation between individuals and the state and through which the idea of the state is embodied and felt. This moves the analysis beyond "the apparatus of government to show how the magic and power of the state are forms in everyday discursive practice" (Crais 2002, 25). An important aspect of state power is the management and appropriation of the symbolic world (Wedeen 1999, 30). The power of the unity-generating Rwandan state is its ability to force individuals to reconcile according to predefined roles and in the dissemination (largely through elected local power brokers) of credible threats of punishment for noncompliance. Individuals behave as if they are being watched because they are—*gacaca* is a public and compulsory spectacle (see fig. 12). Most ordinary Rwandans also understand that the appearance of compliance is an important aspect of performing national unity and reconciliation. Thus, the state commands orchestrated displays of individual obedience to the policy of unity and reconciliation while also producing tactical compliance through the actual or anticipated use of punishment. Another important aspect of the culture of the state is the climate of fear it produces and the self-sanctioning behavior that individuals adopt for fear of being punished for noncompliance.

In spite of this strong state presence and the ubiquity of local officials who work to ensure that as many individuals as possible participate to uphold the façade of national unity and reconciliation that the *gacaca* courts sought to create, many ordinary Rwandans exercise their agency in strategic and creative ways to show their opposition or indignation to what they perceive as unjust actions against them or members of their family. As we saw in chapters 4 and 5, the risks associated with direct action—losing access to social benefits, social outcasting, disappearance, and, in extreme cases, death—can be severe. As a result, ordinary Rwandans practice minute everyday acts of resistance. They include some combination of persistence, prudence, and individual effort to accomplish a specific goal that benefits the individual resister against a local official or other state agent who is unaware that the individual is attempting to resist or subvert the demands of national unity and reconciliation. An analytical focus on the everyday acts of resistance to *gacaca* trials reveals the subtle, indirect, and nonconfrontational ways in which ordinary Rwandans do more than mitigate the demands of their mandatory participation. They also creatively and strategically expressed dissatisfaction with their inability to discuss RPF war crimes, land conflicts, and their continued poverty in the presence of government officials during *gacaca*. Before examining in further detail the specific everyday acts of resistance of Tutsi survivors to illustrate the extent to which *gacaca* is a mechanism of state power, the next section demonstrates how individuals are expected to perform certain roles before the *gacaca* courts in accordance with the script of national unity and reconciliation.

The *Gacaca* Courts in the Promotion of National Unity and Reconciliation

The *gacaca* courts are at the heart of government efforts to achieve national unity and reconciliation since the 1994 genocide "ruptured the social fabric" (interview with NURC official 2006). Little is known about the actual functioning of the *gacaca* courts in pursuit of the goal of promoting national unity and reconciliation despite a voluminous academic literature (for analysis see Ingelaere 2012). This is largely because researchers have focused predominantly on the protection of human rights and the ability of *gacaca* courts to uphold international standards of criminal justice and legal accountability, rather than on outcomes at the level of the individual. Political psychologists and trauma specialists have focused on the healing potential of the courts and the importance of justice as a precondition for reconciliation but are silent on how unity and reconciliation play out in the lives of ordinary Rwandans.

A common thread in these analyses of the *gacaca* process is the assumption that ordinary Rwandans are willing participants. Schabas (2005, 897) claims, without any reference to his methodology or sources, that "Rwandans have consistently rejected any compromise with full accountability, insisting upon criminal prosecution for all alleged perpetrators." Pham et al. (2004, 603) provide more information about their methods but do not state the specifics of their sample or the circumstances in which their survey was completed: "More respondents supported the local judicial responses (90.8 percent supported *gacaca* trials and 67.8 percent the Rwanda national trials) than the ICTR (42.1 percent in support)." Official government documents contend that "the autocratically divisive political structures that once denied minorities a political voice have been replaced, for instance with the implementation of democratic cellular councils that involve local communities in important decisions at grassroots level" (interview with NURC official 2006; NURC 2010, 30–32). What these sources obscure is the extent to which *gacaca* represents yet another "state space" where individual Rwandans are observed and monitored for their compliance with the script of national unity and reconciliation.

Gacaca started as a pilot project in June 2002 and was later refined in 2004. The most notable refinement was the merging of categories 2 and 3 (intentional murder, attempted murder, manslaughter, and assault cases) into a single category. *Gacaca* was launched nationwide in January 2005, with the government estimating that it would take ten years for the courts to complete the process. In fact, the government declared the process completed in 2012, with an estimated few thousand rape cases remaining to be tried in the regular domestic courts. In 2006, during the period of my fieldwork, the *gacaca* trials at the sector and cell levels were taking place throughout the communities where the ordinary Rwandans who participated in my research lived. Trials in these communities had already passed the first stage of *gacaca*, the information-gathering stage, and the courts were involved in the second and final stage of judgment and sentencing.

The *gacaca* process is a top-down and highly centralized process that is overseen by the National Service of Gacaca Jurisdictions (NSGJ), which is a chamber of the Supreme Court of Rwanda. Its primary task is to coordinate the transmission of prisoner dossiers between the cell- and the sector-level courts and to connect these courts to the local offices of the NSGJ, which are housed in the capital of each province (NSGJ 2005/6, 2006). Each district-level office is linked with other government offices, including the prosecutor's office, the prison, and the relevant line ministries, and with the central coordinating office in Kigali (NSGJ/ASF 2002, 3–5). The NSGJ also has the legal authority to monitor and advise the *gacaca* courts, including overseeing the election process for judges, and to intervene at the local level when judges "are not in control of the proceedings" (interview with local NSGJ official 2006). NSGJ staff at the lower levels of the bureaucracy must remain abreast of activities at the level of the cell and the sector and report these to authorities at the provincial and the national levels. They must also complete weekly and monthly reports for transmission to authorities at MINIJUST (NSGJ 2005, 7).

Local NSGJ staff also work with senior government officials from the Ministry of Justice and NSGJ in Kigali to "sensitize the population" and to ensure that *nyumbakumi* ("responsible for ten houses")—the lowest administrative official—assist *gacaca* judges to investigate any involvement of individuals in committing acts of genocide in 1994 (interview with local NSGJ official 2006). Sensitization campaigns target rural populations to encourage people to participate out of self-interest and to further national unity and reconciliation. This quotation from a local official reveals the extent to which the full participation of the population is required: "As for you saying you will not forgive him or that you will not do this or that, that is very bad. Whether you like it or not, that is the law" (quoted in PRI 2002, 23). Mass participation is crucial to the Rwandan state's ability to generate an image of national unity and reconciliation: perpetrators (*génocidaires*) must provide truthful information about what they and their accomplices did during the genocide or go to prison for at least fifteen years. Before any truth telling takes place, a panel of nine judges (*inyangamugayo*) has already amassed a dossier of evidence against which the truth is adjudicated. Witnesses corroborate, revise, or reject the evidence presented by the *inyangamugayo* or the testimony of survivors and/or *génocidaires*. Citizen spectators observe the proceedings, and their en masse presence adds an air of credibility and legitimacy to the proceedings, as it shows external observers (i.e., Westerners) that the government at least tries to treat its citizens fairly in the pursuit of justice for crimes committed during the genocide. The performance of survivors is critical to the spectacle; survivors act both as accusers and, once the truth has been established, as magnanimous individuals who are able to forgive. Tutsi survivors bear the brunt of the burden of providing the truthful record of how the genocide happened, and they can be punished if they fail to "tell all of their truth" (interview with local NSGJ official 2006).

In practice, however, *gacaca* courts are a contested and conflicted state space and are characterized by discord and tension between the various actors. Citizen spectators I consulted spoke of the ways in which local authorities, usually one or more of the *nyumbakumi*, the cell or sector coordinators, demand individual attendance, with the threat of official sanction. Witness this from Béatha, a destitute Hutu widow with children:

> He [the cell coordinator] came, and he asked me why I didn't attend the *gacaca*. He came on a motorcycle, so everyone [in the community] knew. I told him because my son is sick and I stayed home with him. He wrote something in his book and said, "Next time you have to come. I don't care the reason." So I got scared because my son wasn't sick at all! It was that I had no money to spare for transport, but I didn't tell him because I know that is no excuse. The radio says we have a responsibility to participate. Last time we had a meeting [at the office of the cell coordinator], the official said that there was no excuse for not participating. . . .
>
> But I didn't see anything, so what can I say? I heard people getting killed, but I was in hiding. I mean, I hid when they [the killers] came. Who didn't? We all hid in those days [during the genocide]. I don't know who saw what, but I say that I saw nothing. I heard the official tell someone whose name I know to kill, but I didn't see it. If he killed, I don't know. So why go if I have nothing to say and if I have no money? How do I get money to go? I am not a survivor so am not a member of an association; money for school uniforms is now due. Now I have a big headache because he knows I did not go and *gacaca* is again next week. Next week! And now my neighbors know he [the cell coordinator] has come, so I have to go.
>
> I also fear because if my neighbors find out that I said my son was sick they might use that information to denounce me [to the cell coordinator]. What will I do then? (Interview 2006)

Béatha's experience as a Hutu woman is emblematic of the stresses and strains experienced by those who, in the eyes of the government, are peripheral to the success of *gacaca* as a tool to generate national unity and reconciliation. As a Hutu woman, she has a limited role in the *gacaca*, since she is not expected to testify as a Tutsi survivor or to tell her truth as a perpetrator. Instead, her role is to act as a citizen spectator to give the appearance of popular support for the courts. Her words are also symbolic of the self-monitoring behavior that characterizes postgenocide processes of justice and reconciliation. In addition to the strain of meeting the official requirements of *gacaca*, Béatha refers to her neighbors' awareness of her reason for not attending the *gacaca* session. Official state-based sanctions (fines, imprisonment) for nonparticipation matter, but so do the watchful eyes of friends, neighbors, and, in some instances, family in ensuring the full participation of the population at *gacaca*. There may indeed be other reasons why Béatha prefers not to attend the weekly *gacaca* session. She may want to avoid being falsely accused by neighbors, or she may know more than she is willing to share and prefer not to participate to avoid forced contact with her neighbors. The point is that the *gacaca* process is for many ordinary Rwandans an oppressive form of state power that forces them to participate in ways that are not necessarily in line with their own lived realities.

Key actors in ensuring the smooth operation of the *gacaca* courts are the judges, the *inyangamugayo*. Judges are officially "elected" by members of the communities they are to serve under local authorities. Judges are constantly balancing their privileged role as elected (although unpaid) officials against the requirements of living as a member of the community they are to serve. Judges have little autonomy when it comes to rendering judgment. NSGJ official in Kigali resolve any confusion about the scope of the *gacaca* law or the relevant procedures. Judges simply conduct the *gacaca* trial in a fair and impartial way. In theory, "fair and impartial" means that, in the course of assessing evidence, weighing individual testimony from survivors or *génocidaires*, and ensuring the procedural integrity of the trial, judges can draw on their own personal experiences and insights. In practice, it means that judges are under constant surveillance by both local government authorities and community members, both of whom can report any wrongdoing, real or perceived, to state authorities. The *gacaca* law itself is also a constraint, as judges are duty bound to respect its rules and regulations at all times, even though they receive minimal training and support in how to do so. Judges, because of the important role they play in facilitating the smooth operation of the *gacaca* courts, are expected to spur *génocidaires* to tell the truth and also to ensure that survivors are able to offer an act of forgiveness. Because of this power, judges are often reminded by the state of their duty to ensure the active participation of the population at *gacaca*.

Ensuring the active participation of the population is not without its risks. Didier's lament is emblematic of the thoughts of the judges with whom I spoke:

> It is a most difficult thing to be a judge. And no one understands. There is no one I can share my difficulties with. I am a survivor like the other survivors, but even they look at me differently. I feel isolated since I became a judge. And because I have a family, I have responsibilities to them. My wife even asked how I could let my family starve when it was time to harvest. But I couldn't do that work because it [being a judge] takes at least two days a week, sometimes more. . . . If I don't undertake my duties as a judge, I can get into serious problems with [the appointed local government official that he reports to]. And I can also get into serious problems with other survivors.
>
> Last year, we acquitted a Hutu who was accused. We didn't have enough evidence or information to do anything but let him go. So we did.

I truly before God did not think he was guilty. And no one spoke up about his role. It didn't sound like he did anything. And he was sorry. He fell on the ground [in front of his accuser] and said, "I'm sorry, I'm sorry, I'm sorry." The survivor accepted, and we all felt happy about the power of *gacaca* at that moment. I was proud to be a judge, you know, really proud. Then, the day after, the IBUKA lady requested to see all of us judges.[4] I was in my field trying to feed my family the few beans we had left. She said that the survivors around me [in his community] were so angry with us. Then she raged against me, and I felt like I did the best I could in deciding how the accused was telling his truth. I said I was sorry but I don't think it [the evidence against the accused] was enough. I fear now that I am going to be denounced because I was told [by the other judges] that she [the IBUKA representative] is very powerful with many connections in Kigali. . . . What if something happens to me? Who will take care of my family? (Interview 2006)

Didier's narrative is reflective of the additional challenges that judges face in the performance of *gacaca*; judges must uphold its rituals while ensuring that their behavior does not compromise the ability of others to participate. Indeed, the penalties for falling afoul of the postgenocide order of national unity and reconciliation are too high. The most marginal individuals, judges and peasants alike, seek to avoid contact with local officials and other Rwandans. Fear of being "denounced" and the threat of denunciation are common survival strategies under the policy of national unity and reconciliation. Denouncing someone requires both the imagination to craft an appropriate story that the authorities will believe and enough showmanship to deliver the tale successfully. If poorly rendered, a denunciation can result in the shunning or outcasting of the teller by his or her community.

Women are more likely to denounce as the result of the poking and prodding of a male member of her family. For example, male relatives force many Tutsi survivor women to testify in ways that support interests beyond those of delivering justice or promoting reconciliation. In one case, the appointed local official, an individual who has business relations with the brother of a Tutsi survivor, instructed a Tutsi woman on how to deliver her testimony. The accused was detained on allegations of committing genocidal crimes "only" in 2001, which suggests that he was targeted for economic reasons other than his actual involvement in the genocide:

My brother was in business with [the local official]; they knew [the accused] had a house and a good job [as a translator for an international organization]. [The official] told me to denounce [the accused during testimony].

> [The official] said if I didn't, I would end up dead or in prison, even
> though [X] is my brother! I didn't know what to do; he is my blood
> brother, but he grew up outside. He wasn't even here during the war! I
> denounced him [the accused]. He got life [in prison]. I never saw him
> before, but I denounced him. I am an unmarried widow, so I have to do
> what I am told. What would happen to my children? (Interview with Esther,
> a poor Tutsi widow, 2006)

Male survivors, as well as Hutu and Twa women, rarely practice denunciation, as they are not subject to the same levels of surveillance as are Hutu men.
Hutu men in any of three classifications are subject to surveillance by both officials and other Rwandans: (1) those who have been tried and convicted of acts
of genocide, either through the regular domestic or *gacaca* courts, leading to
imprisonment for twenty-five years to life, in which case their economic and
social networks, particularly those who visit them in prison, are watched; (2)
those who have never been imprisoned for committing acts of genocide but
who remain under surveillance to detect any evidence that they harbor genocidal
ideologies or have made revisionist or negationist statements about the genocide; and (3) those who have been imprisoned on charges of committing acts of
genocide and have been released, either following acquittal (domestic courts)
or following judgment at *gacaca* (some individuals remain subject to suspicion in
their communities, particularly those who are seen "to have it too easy"). At
the level of the ordinary rural and peasant Hutu, the third scenario is the most
likely, as the other two apply to urban, educated, and well-resourced individuals.
For ordinary Hutu men, the surveillance tends to be performed by friends and
neighbors. Witness this statement from Félicien, an imprisoned Hutu man:

> I returned to [my community] after *gacaca*, and I confessed everything I
> did. I even told them about things some others did because I was told this
> would help me get home. . . . When I got home, my wife and kids were
> living with a survivor! He wouldn't let me talk to her, but I was her
> husband! I didn't know what to do because he was in my house. I had
> nowhere to go. So I stayed where my parents stayed. Then his relative
> denounced me! She said I didn't tell my truth. But I did. I know I did. I did
> what I said. But I ended up back in prison for life. (Interview 2006)

For perpetrators, the challenges and constraints of participating in *gacaca*
are multiple. There are Tutsi women who have testified against their Hutu husbands. There are Hutu who admit to killing under pressure from the authorities
of the previous regime. There are Hutu who proclaim their innocence despite
sometimes overwhelming evidence that they actively participated in the genocide. Hutu who voice concerns about the impartiality of *gacaca* can be imprisoned

for providing false testimony or for harboring genocidal ideology. Hutu who
question why members of the RPF who killed civilians during and after the
genocide are not being tried in the *gacaca* courts also run the risk of life in prison
or other unpleasant fates, including forced exile, disappearance, or death
(Tertsakian 2008, 2011). That Tutsi might be guilty of serious crimes against
Hutu is publicly unimaginable and something that is rarely discussed among
Rwandans in private, let alone in a public space like *gacaca*. Joseph U. looked at
me wide-eyed when I asked him if he thought the RPF or any other Tutsi had
committed any crimes in 1994. He hushed me and said, "I thought you understood this country! You better just stop talking with questions like that!" Many
individuals invoked the historical oppression of Hutu by Tutsi and scoffed at
the idea that there could be national unity and reconciliation delivered by a
practice as skewed as *gacaca*. Another common theme in the narrative of Hutu
adults, men and women, is the idea that *gacaca* was a pretext to persecute Hutu
for the genocide of Tutsi. The remarks of Anselme, the teenage nephew of one
of my research participants, are revealing:

> You know, I don't think there is an adult Hutu inside this country that
> doesn't fear the *gacaca*. I don't fear it because I was only four years old at
> the time of genocide, but my uncles fear it, and so does my older brother.
> And I fear for them because if something happens to them, what will
> happen to me? I haven't even finished school yet. How will I make my
> living? I wouldn't be surprised if something happened to one of them
> though. . . . That is how things work around here. My people don't know
> anyone important, so who will stand up for us if something goes wrong at
> *gacaca*?
>
> One of my uncle's friends was denounced [for acts of genocide], but he
> knows people in Kigali and his wife's brother is important in our local
> church [a priest]. He knows people, you know. That, and he is already
> important to the community because his brother [the priest] will protect
> him. Not because he is religious but because he also knows people. Right
> after our return [in 1996 in the mass repatriation of Hutu refugees from
> Zaïre by the RPF], he denounced many of us [Hutu]. We don't know
> anyone important. For me, *gacaca* is just a way for the government to put
> us Hutu in prison and to make sure we don't make more genocide for
> them. It [genocide] could happen because Hutu are no longer welcome
> here. My uncle says that he thinks even there could be genocide but the
> RPF won't allow it! (Field notes 2006)

Several participants spoke at length about the onerous demands placed on
Hutu who stand accused before the *gacaca* courts. Chantal, a Hutu woman who
was called to act as a witness but soon found herself in prison accused of acts of

genocide, said, "And then I got denounced. I mean I am telling the truth, and I get denounced from someone in the audience. He said that all Hutu are killers and challenged my version [of events]. I was truly amazed. Really amazed, you know. No one, not the judge, not the survivor, no one said anything. Someone said that Hutu are all in it together. I didn't even know what that person meant when he said that. . . . I am innocent but am in prison now. I have no way out" (interview 2006).

Survivors are just as constrained in their action and speech as are *génocidaires*, if not more so. The role of survivors in the *gacaca* process is critical to the promotion of national unity and reconciliation. The deep well of hope and resilience that survivors, particularly female survivors, display on a daily basis is "an inspiration to all Rwandans and evidence that unity is within reach" (interview with NURC official 2006). A common thread I noted in the narrative of survivors when speaking about *gacaca* was the constant sense of insecurity they felt. Such feelings were widespread, particularly with regard to the act of testifying against the accused at a *gacaca* session and in their daily lives as they came into contact with family, friends, and neighbors of the accused. Witness this statement from Jeanne, a destitute Tutsi survivor, who was required by the cell coordinator to testify against the individual accused of killing her entire family:

> I had a visit from [the *nyumbakumi*] who told me that [the accused] had made a statement that he killed my family. I was amazed. It was like God struck me down. How could this be? I was very nervous but also very excited. I wanted to know what happened to my family but not really. I mean I am alone now. I was raped, and I know that I will not remarry. I am too old. And by this time even barren. Who would marry me?! So I know that I am alone, and I try my best to stay silent so that I can live the rest of my days in peace. I just want peace. I am a member of [survivors' organization], and they give me some small money, and I still have my land. So I was as happy as I could be after genocide.
>
> Then! Then! Then! I am told they found the man who did this to my people. I was horrified. Now I have to relive all of that bad memory. I know how my people were killed. I was there! I was younger then and was able to run away, you know. I just ran into the [banana] grove. Other women talk about how they made efforts to protect their children. Me? I just ran. I guess that means I didn't love my children as much as those other women. I just didn't want to confront the man. I really couldn't remember what he did. I would like to have the remains of my people buried at home, but I would rather stay out of the way of *gacaca* if I could.
>
> Of course, I could not say no because it is my duty to forgive. So he [the accused] stood up, and I recognized him as the husband of my sister!

It was not the man I thought it was at all. No! I just broke down then. I just stopped moving, and I don't think I have moved since. This is why I am not afraid to speak to you, because my life is over. I don't know why they call us "survivors." How can I get peace like this? Really. I wish I never learned the "truth" as the *gacaca* says it is. I had some peace, as much peace as an old woman like me can have, and now I am supposed to live with his news? I wish I was never told to go to *gacaca* that day. I hardly sleep or eat since. . . . Participating comes with nothing for nothing. Maybe I would accept more easily if I could get some kind of [monetary] settlement. (Interview 2006)

Equally, non-Tutsi women thought of themselves as survivors but were unable to be recognized as such. For example, Hutu women bristle at the thought that they are not also considered survivors. As Aurelia, a poor Hutu widow, noted caustically: "I was married to a Tutsi man. He died trying to save me and the children. We all survived but one. I was targeted because my kids are Tutsi because their father is Tutsi. I mean how can I not be considered a 'survivor'? The authorities say it is because I am a Hutu. But my people [male members of her family] are gone; who cares for me? And I have these kids to feed, to send to school" (interview 2006). Adult male survivors felt unwilling to forgive in any sincere way, and many reported feeling culturally bound to reconstitute their family life as husband and head of household as quickly as possible. Participation in *gacaca* had the possible effect of upending the relative stability and peace they had been able to recapture in their private lives. Emmanuel's words are representative:

I remarried as soon as she [the new wife] said yes. She is also a [Tutsi] survivor but is deeply traumatized. She needs a lot of support. So I care for her and our home. We have no children because she is unable to carry any since she was damaged [by rape]. But I don't care. Together, we are a family. I fear *gacaca* because what if someone says something to release her trauma? What if someone accuses me of being an accomplice? I am a man who survived the genocide. For some people, that means I am an accomplice of the *génocidaires*! If I was a "real" Tutsi, I would be dead right now! The people who say that are Hutu, but they are powerful. One of them even drives a taxi. How can I stand [and testify] before such people if they were to ask me to? (Interview with Emmanuel, a poor Tutsi survivor, 2006)

This brief survey of individual experiences with the *gacaca* process from a variety of subject positions reveals the climate of fear as well as the distrust of the government that the courts have created in the lives of many ordinary Rwandans. Individual action before the *gacaca* courts is a performance that does not constitute or even indicate the presence of actual unity and reconciliation in the daily lives of most people. Instead, individual performances of *gacaca* highlight the extent to which the policy of national unity and reconciliation creates an atmosphere of fear and distrust with regard to the RPF-led government. Instead of creating "one Rwanda for all Rwandans," which is the stated goal of the policy of national unity and reconciliation (discussed in chapters 2 and 5), *gacaca* is a mechanism of state power that helps the government consolidate its hold over the country, albeit in a highly coercive and thus unstable manner. In instrumentalizing the courts and individual performances of *gacaca*, the government places the responsibility of appearing to embrace the demands of national unity and reconciliation squarely on the shoulders of ordinary Rwandans. The government has also carefully crafted a state space that makes individual noncompliance difficult. This does not mean that some ordinary Rwandans do not resort to creative and subtle forms of everyday resistance to make their lives more sustainable. Instead, it means that they need to be strategic in enacting their resistance. This is something that Tutsi survivors do most often as key actors in the *gacaca* process, and their everyday acts of resistance express their dissatisfaction with the postgenocide policies of the RPF. It is to their everyday acts of resistance that we now turn.

Everyday Acts of Resistance to *Gacaca*

In carefully scripting individual performances before the *gacaca* courts and in providing repressive sanctions for those who choose to transgress the boundaries of their scripted role, the government does more than affirm its authoritarian tendencies through a dense administrative structure built on a bedrock of state surveillance and individual fear. It also highlights the extent to which individuals are "severely constrained in their ability to openly discuss the social and political situation in Rwanda" (Longman and Rutagengwa 2004, 176). This section draws on the acts of everyday resistance of Tutsi survivors to illustrate the subtle, tactical, and nonconfrontational ways in which some ordinary Rwandans are able to express their discontent with the postgenocide policies of the RPF. Specifically, the section examines the two common ways that many Tutsi survivors show their opposition to and express their indignation about the RPF-led government: (1) they strategically speak out against RPF excesses, and (2) they indirectly criticize the government in voicing the hardships that compliance with new postgenocide policies have created in their everyday lives.

Speaking against RPF Excesses

For some survivors, the *gacaca* courts represent an opportunity to subtly speak out against RPF excesses. Their goal is not to overthrow the *gacaca* court system or even actively subvert its demands. Instead, their everyday acts of resistance are an attempt to live within their own truth—to have their lived experiences of violence during and after the genocide acknowledged and respected by local authorities, not crafted for them as they are by the policy of national unity and reconciliation and implemented by disrespectful appointed local officials. As we saw in the preceding section, participants in the *gacaca* process are expected to act according to script in ways that accord with the ideas, practices, and culture of the postgenocide Rwandan state. The RPF presents the appearance of individual compliance with the *gacaca* process as reality by scripting the ways in which individuals must participate in *gacaca* as a key mechanism of the policy of national unity and reconciliation.

In practice, some survivors strategically criticize the excesses of the RPF in ways that seek to restore their individual dignity. For example, a judge in one of the communities where I regularly observed *gacaca* started proceedings with a brief comment. He sometimes criticized the continued disappearances of residents in his community. He did not look directly into the audience before him or at the observers who were always seated to the side of the judges' bench. Instead, he stood up and looked up toward the sky to lament the disappearances, implying that they were sanctioned by the government but offering no firm statement of accusation. At another trial, a perpetrator stood before the judges' bench, awaiting sentencing after proceedings had finished. He began to speak, to no one in particular, about the poor living conditions in prison and about how the "new government" was "getting rid of all Hutu." Some people in the audience applauded. He was then sentenced to thirty years in prison. It was not clear if the sentence was imposed because of the available evidence (many accused at that particular session received the maximum sentence of thirty years) or because he had spoken out. The government observer then got up and reminded the audience members of their duty to "honor the truth." He continued, "If someone is sentenced, he is no longer part of society. He is not to be applauded" (field notes 2006).

Tutsi survivors, as individuals who regularly stand before the bench of judges, are best positioned to speak out about RPF excesses and do so in ways that are aimed at regaining their personal dignity while offering a subtle critique of the excesses of appointed local government officials. *Gacaca* judges are required to hear all individuals who ask to speak before the courts. Tutsi survivors are the backbone of the *gacaca* process, since its legitimacy is largely contingent on their ability and willingness to speak about what they saw during the 1994 genocide. Many Rwandans told me that they did not see much because they were hiding to save themselves. This may or may not be true, as such statements may be driven by a wish to avoid testifying. Vianney offers this insight:

I mean they [local officials] do what they do because they must react to what Kigali tells them to do, but they do it in ways that are offensive to us and how we [peasants] live our lives. We must be very smart about how we protest their treatment of us. All they care about is power and money. We [peasants] know that if you have power and money, you can do more, enjoy life more.

Of course, for our [local] officials, they do well anyway because very few of them experienced genocide. They can be very cold to our experiences of surviving the genocide, which makes *gacaca* more difficult to experience because they have no feelings for our pain. Reconciliation means respecting officials, not making amends in your heart. At least I am not a former Hutu. I can act out, and if they catch me, I will just say I am having trauma. I notice that when survivors bring up their trauma, the officials sometimes get very uncomfortable, which means it is probably a good way to avoid their punishments. (Interview 2006)

Vianney's narrative illustrates the extent to which he had thought through and considered carefully what acts of resistance he might possibly attempt and how. As a Tutsi survivor, he testified several times at *gacaca* and quickly realized that when he spoke "before the judges, everyone is listening to me. In those moments, I have some possibility to do something clever. I can plead trauma if they treat me too harshly." So Vianney had considered how he would express his act of everyday resistance and assessed its risks. He believed if he got caught, he would invoke his diagnosis as a survivor who was in government-sponsored treatment for trauma. Vianney concluded that any "small protest" he made before the *gacaca* courts had to be carefully considered if it was to accomplish his goal of regaining his dignity and restoring his pride. Indeed, Vianney understood that in appearing before the *gacaca* courts, he had an opportunity to exploit his role as a traumatized survivor who testified before the bench of judges and in front of members of his community. It is also clear that such an opportunity required subtle subterfuge. His everyday act of resistance was strategically directed at what he perceived to be the excesses of the RPF:

At the moment of testifying, I stand up and just begin to talk. Talking about how hard it is since the genocide. How I have no prospects for a wife. How I will never get someone to take care of me and that I will die lonely. How I have no land because that which belonged to my family was redistributed [under the 2000 land policy]. Am I not the head of a household? Am I not the sole living person in my family? How can they take my land? True, I care for no orphans but still, am I not a real survivor?

When I see that the observers are not really paying attention or have decided they don't care about me and that the President [of the *gacaca* court] has decided to let me speak, I go on to say, I have these problems because of the way that government is now working. They say democracy means peace. But I have no peace, and I can't live my life. If the judge looks at me in an unusual way, I stop. But if I feel like I can continue, I turn away [from the judges' bench] and turn out to the audience to see how they are reacting. Some brave souls will applaud or give a laugh to show how they support me.

Up until now, the observers have yet to punish me, and the judge continues to allow me to speak like this. I am known around [his community] as someone who speaks his truth. It doesn't change my life very much; I am still poor and alone. But it somehow makes this life more bearable. It is also that I feel more protected because I am voicing what others will not say. What I say at *gacaca* gives me a reputation as *ibyihebe* [fearless], and I feel respected by the elders [in his community]. They leave me alone, which is what I want because then I can go to *gacaca*, say a few words [against the local authorities and government observer], and make a small protest without getting in much trouble. My neighbors can see I know what I am doing because I've yet to go to *cachot* [detention] or even get a visit [from the local official].

Vianney's seemingly open act of defiance of his scripted role as a survivor of the genocide who must tell his truth reveals more than just his disrespect for the demands of the policy of national unity and reconciliation and the local officials who implement it. Through repeated participation as well as careful analysis of the atmosphere and mood of different actors—judges, local officials, government observers, citizen spectators—to the *gacaca* process on any given day, Vianney performs an everyday act of resistance that demonstrates his dissatisfaction with the process. His speaking out also wins him favor in his community as someone who is able and willing to speak out against the government. What specific excesses he speaks against are contingent on the atmosphere at *gacaca* on the day in question. On different occasions, Vianney and other Tutsi survivors like him speak against the luxuries their appointed local officials enjoy: their ability to afford to go to the local bar most evenings, as well as their "fancy clothes and covered shoes," their access to land and other perks of RPF membership, notably house servants and private vehicles, which "we peasants will never have," their ability to "move around and have the means to do what they want while we basically starve."

Vianney's act of everyday resistance also highlights the gap that local authorities and government observers are supposed to mitigate, between the appearance of broad-based and willing participation at *gacaca* and the actual ability of the government to promote an internalized and sincere belief in the ability of the *gacaca* courts to promote justice, national unity, and reconciliation.

The power of the state, through local officials who carry out its sanctions, seeks to eliminate individual attempts to subvert the demands of the policy of national unity and reconciliation. The policy, as shown in the previous section, requires conformity and discipline—ordinary Rwandans must not step beyond their scripted role. Vianney's carefully constructed statements of dissent illustrate more than the lack of legitimacy that the courts enjoy among ordinary Rwandans. They also highlight the yawning abyss between the aims of the policy and the aims of everyday life. Vianney and others like him who decide to speak out take great risks, albeit calculated ones, in efforts to make their lives more bearable. Everyday acts of resistance in front of the *gacaca* courts also demonstrate that some ordinary Rwandans, despite the demands and concomitant sanctions of the policy, strive to think independently and express their politics as part of their attempts to live within their truth.

Protesting Hardship

The *gacaca* courts are also a site for survivors to protest the economic strains of complying with the new postgenocide policies of the government. In addition to demanding that Rwandans participate in social and political life, the postgenocide government has instituted ambitious policies designed to reengineer rural society, most notably land and agricultural policy. There is a sizable disconnect between government policy and the lived realities of peasant Rwandans, as analyzed in chapters 3 and 5. Rwanda's postgenocide leadership places the responsibility for one's well-being on citizens themselves, proclaiming that "good citizens work hard, and working hard means following government directives. Our job is to work with peasants to make sure they work to overcome their poverty" (interview with MINALOC official 2006, corroborated by Purdeková 2012a, 2012b). Poverty, according to the postgenocide government, is "partly due to the 'wrong peasant mentality'" (Ansoms 2009, 298).

Espérance, a poor Tutsi survivor, sums up the impact of this "wrong mentality" on her daily life: "Being 'good' and 'productive' often means I go to sleep hungry. At least I am mostly alone. But for some [neighbors] it is too much to bear. They struggle even more than me, and I struggle a lot. At least I benefit from membership [in a local survivors' group]. There I can join with others and we can strategize how to be 'good.' For others [nonmembers], their chances are few. I tell you, if they gave food at *gacaca*, everyone would go!"

Espérance's narrative highlights the primary source of tension for many ordinary Rwandans—the need to participate fully at *gacaca* while fulfilling the demands of being a "good" and "productive" citizen without the resources to do so. The government has instituted significant changes to the peasant way of life through its drive to modernize Rwanda's agricultural sector, with a view to reducing the number of households that rely on subsistence farming for their livelihoods without offering another form of income and without consideration of the impact of new institutional arrangements on rural farmers and other un-skilled laborers (MINECOFIN 2000, 17; for analysis see Ansoms 2009; Huggins, 2012; C. Newbury 2011). With little opportunity to protest government efforts to reduce the proportion of the population that relies on subsistence agriculture, ordinary Rwandans like Espérance use the *gacaca* courts to subtly and strategically show their disapproval of such policies: "I really can only speak about land policy when there are no military observers. They come with weapons, and they are not afraid to use them. So if they are there, I say nothing. Land is very contentious because the government is trying to get us to modernize and to produce 'strategically.' If only modernization could benefit us [peasants]. . . . It does not, so speaking out needs to be done very carefully. Me, I am alone, and I am old, too old to remarry. So I speak out to get some respect, and, if I am lucky, I will get some peace and quiet. I have thought about it and am prepared to suffer the consequences. I have nothing left to lose."

Espérance's narrative illustrates more than the extent to which she has considered the room she has to maneuver when testifying before the *gacaca* courts and how this room in turn shapes what she hopes her speaking out will accomplish. Her ultimate goal is to gain "some peace and quiet," by which she means being left alone to cultivate her land in her own way, not according to government dictates. It also illustrates the extent to which she has carefully considered how she can behave before the *gacaca* courts in ways that protest against new land and agricultural policies (introduced in chapter 5)—this is her everyday act of resistance, and it is grounded in both her political acumen and the government's recognition of her status as a Tutsi survivor. As a survivor, she is expected to testify before the *gacaca* courts, and she does so regularly. She does not worry about getting caught because she is "alone and old, too old to remarry." Espérance's narrative illustrates that she seeks to limit the ways in which the rules and regulations of the postgenocide government enter her life, while she attempts to make life more livable by cautiously criticizing government efforts to "modernize" her life:

> I only decide to speak out or not that [particular] day. I never make a clear statement that I disagree with [the policies of] this government. Sometimes I am too weak to go to *gacaca*; maybe I am sick. Other times, I am thinking in my head for days before about what I might say. Then I arrive [at *gacaca*], and I lose my strength to do it. Once militaries came up over the hill in a most unexpected way. We all froze. I testified that day, but what I said was mostly lies. I was too scared to tell the truth. Speaking lies is less risky than being truthful. The government likes to hear our lies because they think it's our truth.

When I do speak out, it is important to speak in ways that are not obviously wrong. I would never say "this policy is useless." That would get me in big trouble, probably in *cachot* [detention]. So, I plan how I will make my protest. If something feels wrong, I don't react. For example, if the prisoner is the relative [of a friend or a member of the cooperative], I will speak but in ways that make him look innocent, even if it really looks like he is not.

So when I get the chance, I talk about how hard we [peasants] work to survive. I mean, we are all survivors of the genocide. Even some former Hutu! I try to show how we are not lazy. I say, "I wake up early to harvest so we can come to *gacaca* on time." I say, "I work hard to produce enough to share with others." I once said, "I can't eat flowers, so why would I tear out my banana trees?" That one got me in trouble when [the local official] came to tell me that if I don't produce what is expected they will take my land, and then I will have to work for someone whose land is working for the nation. So I learned that it is important not to say too much. I just want to say that forced cultivation is not going to work. (Interview 2006)

Espérance's narrative demonstrates the subtleties in her act of everyday resistance. Nowhere does she openly criticize government policy. She understands that the associated risks are too high. Instead, she prudently makes her criticism in ways that express her discontent over the new land and agriculture policy. She prudently waits for the appropriate time to voice her discontent. Espérance assesses both her mood and the general atmosphere before speaking, and she considers other actors who will participate or observe the *gacaca* proceedings. She is also careful to speak when military observers are not present, as she appreciates the added difficulty that their presence brings. Espérance's everyday act of resistance demonstrates the hardships that most ordinary Rwandans experience as a result of the new rules and regulations that have been imposed since the 1994 genocide. It also illustrates the ways in which some ordinary Rwandans seek to strategically confront the postgenocide government.

Ordinary Rwandans like Espérance understand that local officials perceive their overstepping their scripted role as an attack on the government. The policy itself, as a mechanism of state power, is structured in such a way that it leaves nothing to chance. The task of local officials is to ensure the integrity of the policy, and ordinary Rwandans are expected to conform to its demands. Any action that ordinary Rwandans take to express their dissatisfaction with the policies of the postgenocide government may be perceived as criticism of the government, which limits individual options to resist. A focus on the everyday acts of resistance of Tutsi survivors also illustrates how the ordinary peasants that I consulted hardly believe in and support the policies of the government. Instead, they reveal the contours of the system of power that is the policy of

national unity and reconciliation to shape how individuals are forced to participate in state spaces like the *gacaca* courts, as well as the limitations of the policy
in actually commanding a meaningful belief in its ability to make the lives of
ordinary Rwandans more bearable since the genocide.

Conclusion

This chapter focused on the everyday acts of resistance of Tutsi survivors to
illustrate how the requirements of participating at *gacaca* represent a source of
insecurity and fear in their everyday lives. It also showed that some individuals,
notably Tutsi survivors, are able to express their dissatisfaction with the postgenocide regime and its policies by examining their everyday acts of resistance
before the *gacaca* courts. Specifically, the chapter demonstrated how the policy
of national unity and reconciliation seeks to eliminate individual expressions of
nonconformity to its demands. Instead of accepting wholesale the requirements of the policy, some ordinary peasants are creatively resisting its demands
through subtle and thoughtful acts of everyday resistance. The evidence was
largely drawn from the acts of resistance of Tutsi survivors, as they have the
greatest latitude to speak out while providing evidence against *génocidaires* during
the *gacaca* trials.

The chapter also illustrates the mixture of conformity and discipline that is
needed to successfully render an act of everyday resistance. Both Vianney and
Espérance understand the extent to which the *gacaca* courts represent a form
of state control in their everyday lives; they recognize the continuous threat
of sanction and modify their behavior accordingly. Their everyday acts of resistance are, as a matter of necessity, subtle and nonconfrontational. The goal is not
to overthrow the state or even to alter their participation at *gacaca*. Instead, they
seek to make their lives more sustainable in limiting their contact with local
officials. The decision-making process about whether to speak out at *gacaca* is
carefully strategized and cautiously crafted so as not to raise the suspicion of
local government authorities and government observers of the *gacaca* process.
Their everyday acts of resistance illustrate that the courts are not only a site of
national unity and reconciliation but also represent another mechanism that
helps the government maintain its grip on power. A focus on the everyday
acts of resistance of the ordinary Rwandans who participated in my research
also indicates the extent to which the demands of the policy conflict with the
aims of their daily lives—to live peacefully away from the watchful eye of local
officials who do the bidding of the state in the name of national unity and
reconciliation.

Conclusion

Explaining Systems of Power through Acts of Everyday Resistance

This book is a political ethnography of relations between state and society in postgenocide Rwanda. It challenges much of the conventional postgenocide literature, most of which focuses on the behavior and practices of urban elites, provides a top-down perspective on the sociopolitical climate in contemporary Rwanda, and treats the RPF regime as a unitary actor in its efforts to promote "one Rwanda for all Rwandans" in the name of national unity and reconciliation (introduction). It analyzes the policy of national unity and reconciliation and examines in detail the disciplinary mechanisms deployed by the RPF to generate compliance with its demands while seeking to eliminate possible expressions of nonconformity among Rwandans, elites and ordinary folk alike (chapters 3 and 4). It then analyzes the everyday acts of resistance of peasant people resident in southern Rwanda to demonstrate the extent to which state-led and top-down reconciliation processes of national unity and reconciliation are an oppressive form of state power in their everyday lives (chapters 5 and 6). Specifically, I employ the concept of everyday resistance to identify and analyze the system of state power that ordinary Rwandans navigate daily to show how individuals are positioned in relation to state power and how this positioning affects their life chances in the postgenocide order.

The methodology portrays the thirty-seven Rwandans who participated in the research as "knowers" of their own life stories, rather than building on existing portrayals of peasants as powerless and passive victims (chapters 1 and 2). Life history interviews form the backbone of the research material. I triangulate the evidence gathered through life history interviewing with the data gained through semistructured interviews with government elites, a detailed deconstruction of the structural and discursive elements of the policy of national unity and reconciliation along with careful analysis of its historical bases, and participant observation. The methodology allows for analysis of the postgenocide political order from the perspective of ordinary Rwandans who occupy the lowest positions in the country's socioeconomic hierarchy. The purpose is to privilege their locally situated knowledge by employing methodological tools that uncover, rather than presuppose, individuals' motivations and behaviors.

In focusing on the everyday interactions of ordinary peasant Rwandans with the policy of national unity and reconciliation, the research uncovers six key findings. First, the policy constitutes a system of state power that presents a self-serving version of history and manipulates the language of ethnicity to justify and maintain policies of exclusion in much the same way that previous regimes in Rwanda have done. According to the official version of Rwandan history found in the policy of national unity and reconciliation, ultimate blame for the 1994 genocide lies with Rwanda's colonial powers, which instituted divide-and-rule policies that made all Hutu hate all Tutsi. The policy aims to undo the effects of colonial rule in creating "one Rwanda for all Rwandans" (Office of the President 1999). The government exhorts Rwandans to no longer see themselves as Hutu, Tutsi, or Twa because ethnicity is a fiction that was created by Rwanda's colonizers. The policy asserts that for peace and security to prevail, an imagined and romanticized ethnic unity that Rwanda enjoyed prior to the arrival of the Europeans must be reasserted and taught to all Rwandans.

Careful analysis of the historical record finds that violence in Rwanda, whether that of the 1994 genocide or the 1959 social revolution or that which occurred during colonial times, is part of everyday life for many ordinary peasant Rwandans. However, it has not been driven by atavistic tensions between Hutu and Tutsi. Instead, history shows that the political elites have strategically manipulated ethnic identity to justify resorting to violence. Elites have consistently presented violence as the result of ethnic hatred, when in fact its organizers and sponsors have invoked an alleged age-old ethnic animosity to seize, gain, or consolidate political power. For most ordinary peasants, ethnicity actually plays only a minor role in their daily lives; instead, their everyday realities are shaped by their socioeconomic position. The tactics of ethnic control found in the policy of national unity and reconciliation differ from those of previous regimes in that they deemphasize rather than emphasize individual ethnic identities to justify the policy's policies of exclusion.

Second, the policy of national unity and reconciliation polices the boundaries of accepted public speech about the causes and consequences of the 1994 genocide in ways that reify and reinforce the hero status of the RPF in stopping it. Rwandans—elites and ordinary folk alike—can speak only of being "Rwandan" in state-sanctioned settings—for example, in *ingando* reeducation camps, at *gacaca* justice trials, and during genocide mourning week. And yet this reality is starkly contradicted by the fact that the roles played in state-sanctioned spaces and events are determined by ethnic status. There has been no official recognition of different lived experiences of the 1994 genocide beyond the assertion that only ethnic Tutsi were victims of violence during the genocide and only ethnic Hutu killed. The RPF also does not allow for public discussion of violence that individual Rwandans experienced before and after the genocide, particularly the violence they experienced at the hands of RPF soldiers.

Instead, the postgenocide government uses the apparatus of the state to ensure that ordinary Rwandans respect the rules of which individuals can speak about their experiences of the genocide and how they do so through its policy of national unity and reconciliation. From the perspective of many ordinary Rwandans, the official version of how the genocide happened does not recognize the continuum of everyday violence that Rwandans of all ethnicities experienced, albeit to varying degrees of intensity, before, during, and after the genocide. The research finds that the policy of national unity and reconciliation is a mechanism of state power that reinforces the power of the RPF rather than alleviating Rwandans' deep-rooted feelings of fear, anger, and despair as they struggle to rebuild their lives and reconcile with friends, neighbors, and, in some cases, family.

Third, in the name of national unity and reconciliation, the RPF continues to tighten its control over the sociopolitical landscape. Since taking power after effectively stopping the genocide in July 1994, the RPF has aggressively sought to consolidate its grip on state power. The RPF uses its version of how the genocide happened to exclude its political opponents, Hutu, Tutsi, and Twa alike, from education, higher-status jobs, and positions of responsibility in the bureaucracy of the state. All Rwandans, elites and ordinary folk alike, are careful about how and whether they speak about life since the genocide. The RPF considers unscripted comments to be suspect and interprets them as signs of disobedience. In this way, the power of the policy of national unity and reconciliation lies in its ability not only to orchestrate obedience but also to shape discussion about everyday life before, during, and after the genocide. For example, the policy of national unity and reconciliation has labeled adult male Hutu *génocidaires* (perpetrators) who are guilty of acts of genocide or who must be closely watched for evidence that they harbor genocidal ideologies. In identifying all adult male Hutu as potential *génocidaires*, the policy positions them as potential enemies of the state, which in turn leads to the dissemination of credible threats of punishment—such as loss of socioeconomic status, harassment, imprisonment, disappearance, or perhaps even death. In this way, all adult male Hutu become subjects of suspicion and second-class citizens seen as probable perpetrators.

Fourth, most ordinary folks resident in the south recognize that the policy of national unity and reconciliation goes against their interests as peasants who occupy the lowest positions in the socioeconomic hierarchy. They therefore seek to resist—subtly and indirectly—its many demands. For many ordinary peasants, the policy represents a double bind in that they consider the various mechanisms of the policy itself unjust and illegitimate as its aims do not accord with the exigencies of everyday rural life. For example, appointed and volunteer local officials at the sector and cell levels force them to enact reconciliation in state-sponsored spaces, such as at the *gacaca* courts or during national mourning week activities. Individuals who do not conform to the demands of the policy of national unity and reconciliation can be harassed, intimidated, imprisoned, disappeared, or even killed. Any action (or inaction) that leads some ordinary Rwandans, notably those known as *abasazi* ("foolish"), to step outside their scripted role is perceived as an attack on the policy of national unity and reconciliation and indeed as criticism of the government. Many ordinary peasants understand that the policy is designed to create the appearance of peace and security in ways that reinforce the authority of local officials, notably RPF-appointed ones. Most of the thirty-seven peasants with whom I spoke while conducting life history interviews and many of the more than four hundred ordinary Rwandans I met through participant observation consider the directives of the policy to be a burden in their daily efforts to rebuild their lives and livelihoods in dignified and meaningful ways.

Fifth, many ordinary Rwandans see the ways in which the local authorities implement the policy as an affront to their everyday life since the genocide. This marks a dramatic departure from the interactions of ordinary people with the local officials who mediated their relations with the central government authorities before the genocide. The Habyarimana regime (1973–94) enjoyed considerable support among ordinary peasant Rwandans—Hutu and Tutsi alike—who felt that its development policies served their interests, which in turn gave the regime greater legitimacy at the grass roots than the policy of national unity and reconciliation currently enjoys. This is not to suggest that there was no rural discontent under Habyarimana (cf. C. Newbury 1992). It is only to highlight that the policy of national unity and reconciliation is a different form of state power because of the role of appointed local officials in implementing its many demands. The implementation process of the various aspects of the policy and the strategic ways in which peasant Rwandans seek to resist its demands demonstrate more than its unpopularity and illegitimacy among rural people. They also highlight many ordinary Rwandans' resentment of the RPF regime's lack of concern with protecting rural livelihoods. Thus, for many ordinary Rwandans, the policy of national unity and reconciliation is the product of an illegitimate regime, an opinion that contrasts considerably with elite claims that Rwanda is a "nation rehabilitated" and one that has "put the legacy of the genocide behind it" (ORTPN 2004, 4).

Sixth, many ordinary Rwandans attribute the illegitimacy of the policy of national unity and reconciliation to the mediating role that appointed local officials play in its implementation. Before the genocide, everyday interactions with local officials were not necessarily positive. In many ways the relationship between ordinary Rwandans at the lower levels of the socioeconomic hierarchy and their local officials was as coercive as it has been since the genocide. What is different is that the appointed local officials' unpopularity among ordinary Rwandans before the genocide was mitigated by the latter's overall positive opinion of the Habyarimana regime and its development policies; the local representatives of the state were unpopular, but the center was generally quite popular among Hutu and Tutsi alike. This may appear counterintuitive, given the authoritarian tendencies of the regime and the eventual descent to genocide. Ironically, the Habyarimana regime's popular legitimacy among the grass roots actually helped make the genocide possible. Ordinary Hutu killed their Tutsi friends, neighbors, and family members because the order to kill came from local government officials whose authority was backed by the coercive power of the state that was rooted in Habyarimana's credibility in the countryside.

Under the policy of national unity and reconciliation, appointed and volunteer local officials are the intermediaries responsible for implementing the policies of a largely unpopular and coercive central authority, the RPF. The ordinary Rwandans resident in southern Rwanda whom I consulted do not view the RPF regime as a possible source of remedy for their grievances against the excesses of elected local officials and appointed technocrats, who are responsible to Kigali for effectively and efficiently implementing government policy through *imihigo* (performance) contracts and other imposed top-down measures. This finding also challenges the RPF's assertions, seconded by casual foreign observers such as Crisafulli and Redmond (2012) and Kinzer (2008), that its postgenocide policies enjoy broad-based grassroots support. That the policy of national unity and reconciliation provides few benefits to most poor peasant Rwandans explains both the unpopularity of appointed local officials and the illegitimacy of the policy of national unity and reconciliation among rural people. The superficial appearance of grassroots support also shapes the widely held perception among Western observers and Rwandan elites alike that ordinary peasant Rwandans believe in and therefore voluntarily comply with the demands of the policy. A focus on the everyday acts of resistance of ordinary Rwandans challenges the idea they are obedient and illustrates how they hardly believe in the dictates of the policy of national unity and reconciliation. Quite the opposite—their obedience is tactical. Where the policy forces ordinary Rwandans to live within its official truths, they confront it in ways that seek to restore their personal dignity while subtly attempting to live their own truth of what they experienced before, during, and after the genocide.

Taken together, these findings illuminate the system of state power that structures ordinary peasant Rwandans' everyday lives since the genocide. The analysis demonstrates how Rwanda's rigid sociopolitical hierarchy limits individual opportunities to reconcile according to their position in the social structure and how the policy of national unity further limits their ability and willingness to reconcile with neighbors and friends. Many ordinary peasants perceive the demands of the policy as detrimental to their interests, and this shapes their decision to resist in an attempt to make their lives more sustainable and to restore their sense of dignity. For the ordinary Rwandans I consulted, the policy of national unity and reconciliation forms the panorama of their everyday life, meaning that it constantly and consistently reminds them what they must do. The ordinary Rwandans who participated in the research understand that their appointed local authorities, most of whom have no sense of the impact of the legacy of the genocide on their everyday lives, do the bidding of the RPF regime in the name of national unity and reconciliation.

The remainder of this chapter first summarizes what the everyday acts of resistance of ordinary Rwandans to the policy of national unity and reconciliation say about systems of state power. It then underlines the methodological importance of bringing in the individual lived experiences of ordinary peasant people. Finally, it proposes a few areas for further research that are relevant for the study of politics in Rwanda and elsewhere in Africa.

Understanding and Explaining Systems of Power through Acts of Everyday Resistance

Questions about why and when individuals comply have been central to the study of politics since Max Weber first posed the question (Weber 1946, 78–79). The answer is generally drawn from Weber's ideal types of political authority (traditional, charismatic, and legal-rational). People obey for one of three reasons: (1) because they believe in the values, norms, and standards by which a particular regime operates; (2) because they believe it is in their material interest to do so; or (3) because they fear the coercive threats and sanctions they will face for noncompliance. Though these can be valid explanations for why individuals comply, they do not capture the complete picture. Such approaches to compliance rarely consider the ways that individuals subjected to dominant power resist its demands. When they do, it is to understand and explain moments of significant upheaval like rebellions and revolutions, such as the 1994 genocide and the 1959 social revolution in Rwanda. However, moments of upheaval do not contrast as strongly with "normal" times as many social scientists have assumed. Explanations about when and why individuals comply during periods of so-called normalcy fail to provide adequate explanations for why individuals sometimes do not comply when the situation appears "normal," as it currently does in Rwanda under the policy of national unity and reconciliation. In states characterized by authoritarian forms of domination, "normal" times can involve the intensification of older forms of oppression and the creation of new forms, which can in turn create the conditions for a return to political upheaval. It is therefore important that social scientists identify and consider the everyday practices of resistance of individuals subject to coercive forms of power, such as the practices of direct and indirect control found in the policy of national unity and reconciliation.

Neither domination nor resistance is autonomous. The two are entangled, so it becomes difficult to analyze one without discussing the effects of the other at the level of the individual (Scott 1985; Young 2004). An analysis of everyday periods of "normalcy" through an examination of the everyday acts of resistance of individuals subject to dominant forms of power identifies sites of struggle and other points of weakness in the power of the state by pointing to areas where the demands of the state system conflict with the aims of everyday life. This is the primary contribution of this book; it provides a bottom-up analysis of state power from the perspective of those subject to the state's many demands. In this way, the research adds to the resistance literature in focusing on individual acts of everyday resistance as a means of understanding how the various practices of the state are manifested in people's everyday lives. This is important since the way in which politics affects and is "felt" in the daily lives of people is almost completely absent in the academic literature. When it is discussed, it is presented through the eyes of local elites. Such an approach also illustrates the analytical utility of the concept of everyday resistance to further our understanding of the system of power in which individuals are enmeshed and of the resultant social and political tensions and inequalities.

The everyday acts of resistance of ordinary peasants to the coercive mechanisms of the policy of national unity signal more than their individual agency and the strategic nature of their compliance. The book develops the concept of everyday resistance to point analysts toward the multiple and overlapping structures of power that ordinary people confront in their daily lives. Tracing the subtle and indirect resistance of ordinary Rwandans resident in the south from a variety of subject positions to the demands of the policy of national unity and reconciliation provides more than a bottom-up approach to disentangling the various practices of domination and the myriad forms of subjugation in postgenocide Rwanda. It also facilitates analysis of the ways in which particular forms of subjugation produce the appearance of individual compliance. A careful look at what may appear to be trivial matters—remaining silent, laughing at the wrong moment, or playing dumb—can provide important insights into the dynamics of power in contexts of coercive state authority.

A focus on the everyday acts of resistance of some ordinary Rwandans illustrates how the postgenocide state tries to depoliticize peasant people by orchestrating public performances but, most important, closes off the possibility for individuals to join together to organize politically. Because ordinary Rwandans have no opportunity to express themselves politically in public, their responses to the demands of the policy of national unity and reconciliation show how they tactically conceal or reveal their political opinions. When they express no opinion and therefore appear compliant, many casual observers conclude that ordinary people believe in and support the regime. Their everyday acts of resistance illustrate the opposite. Individuals simulate greater loyalty than they actually feel as a means of coping. A closer analysis of their presumed compliance shows that the proscriptions and limitations of everyday life may serve to intensify and enhance their ability and willingness to engage politically. Thus, even where compliance is coercive and the opportunities for dissent are minimal, peasants continue to express their politics through their acts of resistance. Identification of the individual acts of everyday resistance of the most marginal members of a highly stratified society such as postgenocide Rwanda points analysts toward areas where political life can quickly descend from the appearance of compliance to open protest and perhaps to revolution or even genocide.

Indeed, the power of any regime, including the RPF, is always partial. Studying postgenocide Rwanda from the perspective of those subject to its power reveals the paradoxical effects of the mechanisms of social control found in the policy of national unity and reconciliation. On one hand, the policy invites the political engagement of Rwandans, elite and ordinary folk alike, that it seeks to control in forcing them to participate in state-sanctioned activities of national unity and reconciliation. On the other hand, the methods of resistance available to most ordinary Rwandans, especially if they are subtle and indirect, are by themselves incapable of significantly altering the postgenocide sociopoliti-cal order. Nonetheless, these acts of resistance are important because they point to the hidden spheres of dissatisfaction of individuals who have no opportunity to publically express their politics. Their practices of resistance are indicators of more than individual dissatisfaction with a particular regime. They also provide the foundation for creating alternative spaces for political actions and ideas. It is difficult to predict if and when these individual acts will cascade into a collec-tive movement that may lead to peaceful contestation of power or culminate in riot or rebellion. But they clearly demonstrate the *potential* for such upheavals.

The everyday acts of resistance of ordinary people could be called pre-political, since they are not overtly directed at the state system. Still, these acts made in the face of a strong state power are more than elementary signs of indi-viduals seeking to live their daily lives as best they can; they are indicators of emergent confrontation with the state system in which those who are most marginal in society express their dissatisfaction with the state and its agents.

This book has focused on southern Rwanda, but the approach used here is also relevant for the study of politics in other regions of the country, as well as in other parts of Africa and in other societies where domination is common-place. The everyday acts of resistance show how individuals who are subject to oppressive forms of state power, even the most marginal, work to resist the efforts of the state to make them comply with its demands. In this way, everyday acts of resistance act as indicators of discontent and enable analysts to recognize and examine the importance of pre-political actions as indicative of the locations where collective action for political change may emerge. For, as Norton (2004, 41) notes, because political change often comes from those who are most mar-ginal and on the periphery of state power, it is important to "recognize the power of liminal, or marginal, groups. . . . Because they stand on the boundaries of identity they are often central to debates over those boundaries."

Researching Resistance

From the outset, my research has sought to understand the individual experi-ences of a cross section of ordinary Rwandans resident in the south before, during, and after the genocide. Also shaping my analysis is my own direct experiences of the power of the state in stopping my research and placing me in a "reeducation" camp. This firsthand experience of the tactics used by the post-genocide state to induce compliance informs this research. Some readers may contend that I lack the critical distance necessary for the analysis of the complex interactions between some ordinary peasant Rwandans and the demands of the policy of national unity and reconciliation and that my analysis is unduly biased against the current regime. In order to maintain the integrity of the research, I have combined my analysis of the oral data gained through field-work and the insights of participation observation on the daily rhythms of life in postgenocide Rwanda with careful historical and empirical analysis to under-stand and explain the ways that ordinary Rwandans have attempted to shape their lives since the genocide. Throughout the research process, my purpose remained to bring ordinary people into the frame of analysis in order to provide a nuanced view of contemporary Rwanda that moves academic and policy discussions beyond the congratulatory writings of some observers about the hero status of the RPF as the saviors and moral guardians of the "new" Rwanda (e.g., Gourevitch 1998; Kinzer 2008).

My findings challenge the commonly held beliefs, assertions, and assump-tions about rural life during and after the 1994 genocide and more specifically about ordinary peasant people as supposedly powerless and passive—apolitical actors who willingly obey the directives of their political leaders. Ethnographic vignettes and excerpts from the life history interviews that I conducted with those Rwandans who participated in my research add much-needed texture to our understanding of the policy of national unity and reconciliation from the ground up, rather than privileging a state-centered and top-down perspective. The lived experiences of some ordinary Rwandans before, during, and after the genocide also provide important insights on why it is important to look beyond surface characterizations of "normalcy" that uphold and reinforce the power of political elites. This approach also disputes the rhetoric of the RPF regime and shows how they are using the apparatus of the state for their own benefit in the name of national unity and reconciliation.

More narrowly, the focus on the everyday acts of resistance of individuals contributes to a greater understanding of the power relations in which these ordinary Rwandans are enmeshed. This approach is useful to understand and explain the evolving relationship between state structures and socioeconomic inequality that develops in myriad forms in systems where domination is perva-sive. It is also an important approach in terms of breaking down the crude analytical binary of "elite" and "peasant masses" to accentuate the layering effects of one's location in the social hierarchy, as well as one's regional location, to analyze the disciplinary power of the state from the perspective of those subject to it. It is also an approach that could be fruitfully employed in other regions of Rwanda, notably the northwest of the country, where the government has focused its energies on reeducating Hutu accused of harboring a genocidal ideology. My research in southern Rwanda shows that many ordinary Hutu killed for reasons other than ethnic hatred. Understanding the individual reasons that ordinary Hutu killed in different regions of the country would be invaluable to postgenocide processes of justice and reconciliation as it would allow the government to punish individuals for crimes they actually committed, rather that ones they are perceived to have carried out.

The everyday acts of resistance of some ordinary Rwandans to the policy of national unity and reconciliation reveal more than the abyss between the aims of the policy and those of daily life. It also provides for a bottom-up examination of the practices of the system of state power and control under which many ordinary Rwandans live their daily lives to reveal how social structures are constituted through a variety of contradictory and contested processes rather than as a seamless, functional whole. The act of exposing and explaining the politics of ordinary people through their acts of everyday resistance in the face of a strong and centralized state power illustrates that the assumptions that academics, policymakers, and journalists often make about the politics of ordinary people are ill founded or simply incorrect. Ordinary people are political beings with the capacity to act or not, to resist or not, on the basis of their own sophisticated understandings of the social and political context in which they find themselves. Bringing ordinary peasant people into the picture as individual actors rather than as collective victims is "the surest way to avoid the lethal stereotypes that hinder our understanding of complex situations and produce simplifications that contribute to more injustice" (de Lame 2005b, 133).

The rich narratives of the everyday lives of a cross section of peasant Rwandans living under the system of power that constitutes the RPF regime highlight the tenuousness of the political situation in Rwanda at the time of writing, in late 2012. A bottom-up reading of relations between state and society in contemporary Rwanda suggests that the same social, political, and economic trends that contributed to the 1994 genocide are reemerging. Pervasive and institutionalized racism is as commonplace as it was before the genocide. The unresolved consequences of past episodes of violence and the resultant festering refugee problem are exacerbated by continued grinding poverty, and the despair and hopelessness felt by the majority of Rwandans remain virtually unchanged. The manifest unwillingness of the government to promote genuine improvement in the quality of life for the vast majority of Rwanda's poor is nearly unchanged, despite the "pro-poor" rhetoric and apparent policy successes of the RPF in key areas like health, education, and women's rights. Top-down policies shaped both pre- and postgenocide development policies, and they are at the root of the condescending and authoritarian treatment of the population by successive governments; the RPF regime operates no differently from its predecessors. One key difference is that today there is no civil war like the one between the then government and the then rebel RPF that made the planning and implementation of the genocide a viable option (analyzed in chapter 3). At the moment, there is no external or internal threat to the iron grip of the RPF on

Rwandan politics, despite a vocal opposition operating from the United States and Europe and a reconfiguration of donor relations in wake of a damning UN report documenting RPF human rights abuses and war crimes in the Democratic Republic of the Congo (UNOHCHR 2010; UN GOE 2012).

Areas of Future Research

Through analysis of the everyday acts of resistance of a select group of ordinary peasant Rwandans in 2006, we see that the direct and indirect practices of control and manipulation of the policy of national unity and reconciliation are similar to those used by previous regimes. We also see how the RPF regime has orchestrated the appearance of popular legitimacy and broad-based support for its policy through these mechanisms of control. My research has focused on the everyday acts of resistance of individuals subject to state power to illustrate their usefulness for understanding relations between state and society in Rwanda. The book opens up avenues for future research both in Rwanda and in other societies where layered domination is commonplace and legitimated through practices of coercive compliance. This approach can be applied, for example, in a variety of states across Africa where postconflict reconciliation policies have been instituted following violent conflict to understand and explain the extent to which such policies represent an illegitimate and dominant system of power in the lives of ordinary peasant people.

Fruitful avenues of future research include analysis of postconflict peace and reconciliation policies of countries such as Kenya, South Africa, and Zimbabwe, where the repression of the political opposition has potentially masked deep-rooted resentments that could lead to renewed political violence. An analysis of reconciliation practices where peace is brokered through elite power-sharing pacts and reconciliation policies are implemented from the top down can provide useful and important insights into the legitimacy of such policies from the perspective of the peasantry. A study of whether and how ordinary peasants practice everyday acts of resistance to top-down processes of reconciliation can open up new ways of understanding how these policies play out and are felt in peasants' everyday lives. It also facilitates the identification of the overlapping and intersecting forms of subjugation faced by individuals who are subject to the demands of postconflict reconciliation policies and what this could mean for the stability of state power in countries emerging from political conflict.

Another useful area of future study is to focus on the everyday politics of ordinary people, rural peasant and urban dweller alike. Analysis of the politics of ordinary people addresses an important gap in our understanding of relations between state and society in Africa, as most political science research tends to focus on large-scale structures, macro processes, epochal events, major policies, and "important" people. Rather than taking "the state" as a point of departure, a focus on the effects of state power on the everyday lives of rural people points to a recognition of multiple actors, agencies, organizations, and levels that defies straightforward analysis. For example, research into the practices of local officials is necessary, as it is through these individuals that the majority of rural poor come into contact with "the state" and where their images of the state are forged. More research is needed on the role of local officials, appointed and volunteer alike, in the promotion and enforcement of state policies, since they are the frontline intermediaries between ordinary folk and their central government bosses. Such research would challenge stereotypical portrayals by the Western media and policymakers of African regimes as monolithic entities. It would also buoy the work of Africanist scholars who have long recognized that the apparatus of the state is far from monolithic. Portrayals of African states as monolithic hardly reflect the nuanced interrelationships between individuals and the state apparatus itself, within and across different spatial levels, or the dynamics that govern such interactions. A focus on the politics of ordinary people can stretch beyond the boundaries of sub-Saharan Africa to allow for comparisons with countries in Eastern Europe, Latin America, and Asia.

A final area of future research concerns the analysis of postconflict reconciliation policies, such as Rwanda's policy of national unity and reconciliation, from the perspective of other sets of actors living in southern Rwanda as well as in other regions of the country whose lived experiences with state power are also missing from our analyses of the state. An analytical focus on how state power plays out in the lives of, for example, the middle class, youth, or women can further disaggregate social science conceptualizations of the state in questioning the conditions under which it operates as a cohesive and unitary whole. Such an approach points to the importance of including in our analyses the multiple patterns, processes, political hierarchies, socioeconomic strata, and institutions of state power that shape the lives of individuals subject to its power. A bottom-up approach like the one used in this study, combining theoretical inquiry with historical research and the local-level perspectives of thirty-seven ordinary Rwandans at the bottom of the socioeconomic hierarchy, allows for a look behind the rhetoric of elite claims of Rwanda as a "nation rehabilitated" and permits us to focus instead on how elites use state power, to what ends, to whose benefit, and with what effect for future peace and security.

Appendix

Profiles
of Rwandan Life History Participants

Destitute (*Abatindi*) Rwandans

Augustin (b. 1952) is a Hutu widower who was released from prison after telling his truth about what he did during the 1994 genocide. "Oh yes," he says, "I killed. I feared being killed [by other Hutu], so I killed. I did it after my [Tutsi] wife died so there would be someone to take care of our children." He graduated from an *ingando* reeducation camp in late 2005. Augustin rents land from a wealthy Tutsi who returned to Rwanda in 1995. "It is not so bad in terms of production because I am alone now; there is no one left to care for or to take care of me." He thinks the policy of national unity and reconciliation is a good idea if "it stops another event like the killing [of 1994]. At least there is some peace under this government."

Béatha (b. 1975) is a Hutu widow with nine children to care for, two of her own and seven orphans. She lost her youngest child to disease in the refugee camps in Zaïre. "You cannot imagine how hard it is. I can't mourn for my people and I can't care for the ones I have. Since the government reassigned land, it is very difficult to get enough to survive, let alone live." She hopes that the policy of national unity and reconciliation will provide peace but wonders, "Is it really peace if I can't take care of my kids?"

Gaston (b. 1972) is a released Hutu prisoner who has never been married, a source of shame for him. He graduated from *ingando* in 2004 but feels he will "never be able to reconcile with his neighbors" because they do not accept him "as someone who is innocent." The postgenocide government imprisoned him in 1998 upon his forced return from the refugee camps in Zaïre. He was released for lack of evidence in 2001.

Jeanne (b. 1959) is a Tutsi widow whose Hutu husband died in 1996 of disease in the refugee camps in Zaïre. She lives with three of her five children, as her two oldest sons died in late 1994, after the genocide officially ended. She works part-time as a seamstress and is able to barter with friends and neighbors for food and shelter. "I am too old and too broken to work the fields, but I have arrangements that seem to be working out well enough." She does not think unity and reconciliation are possible

197

among Rwandans who lived through the genocide: "We have seen too much to ever recover."

Joseph B. (b. 1980) is a Hutu man who says he did not kill during the genocide but that he did join "a squad" so that the local official in his community would "think I was part of the plan." "I was very young [fourteen years old], so I got food and water for the Interahamwe. I went to prison for this." He was released after *ingando* in 2002. He was able to find his five brothers and younger sister, all of whom survived the genocide after fleeing into the camps in Zaïre. His parents both died in "the events." He would like to reconcile with his neighbors so that Rwanda "doesn't experience any more storms like the genocide."

Joseph N. (b. 1975) is a Tutsi widower who is the only member of his immediate family to have survived the 1994 genocide. "When the killings started, my father told us it was a food riot, so we didn't hide because we had the possibility for a good harvest and wanted to protect our stocks." He has remarried since the genocide; his wife is another [Tutsi] survivor, and they had two children. Joseph has lost land since the genocide as the government "took away some" of his plot and "gave it to a Hutu in the name of national unity." Providing enough for his family's daily needs is his constant preoccupation. He lost one child to malaria, and the other is weak from malnutrition.

Joseph U. (b. 1962) is a Hutu man who was found innocent at a *gacaca* session in April 2006. "Yes, I killed, but I told my truth, and now I am free [after twelve years in prison]." He graduated from *ingando* and returned to his hill to find that his wife had remarried. He has lost most of his land to his ex-wife's new husband ("a former Tutsi!") and fears there will be violence again in Rwanda. "You cannot promise to reeducate a man then leave him to rot. That is not peace. That is not reconciliation."

Judith (b. 1961) is a Hutu widow. "My husband was a Tutsi and was among the first to die when the genocide started." She has seven children, three of her own and four whose parents were killed in 1995 at the Kibeho camp for internally displaced persons, located in southwestern Rwanda. She thinks national unity and reconciliation are not possible because the "government forces it upon us through officials that didn't even grow up in Rwanda. How do they know what is best? They don't even know how to plant or grow [crops], but they tell us how to work our land."

Marie Claire (b. 1970) is a Hutu widow who considers herself a survivor "even though the new government has taken that away from me." "Soldiers" killed her first husband, a Hutu, in 1996 in the Kibeho camp. She married a Tutsi man in 2003 and has been able to get some support as a survivor of the genocide since the marriage. She hopes the postgenocide government can promote national unity and reconciliation but is not sure that "they [the new local officials] understand what peasants like us need."

Martin (b. 1959) is a Tutsi man who survived, with his immediate family, by hiding "deep in the forest." His life has been "especially hard" since the genocide because neighbors and friends wonder what he must have done or whom he worked with to have survived along with his entire family. He says, "I learned after the genocide that talking is no good if others are not able to listen." For Martin, the policy of national unity and reconciliation is just a way for "the government to keep its power. Local officials tell us how to reconcile and we do it. What else can a [poor peasant] like me do? I agree but only because it is safer than disagreeing!"

Olive (b. 1957) is a Hutu woman who lost most of her immediate family during the genocide. "Only three of us survived; all the children starved to death or got diseases in the
camps [in Zaïre]." She lives with her husband, although "he is traumatized and it is
like having another child in the house." She doubts reconciliation is possible because
"so many RPF soldiers killed us [Hutu]. They say forgive and forget, but really is that
possible after so much has happened [in 1994] and things have not yet improved?"

Pacifique (b. 1992) is a Tutsi girl who hid in a pit latrine for two months until the genocide
ended. Both of her parents died during the genocide. She is responsible for nine
other children under the age of twelve, all of whom are orphans of the genocide. Of
the policy of national unity and reconciliation she says, "If I thought reconciliation
was possible, I would work for it. But I can't feed these kids . . . how can you reconcile
if you are hungry day in and day out?"

Scholastique (b. 1952) is a Hutu woman who was released from prison in 2006 for lack of
evidence. She lost her Hutu husband and children during the genocide and another
three children in the Kibeho camp and "feels dead inside ever since." She does not
believe reconciliation is possible because "the soldiers of this new government killed,
but we are not allowed to talk about that."

Séraphine (b. 1910, d. 2008) is the grandmother of *Prosper* (see later entry), another Twa
participant. She has lost family members, friends, and neighbors to ethnic violence
since the Social Revolution in 1959. "I have seen a lot in my years, but nothing as
dramatic as the [1994 genocide] where people went mad, killing everyone around
them." She has lived alone since 1989, when her third husband died of natural
causes. Of the policy of national unity and reconciliation she says, "Of course I have
heard of it. They [the government] promote it everywhere. Rwanda is a place with
many old and unresolved issues; forcing Rwandans to reconcile is not going to
work." She died of natural causes in October 2008.

Tharcisse (b. 1967) is a Hutu man who was released from prison in 2003. He was not
accused of acts of genocide in his home community until 2001 "by neighbors who
said I killed. I didn't. I fled like everyone else. It was soldiers who killed, and we
[Hutu] tried to avoid getting swept up by them!" He is a widower, having lost his
wife and three children during the flight into the camps in Zaïre. He will never remarry because "the only way forward is to marry a Tutsi, and "not one of these
survivors want me since I spent time in prison." He does not believe that "national
unity and reconciliation is designed for Hutu; it is now a Tutsi government so former
Hutu like me must wait until my people have power again."

Théogène (b. 1957) is a Twa man who saved "at least six Tutsi during the events [the 1994
genocide]." He considers himself a "hero, but those Tutsi don't even acknowledge
me when I pass them in the street." He thinks that the policy of national unity and
reconciliation is a good idea but that it "has to allow everyone to participate and
benefit, not just [Tutsi] survivors."

Trésor (b. 1990) is a Tutsi boy who was separated from his mother during the flight into
the refugee camps in Tanzania. He lives with his aunt, the only remaining adult in
his immediate family. He sold gum, matches, cigarettes, and other sundry items to
supplement his family's income until the government mandated in 2006 that all
businesses have to sell in state-sponsored markets. He is unsure about the utility of
the policy of national unity and reconciliation "because no matter what, I will never
see my mother again."

Poor (*Abakene*) Rwandans

Aimable (b. 1930, d. 2010) is a Tutsi man who survived the genocide by providing food and shelter to the leaders of the killing squads in his community. "I was so fearful and since I am an old man, they said they would spare [my life] if I helped them." He is not convinced that the policy of national unity and reconciliation is going "to create peace and security like the new government says. We [peasants] were hungry before the war and we are hungry now. What is changed is that we can no longer solve our problems in our own way. The government says reconcile and that is said to be enough to bring peace." Aimable died of natural causes in 2010.

Alice (b. 1977) is a Tutsi widow who lost her husband and two of her five children during the genocide on the trek to Zaïre. "One kid died of malaria, and the other was just too weak to keep walking. We left him behind to save ourselves. I don't know what happened to him, but we hoped that someone would save him. Three days later my husband was killed by the militias. I somehow escaped." She hopes that the policy of national unity and reconciliation can "bring Rwandans together. It will be good to know peace. Of course there is a lot of opposition to some of these new ideas about unity, but hopefully this government can help those Hutu see the light."

Aurelia (b. 1967) is a Hutu widow who lost her entire family during the genocide. "Some tried to resist the call to kill, but they just got killed. They are buried [at Murambi memorial], but I cannot go there to visit their remains because the [official] says I have to pay to visit [the memorial center]!" She is skeptical about the prospects for lasting peace in Rwanda and says that the policy of national unity and reconciliation is "for Tutsi. They are the survivors, and they get help from this new government. This is how politics works in Rwanda. Now that Tutsi are in power, they help Tutsi."

Emmanuel (b. 1979) is a Tutsi man who survived the genocide by hiding in the drop ceiling of the local government offices. He has little faith in the government's policy of national unity, saying it is something for "elites while poor people starve."

Ephrem (b. 1974) is a Hutu man who was released from prison in 2001 for lack of evidence. He did not participate in the *ingando* reeducation camps, although he wanted to receive "the training so I would know how to participate in these activities for national unity and reconciliation." He feels isolated in his community since he was released from prison. "My wife left me and married a Tutsi because she thought I would never get out of prison. That Tutsi took my wife and my land. What can I do now but keep quiet until the government changes back to a Hutu one?"

Espérance (b. 1969) is a Tutsi widow who survived by "running every time we heard the killers were coming." She eventually ended up in the Kibeho camp and witnessed the RPF attacks on civilians there. "Many died, but the army of the other side [the RPF] sent their men into the camps to tell us to keep quiet. I told them I was a Tutsi, and they took me to a hospital just outside Butare. There I worked as a nurse's assistant until 1998." She is sole survivor in her immediate family and tries to avoid "getting forced to go to activities that the government says are for unity and reconciliation." She says, "Reconciliation is for people who can afford to eat."

Esther (b. 1966) is a Tutsi widow who survived by "[sexually] servicing the killers." As a result, she is "deeply traumatized" and has been outcast by her immediate family, who do not want the shame of having "a damaged woman" in their midst. She hopes the message of national unity and reconciliation "takes root" in the hearts of Rwandans so that "storms like the genocide" never happen again.

Florence (b. 1960) is a Hutu widow who successfully hid Tutsi friends and neighbors during the genocide. "I fought them [the killing squads] and was able to save at least ten people!" She was raped "many times" but "could not give up because I knew they would die if I told them where those [Tutsi] were hiding." She does not believe that the policy of national unity and reconciliation is "doing anything good for Rwanda because some of us are not even considered human because of what happened during the events. If only we could get recognition [from the government] as victims of genocide, perhaps things would get better."

Janvier (b. 1975) is a Tutsi man who survived the genocide because he had a severe case of malaria when the killers came to his community. "I was slumped on the floor with high fever and fits, so they left me as dead. I saw them kill the rest of my family; when I woke up, I found everyone cut up." He works the fields of more prosperous landowners for his daily needs. He thinks it is only a matter of time before Rwandans "start again with the violence" since "it is just part of our culture." He thinks the policy of national unity and reconciliation is a good idea but that it "probably won't work because who can trust anyone nowadays?"

Joseph M. (b. 1945) is a Tutsi man who survived the genocide by cheering on the killing and "appearing to support their cause. Because you can't know who is Tutsi or Hutu, it was easy for me to join." He doesn't think the creation of a national identity of "being Rwandan" will end violence like the genocide. "Really, issues like national identity and reconciliation are for government officials to fight over, not us peasants who just want to eat every day and send our kids to school."

Prosper (b. 1950) is a Twa widower and is the grandson of *Séraphine* (discussed earlier). He was born into a prominent Tutsi family, and his father was a hill chief under the Belgian administration. "When violence came in 1959, I was a young boy. My parents and everyone around me died. *Maman* took us [Prosper and his younger brother] as her own children; she raised us really. I became a Twa over time because she raised us that way. I look like a Tutsi, but my heart is Twa." He is skeptical about the prospects for national unity and reconciliation since the policy "works for [only] some of us. If you are Tutsi survivor, you can benefit. As a Twa, nothing has come out of it for my people and me. We are not even allowed to say we are Twa!"

Vianney (b. 1981) is a Tutsi man who hid in the marshes during the genocide. He has never married and has no kids. "Since the genocide, I am basically alone. My parents died, and I don't know where my brothers and sister are. I suppose they are dead, but they could be alive. No one has offered the truth about how they died." On the policy of national unity and reconciliation, he says, "If only they [those accused of genocide] would tell their truth, then we survivors could know peace and security. I won't rest until the truth has been shared. I just hope this government can bring peace."

Salaried Poor (*Abakene bifashije*) Rwandans

Didier (b. 1959) is a Tutsi man who survived the genocide by hiding in the chicken coop of a Hutu friend who also killed most of his family. He does not have any of his own land because the new government took over his family home "after the war." Because he works as a cook in a restaurant and earns FRw 18,000 (US$39) a month, he is not eligible for subsidies for school fees or medical care despite his volunteer position as a *gacaca* judge. Of the policy of national unity and reconciliation, he says there are "too many problems in this country; they talk about unity and reconciliation, but I don't see it in the hills."

Thomas (b. 1962) is a Hutu man. At the time of the genocide, he was married to a Tutsi woman with four children. His wife and three of his children died. He remarried in 2005, again to a woman who identifies as a Tutsi. He did not flee to the refugee camps in Zaïre. Instead, he stayed behind in the Opération Turquoise zone and later spent time in the Kibeho camp. He presently works as a taxi-moto driver, and has an average monthly income of FRw 7,000 (US$15). He thinks national unity and reconciliation are possible if "the government stops telling us to tell our truth. We [Hutu and Tutsi] need time to heal."

Rwandan Prisoners

Cécile (b. 1961) is a Hutu woman who confessed to her crimes of genocide and was released under the 1996 confession and guilty-plea procedure. She was accused of genocide a second time in 2002 when the *gacaca* courts were in their evidence-gathering phase. She returned to prison in 2004. She says, "National unity and reconciliation is a joke. I told my truth only to have a [Tutsi] survivor say I didn't tell my whole truth. I confessed to what I did, but now I am in prison for another twenty-seven years. And they say Hutu and Tutsi can live together again? Not if Hutu like me can go to prison for no good reason."

Chantal (b. 1971) is a Hutu woman who went to prison in 2005 for crimes she says she did not commit. "I am here for twenty-five years. Who will raise my kids? My husband is also in prison. I don't even know where those kids are or where they might be. I am sad all the time. Reconciliation will never happen for me because I am an old woman and will die in this prison."

Félicien (b. 1973) is an imprisoned Hutu man. He confessed to his crimes in 1998 and received a fifteen-year sentence. "Yes, I killed. I killed because it was the law at the time. I lost most of my relatives, which means life is extra hard here [in prison] because I have no one to come bring me food or really tell me news about how things are under this new government."

Jean-Bosco (b. 1944) is a Hutu man who worked as a medical doctor before and after the genocide. "I took care of Tutsi and Hutu. It didn't matter, we just worked on those that were injured and who could be saved. I was put in prison in 2005. But, honestly, if I was guilty, wouldn't I have run like everyone else? No. I chose to work in the Butare hospital to help save lives. Prosecuting Hutu for acts of genocide is a weapon of this government to keep itself in power."

Jean-Claude (b. 1967) is Hutu man who was released from prison in 2004 after serving ten years in prison for crimes of genocide. He returned to prison in 2005 when neighbors accused him before the *gacaca* courts of killing the family of a Tutsi neighbor. He is now in prison on a thirty-year sentence and feels that the policy of national unity and reconciliation is "a form of genocide against Hutu."

Valentina (b. 1954) is a Hutu woman who left Rwanda in May 1995 with her husband and their two young children after the RPA attacked civilians at the Kibeho camp. She and her husband were both arrested on charges of genocide in 1998 after they returned to Rwanda from the refugee camps in Zaïre. "I do not know who is taking care of my children. I haven't seen them or my husband [since our return]." Her neighbors alleged at *gacaca* in 2006 that she killed nineteen people, which resulted in her imprisonment; she admits to killing six Tutsi and two Hutu. She is serving a thirty-year sentence and expects to "die here," even though she confessed to her crimes shortly after her arrest and expected to receive a reduced sentence.

Glossary

French Words

cachot: Local detention center.

Conseil supérieur: High Council.

fonctionnaire: Public servant.

gendarmes: Police.

génocidaires: Individuals (almost exclusively ethnic Hutu) who fall into one of two broad categories: (1) those convicted of acts of genocide through formal legal channels (*gacaca*, domestic and international courts), meaning they are bona fide perpetrators of acts of genocide; (2) those who are believed to have participated in acts of genocide (regardless of available evidence).

Pères Blancs: White Fathers.

tigistes: Individuals who perform work in the public interest.

travaux d'intérêt général: Works in the general interest.

Kinyarwanda Words

abacengezi: Infiltrators.

abahinza: Hutu kings.

abiru: Official ritualists, meaning custodian of royal tradition as well as its rituals and secrets.

akazu: Literally, little hut. Used to refer to the inner circle of political power under President Habyarimana before the genocide and to President Kagame's inner circle since 2001.

Bakiga: People from the Kiga region in precolonial northern Rwanda. During the Second Republic, used to mean people of northeastern Rwanda (Gisenyi, Ruhengeri, and Byumba).

Banyamulenge: People of Rwandan origin from the Mulenge hills in southern Kivu (Congo) who follow Rwandan customs and cultural codes.

Banyarwanda: People of Rwanda.

ceceka (from the verb *guceceka*): Shut up or be quiet.

gacaca: Traditionally, the spot where local-level dispute resolution takes place (literally, lawn or grass); the postgenocide meaning is neotraditional community-based courts that are outside the formal judicial system.

ibirongozi: Colonial-era local administrators.

ibyitso: Accomplices.

icyihebe (pl. *ibyihebe*): Fearless. Always used with a negative connotation. Since 2012, has meant "terrorist."

igipinga (pl. *ibipinga*): Literally, people with deep-rooted principles. Since 2011, the term has been adopted by government cadres to name and shame whoever tries to oppose RPF ideology and programs. Generally used to mean Hutu opponents.

imihigo: Performance-based contracts that render local officials accountable to the central government.

Impuzamugambi: Literally, those with a common goal (youth wing of the CDR).

ingando: Reeducation camp.

Interahamwe: Title of the youth wing of the MRND, literally, those who attack together.

inyangamugayo: Title given to *gacaca* judges, literally, those who detest disgrace.

inyenzi: Cockroach (used to identify Tutsi infiltrators in 1960 and again in the 1990s).

inzu: House.

isambu: Large areas of land traditionally administered by hill chiefs to their subordinates. The chief held ownership but allowed the land to be farmed in exchange for tribute and corvée labor.

mabati: Iron roof sheeting.

mwami: King.

nyumbakumi: Literally, ten houses. Refers to both groupings of ten households and the elected official responsible for managing Rwanda's smallest administrative unit.

panga: Machete.

shebuja: One's patron.

ubuhake: Traditional system of vassalage. It designated the system in which cattle owners (usually but not exclusively Tutsi) would give cattle to their clients (usually but not exclusively ethnic Hutu) in usufruct in exchange for services.

ubukonde: Practice of acquiring land through sweat equity.

uburetwa: Manual labor in the service of Tutsi chiefs.

ubwoko: Ethnicity (or clan).

umudugudu (pl. *imidugudu*): Literally, village. *Imidugudu* are communal settlements imposed by the RPF government as part of its program of villagization.

umuganda: Community work.

umugaragu: Servant.

umuhakwa: Client (meaning the one dependent on *ubuhake*).

umuheto: Clientship practice based in reciprocal alliances.

umukuru w'umuryango: Head of a lineage.

umuryango: Lineage.

umusazi (pl. *abasazi*): Foolish or fool.

NOTES

Preface and Acknowledgments

1. Decompression was UN-speak at the time to describe the physical and emotional support provided to staff members after a stressful event.

2. The RPF is made up mainly of Tutsi refugees who had fled Rwanda during earlier waves of politically motivated violence led by the Hutu elite and aimed at Tutsi between 1959 and 1973. The military wing of the RPF invaded Rwanda in 1990 with the purpose of toppling Habyarimana's authoritarian regime and gaining the right of return for Tutsi refugees.

3. The Arusha Accords are a series of accords signed by the then-government of Rwanda and the then-rebel Rwandan Patriotic Front in Arusha, Tanzania, in August 1993 to bring an end to the Rwandan civil war that had started when the RPF invaded Rwanda in October 1990 from neighboring Uganda.

4. International journalists coined the phrase "the 'new' Rwanda" in July 1994 to explain the monumental changes in Rwandan society envisaged by the RPF-led government of national unity and reconciliation (see Pottier 2002). The RPF leadership then picked up the phrase in some of its policy documents and the speeches of senior government officials, notably President Paul Kagame, to justify its policy choices.

Introduction

1. Jeanne is not her real name. All names have been changed to ensure the anonymity of participants.

2. In Rwanda, individual integrity is marked through one's ability to keep secrets. It is also a form of power, linked in particular to the secret rituals and codes of kingship. See de Lame 2004b, 2005a, 14–16, 88–91, 93–94, 382–83; Pottier 1989, 472–74; and Turner 2005, 43–47.

3. The LDF is a government-backed citizens' militia introduced by the government in 1997 with the stated aim of protecting civilians at the community level from insurgent incursions along Rwanda's western border with the Democratic Republic of the Congo. By the end of 1998, LDF commands charged with ensuring peace and security at the lowest administrative levels were in place across Rwanda. In practice, they often harass,

intimidate, rob, rape, detain, and torture citizens. In some of the communities where I worked, the LDF has been called to account for its abuses and is disciplined, while in others it has had free rein, notably in communities where government authorities are afraid of its members or have benefited from their actions.

4. The majority of appointed local government officials I met in the course of my research in 2006 were appointed to their positions by virtue of their RPF membership. Corroborated by Ingelaere 2011, 72.

5. Some 45 percent of Rwandans, living in both urban and rural areas, live at or below the poverty line of 64,000 Rwandan francs (FRw) (roughly US$100) per adult equivalent per year (National Institute of Statistics 2012, 14). In Rwanda's Southern province, where most of the Rwandans I interviewed reside, some 57 percent of the population are poor or destitute (ibid.).

6. In 2006, 87 percent of the population lived in rural areas, 65 percent of which live below the poverty line of FRw 175 (US$0.29) per day (IFAD 2011).

7. In 1994 Rwanda was organized into the following administrative hierarchy: 10 *préfectures* (now provinces), 106 *communes* (now districts), 154 *secteurs* (sectors), and 9201 *cellules* (cells), with each *cellule* being further subdivided into groupings of ten households called *nyumbakumi*. In 2001 Rwanda's administration was reorganized into eleven provinces, plus the city of Kigali, 106 districts, 154 sectors, and 9,201 cells. In January 2006 the government again engaged in a sweeping administrative carve-up that reduced the number of provinces (from 11 to 4) and districts (from 106 to 30) but increased the number of sectors (from 154 to 416). The number of cells remained virtually unchanged (going from 9,201 to 9,165).

8. To reflect this finding, the terms "ethnic Tutsi," "ethnic Hutu," and "ethnic Twa" are used throughout the book to indicate that these identities are imposed upon ordinary Rwandans by the state; they are not necessarily identities that the people themselves embrace.

9. The next presidential election is scheduled for August 2017. According to Rwanda's 2003 constitutional revision, the president can only hold two consecutive terms of office, meaning president Kagame is not eligible to stand again as the RPF's presidential candidate.

10. President Kagame's speeches are available on his website (www.paulkagame .com). Most of them are available in English.

11. The combined works of Alison Des Forges, Danielle de Lame, Catharine Newbury, and David Newbury provide locally grounded and historically contextualized analyses of the ideological uses of competing versions of history, the continued superiority of state authority over local forms of knowledge, the political dynamics of ethnicity, and the evolution of the Rwandan state, and reveal contested elite and local views on the 1994 genocide. See de Lame 1995, 2004b, 2005a; Des Forges 1986, 1995, 1999, 2011; M. C. Newbury 1978, 1980; C. Newbury 1988, 1995, 1998; C. Newbury and D. Newbury 1995, 1999; D. Newbury 1980, 1991, 1994, 1997; and D. Newbury and C. Newbury 2000.

Chapter 1. Bringing in Peasant Rwandans through Life History Interviewing

1. The home in figure 1 was photographed in 2006, before the RPF government instituted its *nyakatsi* program in which residents, regardless of household income, must upgrade their mud-and-thatch homes to ones with both cement floors and tiled or metal

roofs. Such "modern" homes, it argued, were needed for community development (MINALOC 2006, 2007). If one accepts, as Human Rights Watch predicted in its report *Uprooting the Rural Poor* (2001b, 1, 11–13), that some 94 percent of rural residents would have to be resettled under the *imidugudu* policy of villigization, then "the Rwandan state is in a process of forcibly changing the residences of nearly all of its citizens" (Sommers 2012b, 26).

2. During the summer of 2006, the soccer World Cup was shown on communal televisions in bars and at schools and hospitals and was announced on local radio across Rwanda.

3. In postgenocide Rwanda, as in many other African countries, academics require permission from the highest level of government for three reasons: to allow the government to ensure that the research is appropriate to its development or peacebuilding agenda, as a way for the government to register and keep track of foreign researchers, and to provide a letter of introduction to government officials and local partner organizations who work at the local level with individual researchers.

4. At the same time that I was negotiating research relationships with both of my local partners, the government introduced *imihigo* (performance) contracts, in which appointed local government officials commit to specific development goals in their jurisdictions in a formal meeting with President Kagame (Bugingo and Interayamahanga 2010; MINALOC 2006; Versailles 2012). This means that local officials are contractually obligated to develop their bailiwick in accordance with national policy objectives; they are not accountable to the needs of the local populations they are supposed to serve. As Ingelaere (2011, 71) notes, the "implementation of central policies at the local level mostly coerce ordinary peasants."

Chapter 2. The Historical Role of the State in Everyday Life

1. Uvin identifies structural violence as one of the root causes of the 1994 genocide, defining it as "a deep and widening inequality of life chances; corruption, arbitrariness, and impunity; the permanence of social and economic exclusion; lack of access to information, education, health, and minimal basic needs; and an authoritarian and condescending state and aid system" (Uvin 1998, 107).

2. The National Unity and Reconciliation Commission (NURC) was established by an act of Parliament in 1999 (law no. 03/99 of March 12, 1999). The 1993 Arusha Peace Accords provided for the Commission as well as for a national summit on unity and reconciliation.

3. Literally, "the gate to the compound" (Vansina 2004, 31). Lineages are made up of *inzu* (house), made up of three generations: grandparents, their married sons, and grandchildren. They live in the same compound, or near one another. *Inzu* is the basic social unit in Rwandan society and the smallest political unit. Only older married men were the leaders of *inzu*. Younger married men and all women were their dependents. The social position of women was "complex and variable" (Burnet 2012, 76), because their status derived from that of their father, husband, or sons. Age and personality were of considerable importance, and a generous bride wealth could greatly enhance a woman's position, bringing along with it considerable freedom of action within the family.

4. On the various (and contradictory) forms of the hypothesis see Chrétien 1985; Evans 1980; and Sanders 1969.

5. Ethnic Tutsi make up about 15 percent of the Rwandan population, both at the time of colonization and today. For an explanation of these percentages, see Codere 1973.

6. *Ubukonde* is the practice of acquiring land through sweat equity. As Vansina (2004, 40) writes, "whomever cleared a plot of land became its owner because the arable land was the fruit of his labor."

7. Strikingly, this inability to secure land has contemporary parallels, with young men today being unable to secure sufficient land holdings to allow them to grow into adulthood (Sommers 2012a).

8. Under the 2006 territorial restructuring, Rucunshu is a community in South province, just outside of Muhanga (former Gitarama) town. See figure 3.

9. Kinyarwanda uses prefixes to indicate whether a word is singular or plural: "Ba" is plural, while "mu" is singular.

10. For analysis of the political origins of the manifesto and its recommendations for structural change, see C. Newbury 1988, 190–93.

11. Rwanda's first president was Dominique Mbonyumutwa, who served as provisional president from January until October 1961. Kayibanda became president following the September 1961 referendum/election.

12. These public safety committees were similar in form and substance to the local defense forces later introduced by the Kagame regime.

13. It was not entirely bloodless. Approximately fifty members of Kayibanda's regime were killed or later died in prison. Kayibanda himself starved to death in prison in December 1976.

14. For analysis of the coffee economy in the late 1970s and 1980s, see Verwimp 2003.

Chapter 3. A Continuum of Violence, 1990–2000

1. In this instance, the phrase "moderate" refers to a Hutu killer who shared his resources with Tutsi before the genocide. This usage is a modified form of the phrase "Hutu moderate," which has come into popular usage since the 1994 genocide. For analysis, see Eltringham 2003.

2. Making Didier's Hutu friend a likely Category One killer, according to the 2004 *gacaca* law.

3. The Interahamwe were associated with the ruling party, Mouvement révolutionnaire national pour le développement (MRND), of President Habyarimana.

4. The Impuzamugambi were associated with the Coalition pour la défense de la république (CDR), an extremist and hardline satellite of the MRND.

5. This chauvinist statement contradicts the stated goals of the policy of national unity and reconciliation.

6. In no way should readers interpret this sentence to conclude that the RPF was part of the plan to institute and carry out the plan for the 1994 genocide, the responsibility for which rests squarely on the relevant political and military actors within the Habyarimana regime. I am suggesting only that the RPF's strategy to take state power (which it did in July 1994) evolved in the fluid context of the October 1990–April 1994 civil war.

7. Pro-MRND parties were the Parti démocratique (PADE), the Parti progressiste de la jeunesse rwandaise (PPJR), and the Rassemblement travailliste pour la démocratie

(RTD). Other parties "flirted" with the MRND, only to later align with one or more of the opposition parties. These included the Parti démocratique islamique (PDI), the Parti socialiste rwandais (PSR), and the Union démocratique du peuple rwandais (UDPR) (Burnet 2005, 84). In keeping with the times, the MRND added another "D" to its name, becoming the Mouvement révolutionnaire national pour le développement et la démocratie (MRND[D]) (Prunier 1997, 126).

8. Indeed, the unwillingness of the RPF to share political power in the postgenocide period is also well documented, as is analyzed more fully in the next chapter (Amnesty International 2010; Habimana 2011; Longman 2011; Rafti 2004; Reyntjens 2004, 2011; Sebarenzi 2011).

9. "Hutu Power" refers to the coalition of Hutu extremists from within the MRND and CDR, as well as those members of the MDR who defected to join the Power cabal.

10. Old-caseload refugees are individuals, mainly Tutsi, who fled Rwanda during successive waves of violence between 1959 and 1973 and their descendants.

11. Sometime in the late 1990s or early 2000s, the RPF instituted the Oath of Oneness, which is a solemn declaration that individual Rwandans take (many are forced) to publicly demonstrate their commitment to RPF rule. In taking the oath, individuals vow to faithfully serve the party and accept that any attempt to leave the party will be interpreted by party elites as an act of treason. It is believed that acceptance of the oath is required to gain a job in the state bureaucracy, as an appointed or volunteer local government official, or as a *gacaca* judge (field notes 2006).

Chapter 4. Practices of National Unity and Reconciliation

1. "Good governance and a capable state" is the first pillar of the RPFs' economic development policy "Vision 20/20." Neither of these concepts is defined in the policy document, which states: "The country is committed to being a capable state, characterized by the rule of law that supports and protects all its citizens without discrimination" (MINECOFIN 2000, 14).

2. Note that *imihigo* contracts were not yet in effect in 2006, during my period of research.

3. In 2006, during my period of research, Hutu perpetrators were known as *génocidaires* (those who committed acts of genocide). The term *génocidaire* (perpetrator) had two meanings in 2006. It referred to individuals (almost exclusively ethnic Hutu) who fell into one of two broad categories: (1) those convicted of acts of genocide through formal legal channels (via the *gacaca* as well as domestic and international courts), and (2) those who were believed to have participated in acts of genocide (regardless of the available evidence). The term has been less commonly used in public parlance since my fieldwork ended, even less so since the closure of the *gacaca* courts in 2012.

4. The practices of the state power analyzed here were representative of everyday life in 2006. At the time of writing, in 2012, the RPF government had intensified its use of many of the practices identified here (see Freedom House International 2013; United States Department of State 2013).

5. "Genocide ideology" was not defined until the Senate issued its report "Genocide Ideology and Strategies for Its Eradication" in 2007. It is "a set of ideas or representations whose major role is to stir up hatred and create a pernicious atmosphere favouring the implementation and legitimisation of the persecution and elimination of a category of

the population" (Senate of the Republic of Rwanda 2007, 16). The definition was legally defined in a 2007 amendment to the Organic law No. 10/2007 of 01/03/2007 on *gacaca*, article 3, as follows: "Ideology of genocide consists in behaviour, a way of speaking, written documents and any other actions meant to wipe out human beings on the basis of their ethnic group, origin, nationality, region, colour of skin, physical traits, sex, language, religion or political opinions" (MINIJUST 2007). Waldorf (2011) found that individuals were accused of having genocide ideology before the law was passed.

6. The 1996 and 2001 *gacaca* laws included provisions for the use of a "confession and the guilty plea procedure which enables the accused to have a reduced sentence and to finish the second half of the sentence performing community service" (PRI 2004, 3).

7. I cannot confirm if the anthem contains these lyrics, as no RPF leader would discuss the message of the anthem with me. The fact these individuals believe that the lyrics warn Tutsi to protect themselves against Hutu is significant.

8. At the time of my research, in 2006, Fatuma Ndangiza was the executive secretary. At the time of writing, in 2012, the executive secretary was the Right Reverend John Rucyahana. Rucyahana is also a member Rwanda's Presidential Advisory Council (PAC).

9. On the practical difficulties and political constraints of teaching history in post-genocide Rwanda, see Freedman et al. 2011.

10. "Ex-soldier" means any member of the Rwandan Patriotic Army (the military branch of the current government) who demobilized after 1995; "ex-combatant" means any ex-FAR soldier who remained in or returned to Rwanda after July 1994 or any member of an armed group who is a Rwandan national and who returned to Rwanda after May 2001 (World Bank 2002, 5).

Chapter 5. Everyday Resistance to National Unity and Reconciliation

1. The Fonds d'assistance aux rescapés du génocide (FARG) was established by the government in 1998 to provide social services to all victims of the genocide, not just Tutsi survivors.

2. The question of what constitutes an act of resistance and what is a survival strategy runs through the literature. See the edited collection of Scott and Kerkvliet (1986) for an overview of the debates.

3. The average yearly salary is FRw 350,000 (US$780).

4. Several Tutsi survivors told me that they found it particularly difficult to provide evidence to the *gacaca* courts because they were in hiding during the genocide and did not actually see anything. Alice told me, "I heard a lot. The screams. There would be screaming and then some cheering and even some laughter. Eventually the screams would stop, but the laughing continued. I really only heard the genocide, I did not see anyone kill anyone. Even if I did, I wouldn't dare tell the authorities. They would make me tell what I saw. I struggle enough without adding the burden of testifying at *gacaca*" (interview 2006).

5. Since 2011 the term *ibipinga* has been used by RPF cadres to name and shame whoever tries to oppose RPF ideology and policies. At the time of writing, in late 2012, *ibipinga* was used to identify Hutu opponents of the government.

Chapter 6. Everyday Resistance
to the *Gacaca* Process

1. The courts concluded their work in June 2012.

2. Citizen spectators are nonparticipating attendees; all adults over the age of eighteen must attend *gacaca* or risk sanction (MINIJUST 2004, article 29).

3. Despite the appearance of free and fair local elections in Rwanda (starting in 2001 and most recently in 2010), I consciously use the language of "chosen" elected official as the RPF controls the electoral process for all levels of government. At the sector level, Rwandans line up behind their candidate of "choice" after having been told by appointed local officials for whom they should vote, guaranteeing electoral support of at least 90 percent for RPF candidates. For analysis, see Delany 2010; International Crisis Group 2002; Reyntjens 2009, 2011.

4. IBUKA (Kinyarwanda, "to remember") is the umbrella organization of survivor groups. Each sector has its own representative.

References

Abrams, Philip. 1988. "Notes on the Difficulty of Studying the State." *Journal of Historical Sociology* 1 (1): 58–89.

Abu-Lughod, Lila. 1990. "The Romance of Resistance: Tracing Transformations of Power through Bedouin Women." *American Ethnologist* 17 (1): 41–55.

Adamczyk, Christiane. 2011. "'Today, I Am No Mutwa Anymore:' Facets of National Unity Discourse in Present-Day Rwanda." *Social Anthropology* 19 (2): 175–88.

———. 2012. "Independent Actors or Silent Agents: Where to Go for Rwandan Civil Society?" In *Rwanda Fast Forward: Social, Economic, Military and Reconciliation Prospects*, edited by Maddalena Campioni and Patrick Noack, 60–75. London: Palgrave Macmillan.

Adhikari, Mohamed. 2008. "*Hotel Rwanda*—The Challenges of Historicising and Commercialising Genocide." *Development Dialogue* 50:173–96.

Aegis Trust. 2006. *We Survived Genocide in Rwanda: 28 Personal Testimonies*. Edited by Wendy Whitworth. London: Quill Press.

African Online News (AFROL). 2008. "Rwanda Ex-leaders Granted Immunity." July 17. http://www.afrol.com/articles/29858. Accessed April 10, 2013.

African Rights. 1994. *Rwanda: Death, Despair and Defiance*. London: African Rights.

———. 2000. *Confessing to Genocide: Responses to Rwanda's Genocide Law*. Kigali: African Rights.

———. 2003a. *Rwanda: Gacaca Justice: A Shared Responsibility*. Kigali: African Rights.

———. 2003b. *The Gisimba Memorial Centre: No Place for Fear*. Kigali: African Rights.

———. 2003c. *Gishamvu: A Collective Account*. Kigali: African Rights.

———. 2003d. *Nyarugunga: A Collective Account*. Kigali: African Rights.

———. 2003e. *Nkomero*. Kigali: African Rights.

———. 2003f. *Nyange*. Kigali: African Rights.

———. 2003g. *Kindama: A Collective Account*. Kigali: African Rights.

———. 2005. *Gahini: A Collective Account*. Kigali: African Rights.

Alevesson, Mats, and Kaj Sköldberg. 2000. "Language/Gender/Power: Discourse Analysis, Feminism and Genealogy." In *Reflexive Methodology: New Vistas for Qualitative Research*, 200–237. London: Sage.

Allina-Pisano, Jessica. 2007. *The Post-Soviet Potemkin Village: Politics and Property Rights in the Black Earth.* Cambridge: Cambridge University Press.

Alonso, Ana Maria. 1994. "The Politics of Space, Time and Substance: State Formation, Nationalism and Ethnicity." *Annual Review of Anthropology* 23:379–405.

Amnesty International. 1997. *Rwanda: Ending the Silence.* September 25. http://www.amnesty.org/en/library/asset/AFR47/032/1997/en/dom-AFR470321997en.html. Accessed July 21, 2006.

———. 2004. "Rwanda: Government Slams the Door on Political Life and Civil Society." June 9. http://www.amnesty.org/en/library/asset/AFR47/012/2004/en/dom-AFR470122004en.html. Accessed July 29, 2006.

———. 2005. "Rwanda: Human Rights Organisation Forced to Shut Down." January 10. http://www.amnesty.org/en/library/asset/AFR47/001/2005/en/dom-AFR470012005en.html. Accessed July 29, 2006.

———. 2010. "Safer to Stay Silent: The Chilling Effect of Rwanda's Laws on 'Genocide Ideology' and 'Sectarianism.'" August 31. http://www.amnesty.org/en/library/info/AFR47/005/2010. Accessed October 29, 2012.

———. 2011. "Rwanda: Freedom of Expression" *Annual Report 2011: The State of the World's Human Rights.* June 7. http://www.amnesty.org/en/region/rwanda/report-2011#section-120-3. Accessed August 4, 2012.

André, Catherine, and Jean-Pierre Platteau. 1998. "Land Relations under Unbearable Stress: Rwanda Caught in the Malthusian Trap." *Journal of Economic Behaviour and Organization* 34 (1): 1–47.

Ansoms, An. 2008. "Resurrection after Civil War and Genocide: Growth, Poverty and Inequality in Post-conflict Rwanda." *European Journal of Development Research* 17 (3): 495–508.

———. 2009. "Re-engineering Rural Society: The Visions and Ambitions of the Rwandan Elite." *African Affairs* 108 (431): 289–309.

———. 2011. "Rwanda's Post-genocide Economic Reconstruction: The Mismatch between Elites Ambitions and Rural Realities." In *Remaking Rwanda: State Building and Human Rights after Mass Violence,* edited by Scott Straus and Lars Waldorf, 240–51. Madison: University of Wisconsin Press.

Archer, Margaret S. 2003. *Structure, Agency and the Internal Conversation.* Cambridge: Cambridge University Press.

Article 19. 1996. "Broadcasting Genocide, Censorship, Propaganda and State-Sponsored Violence in Rwanda, 1990–1994." October 15. www.article19.org/pdfs/publications/rwanda-broadcasting-genocide.pdf. Accessed August 23, 2005.

Arusha Accords. 1993. August 3. http://www.incore.ulst.ac.uk/services/cds/agreements/pdf/rwan1.pdf. Accessed November 30, 2012.

Bagilishya, Déogratius. 2000. "Mourning and Recovery from Trauma: In Rwanda, Tears Flow Within." *Transcultural Psychiatry* 37 (3): 337–53.

Barahinyura, Jean Shyirambere. 1988. *Le Général-Major Habyarimana (1973–1988): Quinze ans de tyrannie de la tartufferie au Rwanda.* Frankfurt: Izuba Verlag.

Begley, Larissa. 2013. "The RPF Control Everything! Fear and Rumour under Rwanda's Genocide Ideology Legislation." In *Emotional and Ethical Challenges for Field Research in Africa: The Story behind the Findings,* edited by Susan Thomson, An Ansoms, and Jude Murison, 70–83. London: Routledge.

Benmayor, Rina. 1991. "Testimony, Action Research, and Empowerment: Puerto Rican Women and Popular Education." In *Women's Words: The Feminist Practice of Oral History*, edited by Sherna Berger Gluck and Daphne Patai, 159–74. London: Routledge.

Berger, Iris. 1981. *Religion and Resistance: East African Kingdoms in the Precolonial Period*. Tervuren, Belgium: Musée royale de l'Afrique centrale.

Bertrand, Jordane. 2000. *Rwanda: L'opposition démocratique avant le génocide (1990–1994)*. Paris: Karthala.

Beswick, Danielle. 2010. "Managing Dissent in a Post-genocide Environment: The Challenge of Political Space in Rwanda." *Development and Change* 41(2): 225–51.

———. 2011. "Democracy, Identity and the Politics of Exclusion in Post-genocide Rwanda: The Case of the Batwa." *Democratization* 18 (2): 490–511.

Bilbija, Ksenija, Jo Ellen Fair, Cynthia E. Milton, and Leigh A. Payne. 2005. *The Art of Truth-Telling about Authoritarian Rule*. Madison: University of Wisconsin Press.

Bondi, Liz. 2002. "Introduction." In *Subjectivities, Knowledges and Feminist Geographies: The Subjects and Ethics of Social Research*, edited by Liz Bondi et al., 1–11. New York: Rowan and Littlefield.

Borland, Kathleen. 1991. "'That's Not What I Said': Interpretative Conflict in Oral Narrative Research." In *Women's Words: The Feminist Practice of Oral History*, edited by Sherna Berger Gluck and Daphne Patai, 63–76. London: Routledge.

Bourdieu, Pierre. 2001. *Masculine Domination*. Stanford: Stanford University Press.

British Broadcasting Corporation (BBC). 2006. "Rwanda Redrawn to Reflect Compass." January 6. http://news.bbc.co.uk/2/hi/africa/4577790.stm. Accessed July 19, 2006.

Brounéus, Karen. 2008. "Truth-Telling as Talking Cure? Insecurity and Retraumatization in the Rwandan Gacaca Courts." *Security Dialogue* 39 (1): 55–76.

Bugingo, Irenee, and Reverien Interayamahanga. 2010. "A Study on the Development and Use of Governance Indicators in Rwanda: Draft Report." October. Kigali: Institute for Research and Dialogue for Peace (IRDP).

Burnet, Jennie E. 2005. "Genocide Lives in Us: Amplified Silence and the Politics of Memory in Rwanda." PhD diss., University of North Carolina at Chapel Hill, Department of Anthropology.

———. 2007. "Country Report: Rwanda." http://www.freedomhouse.org/uploads/ccr/country-7259-8.pdf. Accessed October 28, 2007.

———. 2008a. "Gender Balance and the Meanings of Women in Governance in Post-Genocide Rwanda." *African Affairs* 107 (428): 361–86.

———. 2008b. "The Injustice of Local Justice: Truth, Reconciliation and Revenge in Rwanda." *Journal of Genocide Studies and Prevention* 3 (2): 173–93.

———. 2009. "Whose Genocide? Whose Truth? Representations of Perpetrator and Victim in Rwanda." In *Genocide: Truth, Memory and Representation*, edited by Alex Hinton and Kevin O'Neill, 80–112. Durham, NC: Duke University Press.

———. 2011. "Women Have Found Respect: Gender Quotas, Symbolic Representation, and Female Empowerment in Rwanda." *Politics and Gender* 7:303–34.

———. 2012. *Genocide Lives in Us: Women, Memory, and Silence in Rwanda*. Madison: University of Wisconsin Press.

Butamire, Pan. 2011a. "'Remaking Rwanda' or 'Wishing to Deconstruct Rwanda.'" *Remaking Rwanda: The Fact and Figures on the Ground*. http://theremakingrwanda

.blogspot.com/2011/04/remaking-rwanda-or-wishing-to.html. Accessed August 4, 2012.

———. 2011b. "Susan M. Thomson: A Fraud PhD." *Remaking Rwanda: The Fact and Figures on the Ground.* http://theremakingrwanda.blogspot.com/2011/04/susan-m-thomson-fraud-phd.html. Accessed August 4, 2012.

Cahiers lumière et société. 1995. *Ethnies au Rwanda en 1995.* Kigali: Association lumière et société.

———. 1996. *Rwanda.* Kigali: Association lumière et société.

Chakravarty, Anuradha. 2006. "State Power, Human Rights and the Rule of Law in Post-genocide Rwanda: An Ethnographic Analysis of a Grassroots Judicial Process." Paper presented at the American Political Science Association Meeting, Philadelphia, PA, August 20.

———. 2012. "'Partially Trusting' Field Relationship Opportunities and Constraints of Fieldwork in Rwanda's Postconflict Setting." *Field Methods* 24 (3): 251–71.

———. Forthcoming. "Navigating Identity: A Metric of State-Society Relationships in Post-Genocide Rwanda." *African Affairs.*

Chaulia, Sreeram S. 2002. "UNHCR's Relief, Rehabilitation and Repatriation of Rwandan Refugees in Zaire (1994–1997)." *Journal of Humanitarian Assistance.* http://reliefweb.int/rw/rwb.nsf/db900sid/ACOS-64DBM5?OpenDocument. Accessed February 19, 2008.

Chrétien, Jean-Pierre. 1985. "Hutu et Tutsi au Rwanda et au Burundi." In *Au cœur de l'ethnie,* edited by Jean-Loup Amselle and Elikia M'Bokolo, 129–65. Paris: La Découverte.

———. 2006. *The Great Lakes of Africa: Two Thousand Years of History.* Translated by Scott Straus. New York: Zone Books.

Clinton Foundation. 2009. "Former President Clinton Announces Winners of the Third Annual Clinton Global Citizen Awards." September 23. http://press.clintonglobal initiative.org/press_releases/former-president-clinton-announces-winners-of-the-third-annual-clinton-global-citizen-awards/. Accessed October 29, 2012.

Codere, Helen. 1962. "Power in Ruanda." *Anthropologica* 4:45–85.

———. 1973. *The Biography of an African Society: Rwanda, 1900–1960.* Tervuren, Belgium: Musée royal de l'Afrique centrale.

Comaroff, Jean. 1985. *Body of Power, Spirit of Resistance: The Culture and History of a South African People.* Chicago: University of Chicago Press.

Communauté des Autochtones Rwandais (CAURWA). 2004. "Enquête sur les conditions de vie socio-économique des ménages bénéficiaires de la Communauté des Autochtones Rwandais." www.forestpeoples.org/pt-br/node/779. Accessed March 29, 2013.

Cooke, Jennifer G. 2011. "Rwanda: Assessing Risks to Stability." A Report of the CSIS Africa Program. June. Washington, DC: Center for Strategic and International Studies.

Crais, Clifton. 2002. *The Politics of Evil: Magic, Power and the Political Imagination in South Africa.* Cambridge: Cambridge University Press.

Crépeau, Pierre, and Simon Bizimana. 1979. *Proverbes du Rwanda.* Tervuren, Belgium: Musée royale de l'Afrique centrale.

Crisafulli, Patricia, and Andrea Redmond. 2012. *Rwanda, Inc.: How a Devastated Nation Became an Economic Model for the Developing World.* New York: Palgrave Macmillan.

Crummey, Donald. 1986. "Introduction: The Great Beast." In *Banditry, Rebellion and Social Protest in Africa*, edited by Donald Crummey, 1–31. London: James Currey.

Dagan, David. 2011. "The Cleanest Place in Africa." *Foreign Policy*, October 19. http://www.foreignpolicy.com/articles/2011/10/19/rwanda_the_cleanest_place_in_africa?page=full. Accessed March 29, 2013.

Dallaire, Romeo, with Brent Beardsley. 2003. *Shake Hands with the Devil: The Failure of Humanity in Rwanda*. Toronto: Random House Canada.

Danish International Development Assistance (DANIDA). 1997. "Synthesis Report. Joint Evaluation of Emergency Assistance to Rwanda. The International Response to Conflict and Genocide; Lessons from the Rwanda Experience." http://www.um.dk/Publikationer/Danida/English/Evaluations/RwandaExperience/index.asp. Accessed February 4, 2007.

Das, Veena. 2004. "The Signature of the State: The Paradox of Illegibility." In *Anthropology in the Margins of the State*, edited by Veena Das and Deborah Poole, 224–52. Santa Fe, NM: School of American Research Press.

de Lame, Danielle. 1995. "Les sens des violences." In Les Verts au Parlement Européen, *Les racines de la violence dans la région des Grands Lacs*, 41–48. Brussels: Parlement européen.

———. 2004. "Mighty Secrets, Public Commensality, and the Crisis of Transparency: Rwanda through the Looking Glass." *Canadian Journal of African Studies* 38 (2): 279–317.

———. 2005a. *A Hill among a Thousand: Transformations and Ruptures in Rural Rwanda* Translated by Helen Arnold. Madison: University of Wisconsin Press.

———. 2005b. "On Behalf of Ordinary People: Bridging the Gap between High Politics and Simple Tragedies." *African Studies Review* 48 (3): 133–41.

Delany, Max. 2010. "Kagame Sees 'No Reason' Why He Shouldn't Win Rwanda Election." *Christian Science Monitor*, August 9. http://www.csmonitor.com/World/Africa/2010/0809/Kagame-sees-no-reason-why-he-shouldn-t-win-Rwanda-election. Accessed November 16, 2010.

Des Forges, Alison Liebhafsky. 1986. "'The Drum Is Greater Than the Shout': The 1912 Rebellion in Northern Rwanda." In *Banditry, Rebellion and Social Protest in Africa*, edited by Donald Crummey, 311–31. London: James Currey.

———. 1995. "The Ideology of Genocide." *Issue: A Journal of Opinion* 23 (2): 44–47.

———. 1999. *Leave None to Tell the Story*. New York: Human Rights Watch.

———. 2006. "Land in Rwanda: Winnowing out the Chafe." In *L'Afrique des Grand Lacs: Annuaire 2005–2006*, edited by Filip Reyntjens and Stefaan Marysse, 353–71. Paris: L'Harmattan.

———. 2007. "Call to Genocide: Radio in Rwanda." In *The Media and the Rwandan Genocide*, edited by Allan Thompson, 19–37. Ottawa: International Development Research Centre.

———. 2011. *Defeat Is the Only Bad News: Rwanda under Musinga, 1896–1931*. Edited by David Newbury. Madison: University of Wisconsin Press.

Desrosiers, Marie-Eve, and Susan Thomson. 2011. "Rhetorical Legacies of Leadership: Projections of 'Benevolent Leadership' in Pre- and Post-genocide Rwanda." *Journal of Modern African Studies* 49 (3): 431–55.

d'Hertefelt, Marcel. 1964. "Mythes et idéologies dans le Rwanda ancien et contemporain." In *The Historian in Tropical Africa*, edited by Raymond Mauny, Jan Vansina, and Louis Vincent Thomas, 219–38. London: Oxford University Press.

Dialogue. 2004. "Le génocide des Tutsi du Rwanda: Dix ans après." No. 178 (April–June).

Eltringham, Nigel. 2003. *Accounting for Horror: Post-genocide Debates in Rwanda.* London: Pluto.

Eltringham, Nigel, and Saskia Van Hoyweghen. 2000. "Power and Identity in Post-genocide Rwanda." In *Politics of Identity and Economics of Conflict in the Great Lakes Region,* edited by Ruddy Doom and Jan Gorus, 93–118. Brussels: VUB University Press.

Emirbayer, Mustafa, and Ann Mische. 1998. "What Is Agency?" *American Journal of Sociology* 103 (4): 962–1023.

Evans, William McKee. 1980. "From the Land of Canaan to the Land of Guinea: The Strange Odyssey of the 'Sons of Ham.'" *American Historical Review* 85 (1): 15–43.

Food and Agriculture Organization (FAO). 1998. "Improved Food Situation in the Great Lakes Region but Food Outlook Bleak in Eastern DRC." http://www.fao .org/docrep/004/x0696e/x0696e04.htm#E17E5. Accessed December 21, 2008.

———. 2001. "Human Energy Requirements: Report of a Joint FAO/WHO/UNU Expert Consultation." ftp://ftp.fao.org/docrep/fao/007/y5686e/y5686e00.pdf. Accessed February 10, 2009.

———. 2004. "FAO Statistical Yearbook: Rwanda." http://www.fao.org/es/ess/year book/vol_1_2/pdf/Rwanda.pdf. Accessed January 21, 2009.

Foucault, Michel. 1969 [2002]. *The Archaeology of Knowledge.* Translated by Alan Sheridan. New York: Routledge.

———. 1977. *Discipline and Punish: The Birth of the Prison.* Translated by Alan Sheridan. New York: Vintage.

———. 1980. *Power/Knowledge.* Worchester, MA: Harvester Press.

Franche, Dominique. 1997. *Rwanda: Généalogie d'un génocide.* Paris: Mille et une nuits.

Freedman, Sarah Warshauer, Harvey M. Weinstein, K. L. Murphy, and Timothy Longman. 2011. "Teaching History in Post-Genocide Rwanda." In *Remaking Rwanda: State Building and Human Rights after Mass Violence,* edited by Scott Straus and Lars Waldorf, 297–315. Madison: University of Wisconsin Press.

Freedom House International. 2013. *Freedom in the World 2013: Democratic Breakthroughs in the Balance.* Washington, DC: Freedom House International.

Frontline. 2005. "Disappearances, Threats, Intimidation and Co-optation of Human Rights Defenders, 2001–2004." http://www.law.harvard.edu/programs/hrp/clinic /documents/frontline.pdf. Accessed August 24, 2006.

Fujii, Lee Ann. 2009. *Killing Neighbors: Webs of Violence in Rwanda.* Ithaca, NY: Cornell University Press.

Gasana, James. 2002. *Rwanda: Du parti-état à état-garnison.* Paris: L'Harmattan.

Gaventa, John. 1980. *Power and Powerlessness: Quiescence and Rebellion in an Appalachian Valley.* Chicago: University of Illinois Press.

Geertz, Clifford. 1973. *The Interpretation of Cultures.* New York: Basic Books.

Global Integrity, with Ignatius Ssuuna. 2011. "Rwanda Notebook 2011." http://www .globalintegrity.org/report/Rwanda/2011/notebook. December 4, 2012.

Gökgür, Nilgun. 2012. "Rwanda's Ruling Party–Owned Enterprises: Do They Enhance or Impede Development?" Discussion Paper/2012.03/ISSN 2033-7329. University of Antwerp, Institute for Development Policy and Management (IOB).

Gourevitch, Phillip. 1996. "After Genocide: A Conversation with Paul Kagame." *Transition* 72:162–94.

———. 1998. *We Wish to Inform you That Tomorrow We Will Be Killed with Our Families: Stories from Rwanda.* New York: Picador USA.

———. 2009. "The Life After." *New Yorker,* May 4.

Gravel, Pierre B. 1967. "The Transfer of Cows in Gisaka (Rwanda): A Mechanism for Recording Social Relationships." *American Anthropologist* 69 (3–4): 322–31.

———. 1968. Diffuse Power as a Commodity: A Case Study from Gisaka (Eastern Rwanda). *International Journal of Comparative Sociology* 9 (3–4): 163–76.

Gready, Paul. 2011. "Beyond 'You're with Us or against Us': Civil Society and Policy-making in Post-genocide Rwanda." In *Remaking Rwanda: State Building and Human Rights after Mass Violence,* edited by Scott Straus and Lars Waldorf, 87–100. Madison: University of Wisconsin Press.

Guichaoua, André. 2005. *Rwanda 1994: Les politiques du génocide à Butare.* Paris: Éditions Karthala.

———. 2010. *Rwanda de la guerre au genocide: Les politiques criminelles au Rwanda (1990–1994).* Paris: La Découverte.

Habimana, Aloys. 2011. "The Dancing Is Still the Same." In *Remaking Rwanda: State Building and Human Rights after Mass Violence,* edited by Scott Straus and Lars Waldorf, 354–56. Madison: University of Wisconsin Press.

Hatch, J. Amos, and Richard Wisniewski. 1995. *Life History and Narrative.* London: Falmer Press.

Hatzfeld, Jean. 2005a. *Into the Quick of Life. The Rwandan Genocide: The Survivors Speak.* London: Serpent's Tail.

———. 2005b. *Machete Season: The Killers in Rwanda Speak.* New York: Farrar, Straus and Giroux.

———. 2007. *Life Laid Bare: The Survivors Speak.* Translated by Linda Coverdale. New York: Farrar, Straus and Giroux.

———. 2009. *The Antelope's Strategy: Living in Rwanda after the Genocide.* Translated by Linda Coverdale. New York: Farrar, Straus and Giroux.

Himbara, David. 2012. "Britain's Aid to Rwanda Is Funding a 'Repressive Regime' Says Former Kagame Official." November 24. http://www.telegraph.co.uk/news/worldnews/africaandindianocean/rwanda/9700913/Britains-aid-to-Rwanda-is-funding-a-repressive-regime-says-former-Kagame-official.html. Accessed April 2, 2013.

Hintjens, Helen M. 1999. "Explaining the 1994 Genocide in Rwanda." *Journal of Modern African Studies* 37:241–86.

Hobsbawn, Eric. 1983. "Introduction: Inventing Traditions." In *The Invention of Tradition,* edited by Eric Hobsbawn and Terence Ranger, 1–14. Cambridge: Cambridge University Press.

Howe, Gerard, and Andrew McKay. 2007. "Combining Quantitative and Qualitative Methods in Assessing Chronic Poverty: The Case of Rwanda." *World Development* 35 (2): 197–211.

Huggins, Chris. 2011. "The Presidential Land Commission: Undermining Land Law Reform." In *Remaking Rwanda: State Building and Human Rights after Mass Violence,* edited by Scott Straus and Lars Waldorf, 252–65. Madison: University of Wisconsin Press.

———. 2012. "Consolidating Land, Consolidating Control: What Future for Smallholder Farming in Rwanda's 'Green Revolution'?" Paper presented to the

International Conference on Global Land Grabbing II, Cornell University, Ithaca, NY, October 19.

Human Rights First. 2002. "Rwandans May Be Forced to Leave Tanzanian Refugee Camps." http://www.humanrightsfirst.org/media/2002_alerts/1227.htm. Accessed March 1, 2008.

Human Rights Watch (HRW). 1997. "What Kabila Is Hiding: Civilian Killings and Impunity in Congo." http://www.hrw.org/legacy/reports/1997/congo/. Accessed 21 February 2007.

——. 2001a. "Rwanda: Observing the Rules of War?" New York: HRW.

——. 2001b. "Uprooting the Rural Poor in Rwanda." London: HRW.

——. 2003. "Preparing for Elections: Tightening Control in the Name of Unity." http://www.hrw.org/backgrounder/africa/rwanda0503bck.pdf. Accessed June 10, 2006.

——. 2004. "Struggling to Survive: Barriers to Justice for Rape Victims in Rwanda." New York: HRW.

——. 2006a. "The Rwandan Genocide: How It Was Prepared." New York: HRW.

——. 2006b. "Documents Shed New Light on Genocide Planning." New York: HRW.

——. 2007. "World Report 2007. Rwanda—Events of 2006." New York: HRW. http://hrw.org/englishwr2k7/docs/2007/01/11/rwanda14782.htm. Accessed February 19, 2008.

——. 2008. "Law and Reality: Progress in Judicial Reform in Rwanda." http://www.hrw.org/sites/default/files/reports/rwanda0708webwcover.pdf. Accessed July 27, 2008.

——. 2010. "Rwanda: Silencing Dissent ahead of Elections." August 2. http://www.hrw.org/news/2010/08/02/rwanda-attacks-freedom-expression-freedom-association-and-freedom-assembly-run-presi. Accessed August 29, 2010.

——. 2011. "Justice Compromised: The Legacy of Rwanda's Community-Based Gacaca Courts." http://www.hrw.org/en/reports/2011/05/31/justice-compromised. Accessed June 14, 2011.

Hyden, Margareta. 1993. "Women Battering as a Marital Act: Interviewing and Analysis in Context." In *Qualitative Studies in Social Work Research*, edited by Catherine Kohler Riessman, 95–112. Thousand Oaks, CA: Sage.

Ilibagiza, Immaculée, with Steve Erwin. 2006. *Left to Tell: One Woman's Story of Surviving the Rwandan Holocaust*. London: Hay House.

Ingelaere, Bert. 2011. "The Ruler's Drum and the People's Shout: Accountability and Representation on Rwanda's Hills." In *Remaking Rwanda: State Building and Human Rights after Mass Violence*, edited by Scott Straus and Lars Waldorf, 67–78. Madison: University of Wisconsin Press.

——. 2012. "From Model to Practice: Researching and Representing Rwanda's 'Modernized' *Gacaca* Courts." *Critique of Anthropology* 38 (4): 388–414.

Institute of Research and Dialogue for Peace (IRDP). 2008. *Mechanisms to Fight Against the Negation of the Tutsi Genocide*. May. Kigali: IRDP.

Integrated Regional Information Network (IRIN). 1997. "IRIN Special Feature on Rwandan Trials." February 19. http://www.africa.upenn.edu/Hornet/irin_21997.html. Accessed June 4, 2005.

——. 1998. "UN Report Accuses Kinshasa, Kigali." July 1. http://www.africa.upenn.edu/Hornet/irin_7198.html. Accessed February 19, 2008.

———. 2001. "Twa Community Concerned over Gacaca System." June 6. New York: Office for the Co-ordination of Humanitarian Affairs Integrated Regional Information Network for Central and East Africa.

International Crisis Group (ICG). 2002. "Rwanda at the End of the Transition: A Necessary Political Liberalisation." Nairobi and Brussels: ICG.

International Fund for Agricultural Development (IFAD). 2011. "Rural Poverty in Rwanda." http://www.ruralpovertyportal.org/country/home/tags/rwanda. Accessed April 9, 2013.

International Monetary Fund (IMF). 2008. "Rwanda: Poverty Reduction Strategy Paper." http://www.imf.org/external/pubs/ft/scr/2008/cr0890.pdf. Accessed October 30, 2008.

Issacman, Allen F., and Barbara Issacman. 1977. "Resistance and Collaboration in Southern and Central Africa, c. 1850–1920." *International Journal of African Historical Studies* 10 (1): 31–62.

Jackson, Sue. 1998. "Telling Stories: Memory, Narrative and Experience in Feminist Research and Theory." In *Standpoints and Differences: Essays in the Practice of Feminist Psychology*, edited by Karen Henwood, Chris Griffin, and Ann Phoenix, 45–64. London: Sage.

Jefremovas, Villia. 1995. "Acts of Human Kindness: Tutsi, Hutu and the Genocide." *Issue: A Journal of Opinion* 23 (2): 28–31.

———. 2000. "Treacherous Waters: The Politics of History and the Politics of Genocide in Rwanda and Burundi." *Africa* 70 (2): 298–308.

Jessop, Bob. 1990. *State Theory: Putting the Capitalist State in Its Place.* University Park: Pennsylvania State University Press.

Jha, Uma Shakar, and Surya Narayan Yadav. 2004. *Rwanda, towards Reconciliation, Good Governance and Development: In Honour of His Excellency Mr. Paul Kagame President of the Republic of Rwanda.* New Delhi: Association of Indian Africanist.

Jones, Bruce. 1999. "Roots, Resolution, and Reaction: Civil War, Peace Process and Genocide in Rwanda." In *Civil Wars in Africa: Roots and Resolution*, edited by Taisier M. Ali and Robert O. Matthews, 53–79. Montreal: McGill-Queen's University Press.

———. 2001. *Peacemaking in Rwanda: The Dynamics of Failure.* Boulder, CO: Lynne Reinner.

Justino, Patricia, and Philip Verwimp. 2008. "Poverty Dynamics, Violent Conflict and Convergence in Rwanda." MICROCON Research Working Paper 4. Brighton, England: MICROCON.

Kagabo, Jean, and Vincent Mudandagizi. 1974. "Complaintes des gens d'argile: Les Twas du Rwanda." *Cahiers d'études africaines* 14:75–87.

Kagame, Paul. 2011. "Opening Address by H.E. Paul Kagame, at the 9th National Dialogue Council." December 15. http://www.paulkagame.com/2010/index .php?option=com_content&view=article&id=550%3Aopening-address-by-he-paul-kagame-president-of-the-republic-of-rwanda-at-the-9th-national-dialogue-council&catid=34%3Aspeeches&Itemid=56&lang=en. Accessed March 30, 2013.

———. 2012. "Speech by H.E Paul Kagame at the 18th Commemoration of the Genocide Against The Tutsi." April 7. http://www.paulkagame.com/2010/index .php?option=com_content&view=article&id=630%3Aspeech-by-he-paul-kagame-president-of-the-republic-of-rwanda-at-the-18th-commemoration-of-the-genocide-against-the-tutsi-amahoro-stadium-7-april-2012&catid=34%3Aspeeches&Itemid=56&lang=en. Accessed March 30, 2013.

Kayitesi, Annick. 2004. *Nous existons encore*. Paris: Michel Lafon.

Keane, Fergal. 1995. *Season of Blood: A Rwandan Journey*. London: Viking.

Kellehear, Allan. 1993. *The Unobtrusive Researcher: A Guide to Methods*. Sydney: Allen and Unwin.

Kezio-Musoke, David. 2008. "Rwanda: 'Hotel Rwanda' a Myth Created By Hollywood, Says New Book." March 24. http://allafrica.com/stories/200803240593.html. Accessed March 30, 2013.

Kimonyo, Jean-Paul. 2000. *Revue critique des interprétations du conflit rwandais*. Butare: Centre de gestion des conflits/Université nationale du Rwanda.

Kinzer, Stephen. 2008. *A Thousand Hills: Rwanda's Rebirth and the Man Who Dreamed It*. Hoboken, NJ: John Wiley and Sons.

Koff, Clea. 2004. *The Bone Woman: A Forensic Anthropologist's Search for Truth in the Mass Graves of Rwanda, Bosnia, Croatia, and Kosovo*. New York: Random House.

Kouyate, Mamadou. 2011. "Rwanda: Paul Kagame Responds to US Ambassador Susan E. Rice." November 28. http://hungryoftruth.blogspot.com/2011/11/rwanda-paul-kagame-responds-to-us.html. Accessed November 30, 2011.

Kroslak, Daniela. 2008. *The French Betrayal of Rwanda*. Bloomington: Indiana University Press.

Kuperman, Alan. 2004. "Provoking Genocide: A Revised History of the Rwandan Patriotic Front." *Journal of Genocide Research* 6 (1): 61–84.

Lawler, Steph. 2002. "Narrative in Social Research." In *Qualitative Research in Action*, edited by Tim May, 242–58. London: Sage.

Legal and Constitutional Commission, Republic of Rwanda. 2003. "The Constitution of the Republic of Rwanda." Kigali: Legal and Constitutional Commission.

Lemarchand, René. 1970. *Rwanda and Burundi*. New York: Praeger.

———. 1998. "Genocide in the Great Lakes: Which Genocide? Whose Genocide?" *African Studies Review* 41 (1): 3–16.

Ligue des droits de la personne dans la région des Grands Lacs (LGDL). 2004. "Lueur de paix et persistance chronique de l'impunité: Rapport annuel sur la situation des droits de l'homme dans la sous-région des Grand Lacs (Burundi, RD Congo, Rwanda)." Kigali: LGDL.

Ligue rwandaise pour la promotion et la défense des droits de l'homme (LIPRODHOR). 2001. "Rapport final du projet 'Programme de suivi des détentions dans les cachots communaux.'" February 21. Kigali: LIPRODHOR.

Linden, Ian, with Jane Linden. 1977. *Church and Revolution in Rwanda*. Manchester: University of Manchester Press.

Longman, Timothy. 1995. "Genocide and Socio-Political Change: Massacres in Two Rwandan Villages." *Issue: A Journal of Opinion* 23 (2): 18–21.

———. 1998. "Rwanda: Chaos from Above." In *The African State at a Critical Juncture: between Disintegration and Reconfiguration*, edited by Leonardo A. Villalón and Philip A. Huxtable, 75–91. Boulder, CO: Lynne Rienner.

———. 2011. "Limitations to Political Reform: The Undemocratic Nature of Transition in Rwanda." In *Remaking Rwanda: State Building and Human Rights after Mass Violence*, edited by Scott Straus and Lars Waldorf, 25–47. Madison: University of Wisconsin Press.

Longman, Timothy, and Théonèste Rutagengwa. 2004. "Memory, Identity, and Community in Rwanda." In *My Neighbor, My Enemy: Justice and Community in the*

Aftermath of Mass Atrocity, edited by Eric Stover and Harvey M. Weinstein, 162–82. New York: Cambridge University Press.

Louis, William Roger. 1963. *Rwanda-Urundi, 1884–1919*. Oxford: Clarendon Press.

Lyon, Robert, and Scott Straus. 2006. *Intimate Enemy: Images and Voices of the Rwandan Genocide*. New York: Zone Books.

Maina, Chris, and Edith Kibalama, eds. 2006. *Civil Society and the Struggle for a Better Rwanda: A Report of the Fact-Finding Mission to Rwanda Organised under the Auspices of Kituo Cha Katiba*. Kampala, Uganda: Fountain.

Makombo, Angèle N. 1998. "Civil Conflict in the Great Lakes Region: The Issue of Nationality of the Banyarwanda in the Democratic Republic of the Congo." In *African Yearbook of International Law / Annuaire africain de droit international*, vol. 5, edited by Abdulqawi A. Yusuf, 49–62. Leiden: Brill.

Mamdani, Mahmood. 2001. *When Victims Become Killers: Colonialism, Nativism and the Genocide in Rwanda*. Kampala, Uganda: Fountain.

McCabe, Allysa, and Lynn S. Bliss. 2003. *Patterns of Narrative Discourse: A Multicultural Life Span Approach*. Boston: Pearson.

Médecins sans frontières (MSF). 2003. "Release of Genocide Suspects in Rwanda Prompts Concern for Survivors." April 14. http://www.msf.org/article/release-genocide-suspects-rwanda-prompts-concern-survivors. Accessed August 26, 2004.

———. 2004a. "Rwanda: Aiding Civilians Affected by Genocide." August 18. http://www.msf.org/article/rwanda-aiding-civilians-affected-genocide. Accessed August 26, 2004.

———. 2004b. "Rwanda: Providing Psychological and Medical Care." December 16. http://www.msf.org/rwanda-providing-psychological-and-medical-care. Accessed August 26, 2004.

———. 2006a. "'I Try to Stay Unknown as Much as I Can'—Portrait of a Rwandan Seeking Refuge." June 22. http://www.msf.org/article/i-try-stay-unknown-much-i-can-portrait-rwandan-seeking-refuge. Accessed August 29, 2006.

———. 2006b. "I Feel like a Stone—Portrait of a Rwandan Seeking Refuge." June 22. http://www.msf.org/article/i-feel-stone-portrait-rwandan-seeking-refuge. Accessed August 29, 2006.

———. 2006c. "Sheer Fear Forces Rwandans to Take Flight." June 22. http://www.msf.org/article/sheer-fear-forces-rwandans-take-flight. Accessed August 29, 2006.

———. 2006d. "The World Needs to Know What Is Going On—Portrait of a Rwandan Seeking Refuge." June 22. http://www.msf.org/article/world-needs-know-what-going-portrait-rwandan-seeking-refuge. Accessed August 29, 2006.

Meierhenrich, Jens. 2011. "Topographies of Remembering and Forgetting: The Transformation of *Lieux de Mémoire* in Rwanda." In *Remaking Rwanda: State Building and Human Rights after Mass Violence*, edited by Scott Straus and Lars Waldorf, 283–95. Madison: University of Wisconsin Press.

Meschi, Linda. 1974. "Evolution des structures foncières au Rwanda: Le cas d'un lineage Hutu." *Cahiers d'études africaines* 16 (1): 39–51.

Mgbako, Chi. 2005. "*Ingando* Solidarity Camps: Reconciliation and Political Indoctrination in Post-genocide Rwanda." *Harvard Human Rights Journal* 18 (Spring): 201–24.

Migdal, Joel. 2001. *State in Society: Studying How States and Societies Transform and Constitute One Another*. Cambridge: Cambridge University Press.

Minear, Larry, and Philippe Guillot. 1996. *Soldiers to the Rescue: Humanitarian Lessons from Rwanda*. Paris: Organization for Economic Cooperation and Development.

Ministry of Finance and Economic Planning (MINECOFIN). 2000. *Vision 20/20*. Kigali: MINECOFIN.

———. 2001. *Participatory Poverty Assessment*. National Poverty Reduction Program. Kigali: MINECOFIN.

Ministry of Justice (MINIJUST). 2004. "Organic Law No. 16/2004 of June 19, 2004, Establishing the Organization, Competence and Functioning of Gacaca Courts Charged with Prosecuting and Trying the Perpetrators of the Crime of Genocide and Other Crimes against Humanity, Committed between October 1, 1990, and December 31, 1994." http://www.inkiko-gacaca.gov.rw/pdf/newlaw1.pdf. Accessed February 21, 2005.

———. 2007. "Organic Law No. 09/2007 of 16/02/2007 Law on the Attributions, Organisation and Functioning of the National Commission for the Fight against Genocide." http://www.cnlg.gov.rw/commission.htm. Accessed February 19, 2008.

Ministry of Lands, Environment, Forestry, Water and Natural Resources (MINITERRE). 2004. *National Land Policy*. Kigali: MINITERRE.

Ministry of Local Government, Community Development and Social Affairs (MINALOC). 2002. *Dénombremement des victimes du génocide: Rapport final*. Kigali: MINALOC.

———. 2004. *Rwanda Five-Year Decentralisation Implementation Program: Poverty Reduction and Empowerment through Entrenchment of Democratic Decentralisation*. Kigali: MINALOC.

———. 2006. *Making Decentralized Service Delivery Work in Rwanda: Putting the People at the Center of Service Provision*. Kigali: MINALOC.

———. 2007. *Rwanda Decentralization Strategic Framework: Towards a Sector-Wide Approach for Decentralization Implementation*. Kigali: MINALOC.

Mironko, Charles K. 2004. "Social and Political Mechanisms of Mass Murder: An Analysis of Perpetrators in the Rwandan Genocide." PhD diss., Yale University, Faculty of Graduate Studies.

Mitchell, Timothy. 1991. "The Limits of the State: Beyond Statist Approaches and their Critics." *American Political Science Review* 85 (1): 77–96.

Mujawayo, Esther, and Souâd Belhaddad. 2004. *Survivantes: Rwanda, dix ans après le génocide*. Paris: Editions de l'Aube.

———. 2006. *La fleur de Stéphanie: Rwanda entre reconciliation et déni*. Paris: Flammarion.

Mukagasana, Yolande. 1997. *La mort ne veut pas de moi*. Paris: Laffont.

———. 1999. *N'aie pas peur de savoir*. Paris: Laffont.

———. 2001. *Les blessures du silence*. Arles, France: Actes Sud.

Mukasonga, Scholastique. 2006. *Inyenzi ou les cafards*. Paris: Gallimard.

National Commission for the Fight Against Genocide (CNLG). 2013. "About Us," "Education." http://cnlg.gov.rw/. Accessed April 23, 2013.

National Institute of Statistics. 2006. "Preliminary Poverty Update, Integrated Living Conditions Survey 2005/6." Kigali: National Institute of Statistics.

———. 2012. "The Evolution of Poverty in Rwanda from 2000 to 2011: Results from the Household Surveys (EICV)." Kigali: National Institute of Statistics.

National Service of Gacaca Jurisdictions (NSGJ). 2005. "Instruction No. 04/2005 of 16-02/2005 from the National Secretary of the Gacaca Courts Related to Conditions

Required from Observers, Researchers and Journalists in the Gacaca Court Process." Kigali: MINIJUST.

———. 2005/06. "Gacaca Process: Achievement, Problems and Future Prospects." Kigali: MINIJUST.

———. 2006. "Achievements in Gacaca Courts." Kigali: MINIJUST.

———/Avocats sans frontières (NSGJ/ASF). 2002. "Formation of Decentralized Agents Intervening in Processes Put in Place by the NSGJ—Administrative and Logistic Module." Kigali: MINIJUST.

National Unity and Reconciliation Commission (NURC). 2000. "Nation-Wide Grassroots Consultations Report: Unity and Reconciliation Initiatives in Rwanda." Kigali: NURC.

———. 2003. "Opinion Survey on Participation in Gacaca and National Reconciliation." Kigali: NURC.

———, under the direction of Anatase Shyaka. 2004. "The Rwandan Conflict: Origin, Development, Exit Strategies." Kigali: NURC.

———. 2006a. "The Ingando Concept and It's [*sic*] Syllabus Reform." Kigali: NURC.

———. 2006b. "The Themes Meant to Be Discussed during "Ingando" Workshop for Leaders." Kigali: NURC.

———. 2006c. "The A–Z of Ingando." Kigali: NURC.

———. 2007a. "Background of the NURC." http://www.nurc.gov.rw/index.php?back. Accessed September 24, 2007.

———. 2007b. "Mission and Vision." http://www.nurc.gov.rw/index.php?MisViv. Accessed September 24, 2007

———. 2007c. "Programs: Civic Education." http://www.nurc.gov.rw/index.php?Civi. Accessed September 24, 2007.

———. 2007d. "Programs: Conflict Management." http://www.nurc.gov.rw/index.php ?Confl. Accessed September 24, 2007.

———. 2007e. "Tools of Reconciliation: Ingando." http://www.nurc.gov.rw/index.php ?Init. Accessed September 24, 2007.

———. 2007f. "Tools of Reconciliation: Community Based Initiatives [*sic*]." http:// www.nurc.gov.rw/index.php?Init. Accessed September 24, 2007.

———. 2007g. "Tools of Reconciliation: National Summit." http://www.nurc.gov.rw /index.php?Nat. Accessed September 24, 2007.

———. 2007h. "Tools of Reconciliation: Community Festivals." http://www.nurc.gov .rw/index.php?Comm. Accessed September 24, 2007.

———. 2007i. "SCUR: Students' Club for Unity and Reconciliation." http://www .nurc.gov.rw/index.php?scur. Accessed September 24, 2007.

———. 2010. "Rwanda Reconciliation Barometer." Kigali: NURC.

———. n.d. "The National Unity and Reconciliation Commission at a Glance." Kigali: NURC.

Ndahiro, Alfred, and Privat Rutazibwa. 2008. *Hotel Rwanda or the Tutsi Genocide as Seen by Hollywood*. Kigali: Office of the President.

Ndayambaje, Jean Damascène. 2001. *Le génocide au Rwanda: Un analyse psychologique*. Butare: Université nationale du Rwanda/Centre universitaire de santé mentale.

Newbury, Catharine. 1988. *The Cohesion of Oppression: Clientship and Ethnicity in Rwanda, 1860–1960*. New York: Columbia University Press.

———. 1992. "Rwanda: Recent Debates over Governance and Rural Development." In *Governance and Politics in Africa*, edited by Goran Hyden and Michael Bratton, 193–219. Boulder, CO: Lynne Reinner.

———. 1995. "Background to Genocide: Rwanda." *Issue: A Journal of Opinion* 23 (2): 12–17.

———. 1998. "Ethnicity and the Politics of History in Rwanda." *Africa Today* 45 (1): 7–25.

———. 2011. "High Modernism at the Ground Level: The *Imidugudu* Policy in Rwanda." In *Remaking Rwanda: State Building and Human Rights after Mass Violence*, edited by Scott Straus and Lars Waldorf, 223–39. Madison: University of Wisconsin Press.

Newbury, Catharine, and Hannah Baldwin. 2001. *Aftermath: Women in Postgenocide Rwanda*. Washington, DC: USAID, Department of Information and Evaluation.

Newbury, Catharine, and David Newbury. 1995. "Identity, Genocide, and Reconstruction in Rwanda." In Les Verts au Parlement Européen, *Les Racines de la violence dans la région des Grands Lacs*, 15–40. Brussels: Parlement européen.

———. 1999. "A Catholic Mass in Kigali: Contested Views of the Genocide and Ethnicity in Rwanda." *Canadian Journal of African Studies* 33 (2/3): 292–328.

Newbury, David. 1980. "The Clans of Rwanda: An Historical Hypothesis." *Africa* 50 (4): 389–403.

———. 1991. *Kings and Clans: A Social History of the Lake Kivu Rift Valley*. Madison: University of Wisconsin Press.

———. 1994. "Trick Cyclists? Recontextualizing Rwandan Dynastic Chronology." *History in Africa* 21:191–217.

———. 1997. "Irredentist Rwanda: Ethnic and Territorial Frontiers in Central Africa." *Africa Today* 44 (2): 211–22.

Newbury, David, and Catharine Newbury. 2000. "Bringing the Peasants Back In: Agrarian Themes in the Construction and Corrosion of Statist Historiography in Rwanda." *American Historical Review* 105 (3): 832–78.

Newbury, M. Catharine. 1978. "Ethnicity in Rwanda: The Case of Kinyaga." *Africa* 48 (1): 16–29.

———. 1980. "Ubureetwa and Thangata. Catalysts to Peasant Political Consciousness in Rwanda." *Canadian Journal of African Studies* 14 (1): 91–111.

Nordstrom, Carolyn. 2004. *Shadows of War: Violence, Power, and International Profiteering in the Twenty-First Century*. Berkeley: University of California Press.

Norton, Anne. 2004. *Theses on Politics, Culture, and Method*. New Haven, CT: Yale University Press.

Nzongola-Ntalaja, Georges. 1996. "Conflict in Eastern Zaire." http://www.africa.upenn.edu/Urgent_Action/apic_12106.html. Accessed February 19, 2008.

Office of the President of the Republic. 1999. "The Unity of Rwandans: Before the Colonial Period and under the Colonial Rule under the First Republic." Kigali: Urugwiro Village.

Office Rwandaise du tourisme et des parcs nationaux (ORTPN). 2004. *Rwanda*. Kigali: ORTPN.

Olson, Karen, and Linda Shopes. 1991. "Crossing Boundaries, Building Bridges: Doing Oral History among Working-Class Women and Men." In *Women's Words: The Feminist Practice of Oral History*, edited by Sherna Berger Gluck and Daphne Patai, 189–204. London: Routledge.

Ortner, Sherry B. 1995. "Resistance and the Problem of Ethnographic Refusal." *Comparative Studies in Society and History* 37 (1): 173–93.

Overdulve, Christian M. 1975. *Apprendre la langue Rwandaise.* The Hague/Paris: Mouton.

Pader, Ellen. 2006. "Seeing with an Ethnographic Sensibility: Explorations beneath the Surface of Public Policies." In *Interpretation and Method: Empirical Research and the Interpretative Turn,* edited by Dvora Yanow and Peregrine Schwartz-Shea, 161–75. Armonk, NY: M. E. Sharpe.

Penal Reform International (PRI). 2002. "PRI Research Team on Gacaca Report III." April–June. Kigali: PRI.

———. 2004. "PRI Research on Gacaca Report. Report IV. The Guilty Plea Procedure, Cornerstone of the Rwandan Justice System." Kigali: PRI.

———. 2007. "Annual Report 2006." London: PRI.

Pham, Phuong N., Harvey M. Weinstein, and Timothy Longman. 2004. "Trauma and PTSD Symptoms in Rwanda: Implications for Attitudes towards Justice and Reconciliation." *Journal of the American Medical Association* 292 (5): 602–12.

Plummer, Ken. 1995. *Telling Sexual Stories: Power, Change and Social Worlds.* London: Routledge.

———. 2001. "The Call of Life Stories in Ethnographic Research." In *Handbook of Ethnography,* edited by Paul A. Atkinson, Amanda Coffey, Sara Delamont, John Laflond, and Lyn Laflond, 395–406. London: Sage.

Pottier, Johan. 1989. "Three's a Crowd: Knowledge, Ignorance and Power in the Context of Urban Agriculture in Rwanda." *Africa* 59:461–77.

———. 1997. "Relief and Repatriation: Views by Rwandan Refugees. Lessons for Humanitarian Aid Workers." *African Affair* 95 (380): 403–29.

———. 2002. *Re-Imagining Rwanda: Conflict, Survival and Disinformation in the late 20th Century.* Cambridge: Cambridge University Press.

———. 2006. "Land Reform for Peace? Rwanda's 2005 Land Law in Context." *Journal of Agrarian Change* 6 (4): 509–37.

Prunier, Gérard. 1997. *The Rwanda Crisis, 1959–1994: A History of a Genocide.* 2nd ed. Kampala, Uganda: Fountain/Broadview Press.

———. 2009. *Africa's World War: Congo, the Rwandan Genocide, and the Making of a Continental Catastrophe.* Oxford: Oxford University Press.

Purdeková, Andrea. 2011. "'Even if I Am Not Here, There Are So Many Eyes': Surveillance and State Reach in Rwanda." *Journal of Modern African Studies* 49 (3): 475–97.

———. 2012a. "Civic Education and Social Transformation in Post-genocide Rwanda: Forging the Perfect Development Subjects." In *Rwanda Fast Forward: Social, Economic, Military and Reconciliation Prospects,* edited by Maddalena Campioni and Patrick Noack, 192–209. London: Palgrave Macmillan.

———. 2012b. "The Everyday Politics of Embodied Domination: Explaining the Production of Disempowerment in a Post-Genocide Authoritarianism." Paper presented at the Rwanda from Below Conference, Institute of Development Policy and Management, University of Antwerp, June 29.

Rafti, Marina. 2004. "The Dismantling of the Rwandan Political Opposition in Exile." In *L'Afrique des Grands Lacs annuaire 2003–2004,* edited by Filip Reyntjens and Stefan Marysse, 23–44. Anvers, Belgium: Centre d'étude de la région des Grands Lacs d'Afrique.

Rake, Alan. 2001. "Rwanda." In *African Leaders: Guiding the New Millennium*, 185–87. Lanham, MD: Scarecrow Press.

Reed, William Cyrus. 1996. "Exile, Reform and the Rise of the Rwandan Patriotic Front." *Journal of Modern African Studies* 34 (3): 479–501.

Reporters sans frontières (RSF). 2002. "President Paul Kagame Has Been Denounced as a Predator of Press Freedom." http://www.rsf.org/article.php3?id_article=13640. Accessed August 26, 2006.

———. 2010. "Around 30 News Media Closed a Few Days ahead of Presidential Elections. http://en.rsf.org/rwanda-around-30-news-media-closed-a-few-02-08-2010,38076.html. Accessed December 13, 2011.

———. 2012. "World Report: Rwanda." October. http://en.rsf.org/report-rwanda,38.html. Accessed October 9, 2012.

Rettig, Max. 2008. "Gacaca: Truth, Justice and Reconciliation in Post-genocide Rwanda." *African Studies Review* 51 (3): 25–50.

Reyntjens, Filip. 1985. *Pouvoir et droit au Rwanda*. Tervuren, Belgium: Musée royal de l'Afrique centrale.

———. 1992. "Les mouvements armés des réfugiés rwandais: Rupture ou continuité?" *Civilisations* 40 (2): 170–82.

———. 1995. *Rwanda: Trois jours qui ont fait basculer l'histoire*. Brussels and Paris: Institut africain/L'Harmattan.

———. 1996. "Rwanda: Genocide and Beyond." *Journal of Refugee Studies* 9 (3): 240–51.

———. 1999. "The Dubious Discourse on Rwanda." *African Affairs* 98 (390): 119–23.

———. 2004. "Rwanda, Ten Years On: From Genocide to Dictatorship." *African Affairs* 103 (411): 177–210.

———. 2006. "Post-1994 Politics in Rwanda: Problematising 'Liberation' and 'Democratisation.'" *Third World Quarterly* 27 (6): 1103–17.

———. 2009. "Rwanda: A Fake Report on Fake Elections." http://africannewsanalysis.blogspot.com/2009/02/fake-report-on-fake-elections.html. Accessed November 30, 2012.

———. 2011. "Constructing the Truth, Dealing with Dissent, Domesticating the World: Governance in Post-genocide Rwanda." *African Affairs* 110 (438): 1–34.

———, and Stef Vandeginste. 2005. "Rwanda: An Atypical Transition." In *Roads to Reconciliation*, edited by Elin Skaar, Siri Gloppen, and Astri Suhrke, 101–28. Lanham, MD: Lexington Books.

Riessman, Catherine Kohler. 1990. *Divorce Talk: Women and Men Make Sense of Personal Relationships*. New Brunswick, NJ: Rutgers University Press.

Ross, Fiona C. 2003. *Bearing Witness: Women and the Truth and Reconciliation Commission in South Africa*. London: Pluto.

Roth, Michael S., and Charles G. Salas. 2001. "Introduction." In *Disturbing Remains: Memory, History, and Crisis in the Twentieth Century*, edited by Michael S. Roth and Charles G. Sala, 1–16. Los Angeles: Getty Research Institute Publication.

Rucyahana, John, with James Riordan. 2007. *The Bishop of Rwanda: Finding Forgiveness amidst a Pile of Bones*. Nashville, TN: Thomas Nelson.

Rusagara, Frank K. 2005. "Gacaca as a Reconciliation and Nation-Building Strategy in Post-genocide Rwanda." *Conflict Trends* 20 (2): 20–25.

Rusesabagina, Paul, with Tom Zoellner. 2006. *An Ordinary Man: An Autobiography*. New York: Viking.

Ruzibiza, Abdul Joshua. 2005. *Rwanda: L'histoire secrète*. Paris: Editions du Panama.

Rwabukumba, Joseph, and Vincent Mudandagizi. 1974. "Les formes historiques de la dépendance personnelle dans l'État rwandais." *Cahiers d'études africaines* 14:12–15.

Sanders, Edith R. 1969. "The Hamitic Hypothesis: Its Origin and Function in Time Perspective." *Journal of African History* 10 (4): 521–32.

Schabas, William. 2005. "Genocide Trials and Gacaca Courts." *Journal of International Criminal Justice* 3 (4): 896–919.

Schensul, Stephen, Jean Schensul, and Margaret LeCompte. 1999. *Essential Ethnographic Methods: Observations, Interviews, and Questionnaires*. Walnut Creek, CA: AltaMira Press.

Scherrer, Christian P. 2002. *Genocide and Crisis in Central Africa: Conflict Roots, Mass Violence, and Regional War*. New York: Praeger.

Schwartz-Shea, Peregrine, and Dvora Yanow. 2012. *Interpretative Research Design: Concepts and Processes*. New York: Routledge.

Scott, James C. 1985. *Weapons of the Weak: Everyday Forms of Peasant Resistance*. New Haven, CT: Yale University Press.

———. 1990. *Domination and the Arts of Resistance: Hidden Transcripts*. New Haven, CT: Yale University Press.

———. 1998. *Seeing like a State*. New Haven, CT: Yale University Press.

Scott, James C., and Benedict J. Tria Kerkvliet. 1986. "Everyday Forms of Peasant Resistance in South-East Asia." *Journal of Peasant Studies: Special Issue* 13 (2).

Scott, Joan W. 1991. "The Evidence of Experience." *Critical Inquiry* 17:773–97.

Sebarenzi, Joseph. 2009. *God Sleeps in Rwanda*. New York: Atria Books.

———. 2011. "Justice and Human Rights for All Rwandans." In *Remaking Rwanda: State Building and Human Rights after Mass Violence*, edited by Scott Straus and Lars Waldorf, 343–53. Madison: University of Wisconsin Press.

Senate of the Republic of Rwanda. 2007. "Rwanda: Genocide Ideology and Strategies for Its Eradication." Kigali: Government of Rwanda.

Shimamungu, Eugène. 1998. *Le Kinyarwanda: Initiation à une langue Bantu*. Paris: L'Harmattan.

Sivaramakrishnan, K. 2005. "Some Intellectual Genealogies for the Concept of Everyday Resistance." *American Anthropologist* 107 (3): 346–55.

Smith, Linda Tuhiwai. 2004. *Decolonizing Methodologies: Research and Indigenous Peoples*. London: Zed Books.

Sommers, Marc. 2012a. *Stuck: Rwandan Youth and the Struggle for Adulthood*. Athens and London: University of Georgia Press.

———. 2012b. "The Darling Dictator of the Day." *New York Times*. May 27.

Stanley, Liz, and Sue Wise. 1991. "Feminist Research, Feminist Consciousness, and Experiences of Sexism." In *Beyond Methodology: Feminist Scholarship as Lived Research*, edited by Mary Margaret Fanow and Judith A. Cook, 265–83. Bloomington: Indiana University Press.

Steedman, Carolyn Kay. 1987. *Landscape for a Good Woman: A Story of Two Lives*. New Brunswick, NJ: Rutgers University Press.

Straus, Scott. 2004. "How Many Perpetrators Were There in the Rwandan Genocide? An Estimate." *Journal of Genocide Research* 6 (1): 85–98.

———. 2006. *The Order of Genocide: Race, Power, and War in Rwanda*. Ithaca, NY: Cornell University Press.

———. 2007. "What Is the Relationship between Hate Radio and Violence? Reexamining Rwanda's 'Radio Machete.'" *Politics and Society* 35 (4): 609–37.

Straus, Scott, and Lars Waldorf. 2011. "Introduction: Seeing like a Post-conflict State." In *Remaking Rwanda: State Building and Human Rights after Mass Violence*, edited by Scott Straus and Lars Waldorf, 3–21. Madison: University of Wisconsin Press.

Tertsakian, Carina. 2008. *Le Château: The Lives of Prisoners in Rwanda*. London: Arves Books.

———. 2011. "'All Rwandans Are Afraid of Being Arrested One Day': Prisoners Past, Present and Future." In *Remaking Rwanda: State Building and Human Rights after Mass Violence*, edited by Scott Straus and Lars Waldorf, 210–20. Madison: University of Wisconsin Press.

Thomson, Susan. 2009a. "'That Is Not What We Authorised You to Do . . .': Access and Government Interference in Highly Politicised Research Environments." In *Surviving Field Research: Working in Violent and Difficult Situations*, edited by Chandra Lekha Sriram, John C. King, Julie A. Mertus, Olga Martin-Ortega, and Johanna Herman, 108–24. London: Routledge.

———. 2009b. "Ethnic Twa and Rwandan National Unity and Reconciliation Policy." *Peace Review: A Journal of Social Justice* 21 (3): 313–20.

———. 2010. "Getting Close to Rwandans since the Genocide: Studying Everyday Life in Highly Politicized Research Settings." *African Studies Review* 53 (3): 19–34.

———. 2011a. "Whispering Truth to Power: The Everyday Resistance of Peasant Rwandans to Post-genocide Reconciliation." *African Affairs* 100 (440): 439–56.

———. 2011b. "The Darker Side of Transitional Justice: The Power Dynamics behind Rwanda's Gacaca Courts." *Africa* 81 (3): 373–90.

———. 2011c. "Local Power Relations and Household Gender Dynamics: Assessing Rwanda's Claim to Universal HIV/AIDS Treatment in Context." *Canadian Journal of African Studies* 44 (3): 552–78.

———. 2011d. "Re-education for Reconciliation: Participant Observations on *Ingando*." In *Remaking Rwanda: State Building and Human Rights after Mass Violence*, edited by Scott Straus and Lars Waldorf, 311–39. Madison: University of Wisconsin Press.

———. 2012. "Peasant Perspectives on National Unity and Reconciliation: Building Peace or Promoting Division?" In *Rwanda Fast Forward*, edited by Maddalena Campioni and Patrick Noack, 96–110. London: Routledge.

———. 2013. "Academic Integrity and Ethical Responsibilities in Post-genocide Rwanda: Working with Research Ethics Boards to Prepare for Fieldwork with 'Human Subjects.'" In *Emotional and Ethical Challenges for Field Research in Africa: The Story behind the Findings*, edited by Susan Thomson, An Ansoms, and Jude Murison, 139–54. London: Routledge.

———, and Rosemary Nagy. 2011. "Law, Power and Justice: What Legalism Fails to Address in the Functioning of Rwanda's Gacaca Courts." *International Journal of Transitional Justice* 5 (1): 11–30.

Turner, Simon. 2005. "'The Tutsi Are Afraid We Will Discover their Secrets'—On Secrecy and Sovereign Power in Burundi." *Social Identities* 11 (1): 37–54.

Umutesi, Marie Béatrice. 2004. *Surviving the Slaughter: The Ordeal of a Rwandan Refugee in Zaire*. Translated by Julia Emerson. Madison: University of Wisconsin Press.

United Nations Development Program (UNDP). 2008. "Human Development Report

2008: Human Development from Theory to Practice." http://hdr.undp.org/en /humandev/. Accessed October 14, 2008.

United Nations Development Program in Rwanda (UNDP Rwanda). 2004. "UNDP Country Cooperation: 2004–2008. Project Profiles. Government of Rwanda/United Nations Development Program." Kigali: UNDP.

———. 2007. "Turning Vision 20/20 into Reality: From Recovery to Sustainable Human Development." http://hdr.undp.org/en/reports/national/africa/rwanda /name,3322,en.html. Accessed August 20, 2013.

United Nations Group of Experts on the Democratic Republic of the Congo (UN GOE). 2012. "Final Report of the Group of Experts on the DRC Submitted in Accordance with Paragraph 4 of Security Council Resolution 2021 (2011)." November 15. S/2012/843. http://www.un.org/sc/committees/1533/egroup.shtml. Accessed November 22, 2012.

United Nations High Commission for Refugees (UNHCR). 1997. "Update on Developments in the Great Lakes Region." EC/47/SC/CRP.38. http://www.unhcr.org /excom/EXCOM/3ae68do61c.html. Accessed March 30, 2007.

United Nations Office of the High Commissioner for Human Rights (UNOHCHR). 2010. "Democratic Republic of the Congo, 1993–2003: Report of the Mapping Exercise Documenting the Most Serious Violations of Human Rights and International Humanitarian Law Committed within the Territory of the Democratic Republic of the Congo between March 1993 and June 2003" ("Mapping Report"). August. http://www.ohchr.org/en/Countries/AfricaRegion/Pages/RDCProjet Mapping.aspx. Accessed September 19, 2010.

United Nations Office of the High Representative for Least Developed Countries, Landlocked Developing Countries and Small Island Developing States (UN-OHRLLS) and United Nations Development Program (UNDP). 2006. "Governance for the Future: Democracy and Development in the Least Developed Countries." New York: UNDP.

United States Committee for Refugees and Immigrants (USCRI). 2004. "World Refugee Survey 2004 Country Report Tanzania." http://refugeesusa.org/countryreports .aspx?id=175. Accessed July 21, 2008.

United States Department of State. 2013. "Country Reports on Human Rights Practices for 2012: Rwanda." http://www.state.gov/j/drl/rls/hrrpt/humanrightsreport /index.htm?year=2012&dlid=204156#wrapper. Accessed April 19, 2013.

Uvin, Peter. 1998. *Aiding Violence: The Development Enterprise in Rwanda.* West Hartford, CT: Kumarian.

———. 2001. "Reading the Rwandan Genocide." *International Studies Review* 3 (3): 75–99.

———. 2003. "Wake Up! Some Personal Reflections and Policy Proposals." http:// fletcher.tufts.edu/faculty/uvin/reports/wakeup.pdf. Accessed March 31, 2007.

Vail, Leroy, and Landeg White. 1986. "Forms of Resistance: Songs and Perceptions of Power in Colonial Mozambique." In *Banditry, Rebellion and Social Protest in Africa,* edited by Donald Crummey, 193–228. London: James Currey.

Vandeginste, Stef. 2003. "Victims of Genocide, Crimes against Humanity and War Crimes in Rwanda: The Legal and Institutional Framework of their Right to Reparation." In *Politics and the Past: On Repairing Historical Injustices,* edited by John Torpey, 184–205. Lanham, MD: Rowman and Littlefield.

van der Meeren, Rachel. 1996. "Three Decades in Exile: Rwandan Refugees 1960–1990." *Journal of Refugee Studies* 9 (3): 252–67.

van Leeuwen, Mathijs. 2001. "Rwanda's Imidugudu Programme and Earlier Experiences with Villagisation and Resettlement in East Africa." *Journal of Modern African Studies* 39 (4): 623–44.

Vansina, Jan. 2000. "Historical Tales (*Ibiteekerezo*) and the History of Rwanda." *History in Africa* 27:375–414.

———. 2004. *Antecedents to Modern Rwanda: The Nyiginya Kingdom*. Madison: University of Wisconsin Press.

Versailles, Bruno. 2012. "Rwanda: Performance Contracts (Imihigo)." Overseas Institute for Development Budget Strengthening Initiative. April. http://www.budget strengthening.org/storage/country-learning-notes/Rwanda%20performance%20 contracts.pdf. Accessed November 19, 2012.

Verwimp, Philip. 2003. "The Political Economy of Coffee, Dictatorship, and Genocide." *European Journal of Political Economy* 19 (2): 161–81.

———. 2005. "An Economic Profile of Peasant Perpetrators of Genocide: Micro-level Evidence from Rwanda." *Journal of Development Economics* 77 (2): 297–323.

Vidal, Claudine. 1969. "Le Rwanda des anthropologues ou le fétichisme de la vache." *Cahiers d'études africaines* 9 (3): 384–401.

———. 1974. "Economie de la société féodale Rwandaise." *Cahiers d'études africaines* 14:52–74.

Vlassenroot, Koen. 2002. "Citizenship, Identity Formation and Conflict in South Kivu: The Case of the Banyamulenge." *Review of African Political Economy* 29 (93/94): 499–515.

Waldorf, Lars. 2006. "Mass Justice for Mass Atrocity: Rethinking Local Justice as Transitional Justice." *Temple Law Review* 79 (1): 1–87.

———. 2009. "Revisiting *Hotel Rwanda*: Genocide, Ideology, Reconciliation, and Rescuers." *Journal of Genocide Research* 11 (1): 101–25.

———. 2011. "Instrumentalizing Genocide: The RPF's Campaign against 'Genocide Ideology.'" In *Remaking Rwanda: State Building and Human Rights after Mass Violence*, edited by Scott Straus and Lars Waldorf, 48–66. Madison: University of Wisconsin Press.

Warren, Rick. 2009. "The 2009 Time 100: Paul Kagame" *Time*, April 30. http://www .time.com/time/specials/packages/article/0,28804,1894410_1893847_1893843,00 .html. Accessed October 29, 2012.

Weber, Max. 1946. "Politics as Vocation." In *From Max Weber: Essays in Sociology*, edited by Hans Heinrich Gerth and Charles Wright Mills, 77–128. New York: Oxford University Press.

Wedeen, Lisa. 1999. *Ambiguities of Domination: Politics, Rhetoric and Symbols in Contemporary Syria*. Chicago: University of Chicago Press.

———. 2003. "Seeing like a Citizen, Acting like a State: Exemplary Events in Unified Yemen." *Comparative Study of Society and History* 45 (4): 680–713.

Weinstein, Warren. 1977. "Military Continuities in the Rwanda State." In *The Warrior Traditions in Modern Africa*, edited by Ali Mazru, 48–66. Leiden: Brill.

Willame, Jean-Claude. 1997. *Banyarwanda and Banyamulenge: Violences ethniques et gestion de l'identitaire au Kivu*. Paris: L'Harmattan.

World Bank (WB). 2002. "Technical Annex—Rwanda Emergency Demobilization and Reintegration Project." http://www.mdrp.org/PDFs/Country_PDFs/Rwanda Doc_TechAnnex.pdf. Accessed March 21, 2008.

———. 2012. "Rwanda: Data and Statistics." http://data.worldbank.org/country /rwanda. Accessed November 20, 2012.

Worthington, Kim L. 1996. *Self as Narrative, Subjectivity and Community in Contemporary Fiction.* Oxford: Clarendon Press.

Young, Iris Marion. 1990. *Justice and the Politics of Difference.* Princeton, NJ: Princeton University Press.

———. 1997. *Interesting Voices, Dilemmas of Gender, Political Philosophy and Policy.* Princeton, NJ: Princeton University Press.

———. 2004. "Five Faces of Power." In *Oppression, Privilege, and Resistance: Theoretical Perspectives on Racism, Sexism and Hetrosexism,* edited by Lisa Heldke and Peg O'Connor, 37–63. Boston: McGraw-Hill.

Zakaria, Fareed. 2009. "Africa's New Path: Paul Kagame Charts a Way Forward." *Newsweek,* July 18. http://www.newsweek.com/id/207403. Accessed October 29, 2012.

Žižek, Slavoj. 1996. "'I Hear You with My Eyes': Or, the Invisible Master." In *Gaze and Voice as Love Objects,* edited by Renata Saleci and Slavoj Žižek, 90–126. Durham, NC: Duke University Press.

Zorbas, Eugenia. 2004. "Reconciliation in Post-genocide Rwanda." *African Journal of Legal Studies* 1:29–52.

———. 2011. "Aid Dependence and Policy Independence: Explaining the Rwandan Paradox." In *Remaking Rwanda: State Building and Human Rights after Mass Violence,* edited by Scott Straus and Lars Waldorf, 103–17. Madison: University of Wisconsin Press.

Zraly, Maggie. 2010. "Danger Denied: Everyday Life and Everyday Violence among Rwandan Genocide-Rape Survivors." *Voices* 10 (1): 18–23.

INDEX

Page numbers in italics indicate illustrations.

Africa and the Diaspora
History, Politics, Culture

SERIES EDITORS

Thomas Spear
Neil Kodesh
Tejumola Olaniyan
Michael G. Schatzberg
James H. Sweet

Spirit, Structure, and Flesh:
Gendered Experiences in African Instituted Churches among the Yoruba of Nigeria
Deidre Helen Crumbley

A Hill among a Thousand: Transformations and Ruptures in Rural Rwanda
Danielle de Lame

Defeat Is the Only Bad News: Rwanda under Musinga, 1896–1931
Alison Liebhafsky Des Forges; edited by David Newbury

Power in Colonial Africa: Conflict and Discourse in Lesotho, 1870–1960
Elizabeth A. Eldredge

Nachituti's Gift: Economy, Society, and Environment in Central Africa
David M. Gordon

Intermediaries, Interpreters, and Clerks: African Employees in the Making of Colonial Africa
Edited by Benjamin N. Lawrance, Emily Lynn Osborn, and Richard L. Roberts

Naming Colonialism: History and Collective Memory in the Congo, 1870–1960
Osumaka Likaka

Mau Mau's Children: The Making of Kenya's Postcolonial Elite
David P. Sandgren